MUDDLING THROUGH

THE REMARKABLE STORY OF THE BARR COLONISTS

LYNNE BOWEN

GREYSTONE BOOKS
DOUGLAS & McINTYRE
Vancouver/Toronto

Greystone Books
A division of Douglas & McIntyre Ltd.
1615 Venables Street
Vancouver, British Columbia V5L 2H1

Canadian Cataloguing in Publication Data

Bowen, Lynne, 1940–
    Muddling through

    "Greystone Books"
    ISBN 1-55054-105-6

    1. Barr Colony (Alta. and Sask.)   2. British—Prairie Provinces—History—20th century.   3. Agricultural colonies—Prairie Provinces—History—20th century.   4. Prairie Provinces—Emigration and immigration—History—20th century.   5. Prairie Provinces—Colonization—History—20th century.   6. Great Britain—Emigration and immigration—History—20th century.   7. Immigrants—Prairie Provinces—History-20th century.   I. Title.
FC3242.9   B37B69   1994   971.242   C94-910044-7
F1060.9.B69   1994

Editing by Barbara Pulling
Design by The Typeworks
Cover design by Eric Ansley and Associates Ltd.
Cover photographs courtesy Provincial Archives of Alberta/A9391 and
    collection of the author
Maps by Andrew Bowen

Printed and bound in Canada by D. W. Friesen & Sons Ltd.
Printed on acid-free paper ∞

The author wishes to acknowledge the generous support of the Canada Council.

To the memory of
Isobel Willis Boyd Crossley
1912-1989

Contents

Preface

THE TELLING OF HISTORY IS THE TELLING OF STORIES. WHETHER THE STORIES are told around a campfire, confided to a diary or written in a memoir or government report, the history of all people on earth is told in stories.

I grew up on the stories of the Barr Colony—the gentle tales told to me by my grandmother and the lively and sometimes outrageous ones told by my grandfather. Grandpa had a way with an audience—he was a good storyteller. In the years since he died, I have come to realize that good storytellers exaggerate, embellish, borrow and even lie. But the embellishments hold the audience, making the story more real for each listener, and I believe that as long as essential truths are told and no one is slandered, more good than harm is done by a good storyteller.

Many storytellers contributed to this book. I have used their stories to tell, as accurately as I can, how over two thousand British clerks, butchers, housewives, ex–Boer War soldiers, saleswomen and remittance men followed a charismatic but inept Anglican minister to the Canadian prairies. Some told their stories to their diaries, probably the best source of raw material. Others wrote letters to parents and fiancées, distorting the truth a little or a lot to spare the recipient. Those who wrote books had more time to consider, and more time to bend and stretch the facts. Government documents told stories too, stories stripped of artistry if not of artifice.

As the writer of two books of coal mining history, I have had to explain on many occasions that it was not necessary to be a coal miner's daughter to tell the miners' story. But it would have been nice to have been able to answer "yes" when asked that question. For this book, I can say, "Yes. I am a Barr colonist's granddaughter, and a grandniece, and a second-cousin-by-marriage-twice-removed."

To track down the stories of my family and of many other families, I returned to the prairies several times to work with the Barr Colony collections in a number of prairie archives. There were Barr Colony descendants and even two survivors to meet. I wanted to see Barr Colony country and refresh my memory of the prairie landscape.

Even prairie dust can be evocative when one is discovering one's roots. My favourite trip was the one during which my husband and I retraced the trek, flirting with the actual route as we followed backroads, encountering trail-blocking fences and stumbling onto recognizable landmarks. I met Barr Colony relatives for the first time, learned how to read a township map, drank the hard water and realized that my twenty years spent on the lush British Columbia coast had only enhanced my appreciation for the subtler beauty of the prairies.

My cousin Mildred was seventy-nine when we visited in the spring of 1990. She asked us to drive her into town to pick up her airplane, which she flew back to the landing strip on her farm. That landing strip runs along a large slough. On the other side of the water is a precious legacy that Mildred has preserved—land that has never been ploughed, virgin prairie. We felt the springiness of the dead grasses, heard the crunch of prairie wool under our feet and felt closer to the people who walked on it ninety years before us. Mildred took us to the site of the family homestead; she scrambled across a muddy ditch and up a small knoll to show us where the sod house used to stand. The land and the sky dwarfed her. When Mildred's father was nineteen, a former clerk in a commercial traveller's office, he took this land on and made it work for him.

My own father died before I began this project, but he left me with a few of his father's treasures—a plough handle, a letter from Isaac Barr and a bill of sale for a pair of oxen. *Muddling Through* is dedicated to my mother. She transcribed the interviews for this book, but she died while I was writing it. I miss her very much.

Not all the descendants of Barr colonists will find their ancestors' names mentioned in this book, but the story belongs to all of them— the children and grandchildren to the fourth and fifth generations. To those generations of my family: Here are some of the stories that made you what you are. And to my grandfather: Thank you for the stories—for the ones that happened just as you told them, for the ones you borrowed from others and for the ones that got better and better as the years went by.

District of Athabasca

District of Saskatchewan

Manitoba

4th Meridian

Colony Site

Battleford

Saskatoon

Regina

North Sask. River

Battle River

Edmonton

District of Alberta

District of Assiniboia

North West Territories, 1903

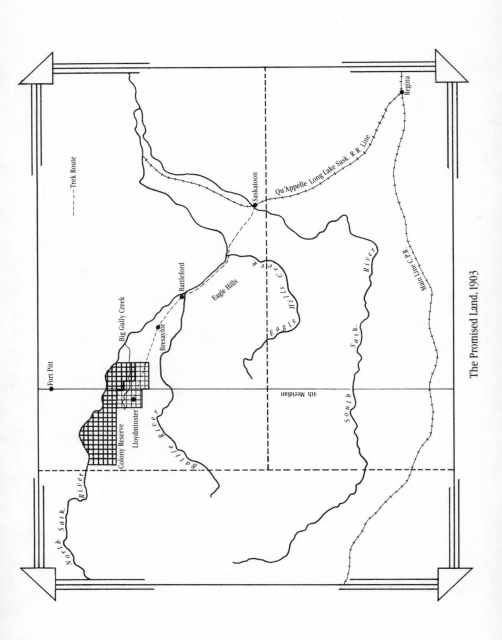

The Promised Land, 1903

- - - - Trek Route

North Sask. River

Fort Pitt

Big Gully Creek

Colony Reserve

Lloydminster

Bresaylor

Battleford

Battle River

Eagle Hills

Eagle Hills Creek

Saskatoon

Qu'Appelle Long Lake Sask. R.R. Line

South Sask. River

4th Meridian

Main Line C.P.R.

Regina

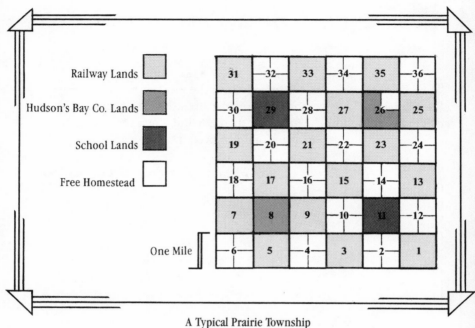

Railway Lands

Hudson's Bay Co. Lands

School Lands

Free Homestead

One Mile

A Typical Prairie Township

"The English race gets continually into the most unheard of scrapes all over the world by reason of its insular prejudices and superiority to advice; but somehow they muddle through and when they do they are on the ground to hold it."

Manitoba Free Press, December 1903

Prologue

IN THE LAST DAYS OF MAY IN THE YEAR 1903, NOAH'S ARK CAME TO REST ON THE mud bottom of a large slough thirty miles from the Promised Land. The remnants of a late spring snowfall lay in patches on the low surrounding hills, blackened by a recent prairie fire. The wind blew, raw and penetrating.

Noah's Ark was not a boat. Spoked wheels, just visible above the surface of the water, gave away its true identity. It was a high and utilitarian Bain wagon topped with a peaked roof of wood and tarpaper. The master of this strange craft was Thomas Edwards. It was whispered around that Edwards was demented and that the Ark was proof of it.

As he eased down off the wagon into the icy water, Edwards might have agreed. A man had to be demented to be in this godforsaken country by choice. The oxen looked back with mournful eyes as he lurched forward to take hold of the harness, the sticky mud pulling at his feet. He tugged at one of their collars, urging them forward, but the Ark did not move.

Edwards and his family were en route from Saskatoon in the Northwest Territories of Canada to the proposed site of the All-British Colony two hundred miles to the north and west. They were part of a group of over two thousand British colonists recruited by the Reverend Isaac Barr to settle in an uninhabited part of the Canadian prairies and save it from all the "foreigners" who were flooding in to claim the free land. "Canada for the British" was their rallying cry.

It looked as if they intended to save Canada by bringing half of Britain with them. All the wagons were overloaded, the piles of boxes, trunks, furniture and farm implements higher than the wagons themselves. The cumbersome vehicles had been stuck in mud and in sloughs many times as they made their way behind plodding teams to the land that Barr said flowed with milk and honey.

In the camp near the slough where the Ark was stranded, there was almost nothing to eat. Someone called it Starvation Camp, and the name stuck. The travellers had used up most of their food. Prairie fires had destroyed the feed for the livestock and the wood for campfires. Snow had fallen more than once, then heavy rains had followed the snow. No one could keep dry or warm. Some of the children had scarlet fever. Even the wild ducks, so abundant at other camps, had disappeared. Someone named the slough Duck Lake. At least someone still had a sense of humour.

Thomas Edwards's wife, Alice, watched from the shore. She had refused to ride in the Ark, choosing instead to walk all the way from Saskatoon. Life with Thomas had not been easy. She had married him in Australia after her first husband died of tuberculosis. He had taken her back to his native Wales, from whence his family had banished him thirteen years before with instructions to make something of himself and thirty pounds to see him through until he did. Alice had borne a daughter when she was forty-one years old, and now here she was, the mother of a six-year-old girl, sitting on the edge of a slough in the middle of a wilderness looking at that joke of a wagon carrying everything that was important to her.

Edwards had tried to find a way around the slough, but all he had seen was more muddy ground, so he risked the direct route through the water. It seemed at first that the plodding pace of the bullocks would carry the wagon across, but then they stopped in the middle to drink and lost their momentum.

Thomas carried his daughter through the waist-deep water to shore, then began the laborious process of unloading the wagon with the assistance of the other colonists. By now everyone knew what to do. An unloaded wagon would be light enough for the oxen to pull out.

But before that could happen, Edwards did a strange thing. He unhitched the team. Liberated from their immovable burden, the oxen headed for dry land—and kept right on going. It was ten days before they were found and brought back. While they were gone, the air temperature rose. The melting snow raised the level of the water until it covered the tops of the wagon's wheels. Noah's Ark, looking more than ever like a misbegotten boat, sat marooned in the middle of Duck Lake.

It was enough to make a man want to quit. It certainly made a man think hard about the circumstances that had brought him there, and it made him want to find someone to blame. For Thomas Edwards and the rest of the colonists it was easy to see who that someone was.

Isaac Barr was the agent of their misfortune. He had lured them to Canada with his overblown descriptions of rich soil and good climate. He had told them that the land was free to anyone prepared to live on it for half of each of three years, build a house and do a little plough-ing, and that was true, but Barr had made it sound so easy. He had promised to set it up for them, make it safe. Free land. And all they had to do was get there.

But Barr's flowery rhetoric and ill-conceived promises were no match for the Canadian prairies and for the greed and ambition of other men. In the years to come, sitting in the comfort of warm, dry homes, the colonists would think back to this time, and many of them would forgive Isaac Barr. But no one thought kindly of him in the last days of May in the year 1903 at Starvation Camp thirty miles from the Promised Land.

CHAPTER

I

Canada for the British

IT WAS IN THE MIND OF ISAAC MONTGOMERY BARR, AN EXPATRIATE CANADIAN parson, that the All-British Colony was born. The idea had been a long time in gestation and for years had been without specific form. Barr was well into middle age before he knew that his dream of establishing a colony somewhere in the British Empire would really happen. Better still, this brain child of his would glorify the Empire at a time when her self-confidence had been severely tested by the unexpectedly fierce determination of the Boers in South Africa to defend what they said was theirs.

Barr was an unlikely champion. By 1902, he had lived outside the British Empire for nineteen years, having left Canada under a cloud in 1883 and resided in various locations in the United States ever since. But somewhere in the recesses of his early life, a grandiose plan had been in the making.

A series of austere Presbyterian manses in Ontario's Halton County had provided the setting for his childhood. Having been educated by his Irish father in Latin, Greek and Hebrew, he looked to the ancient world for refuge from paternal frugality and bad temper. At his mother's knee he had heard of the exploits of her family, which boasted among its antecessors a surgeon on Nelson's ship at Trafalgar. When his mother died young, he clung to the knowledge that he came from adventurous stock. Steeped in real and imagined past glories, Barr grew to manhood and, casting aside his father's church, was ordained as an Anglican minister. A brief posting at Prince Albert in 1875 convinced him that there on the vast prairie a man could do something great.

But any dreams and plans Barr may have had were complicated by a

failing marriage, financial disagreements with congregations, and bish-
ops who insisted on doctrinal purity. He fled Canada for the United
States. During the next nineteen years he moved from parish to parish: now to Michigan, where he shed his first wife; then to Tennessee,
where he not only impressed his bishop but gained the trust of the
local moonshiners, and finally to an obscure parish in Whatcom
County, Washington, where he married again. And always his grand
scheme sustained him.

He was inspired by Cecil Rhodes and boasted that he was planning
a settlement project with the great imperialist and financier. Although
there is no record of his even having met Rhodes, there is ample evidence of Barr's pro-British activities in Whatcom County. Mother
Britain was in dire need of supporters there, many people being sympathetic to the Boers. Barr took it upon himself to defend the Empire.

The death of his son while serving with the Canadian army in
South Africa gave Barr a more personal reason for his renewed interest in things imperial. He organized the British America Club. In
1901, when Queen Victoria died, he delivered an eloquent public trib-
ute to her memory. Late that year he made plans to leave for Britain,
where he would, he said, arrange for a considerable number of Canadians resident in Whatcom County "to take up pastoral pursuits in
South Africa."

Somewhere between Washington and Great Britain, the project
dissolved. Within weeks of arriving in London in January 1902, Isaac
Barr had a new plan. Armed with several impressive letters of recom-
mendation, he launched a written assault on Mr. W. J. White, an official of the Department of Immigration for the Dominion of Canada.

Barr requested that White give him a job promoting American immigration to Canada. In a letter dated February 1902, the cleric presented himself in this fashion.

> I have further had some successful experience in locating
> people on land and have for years taken a deep interest in
> immigration and colonizing. Since my son's death in the
> cause of the Empire, I have had a strong desire to take up
> my abode again under the old flag which I love so well and
> spend the remainder of my years promoting the good of
> the Empire.

Two weeks later, Barr wrote again to White. Now he was suggesting not that he live "under the old flag" but that he return to Washington State and work for bare expenses until the job merited a salary. Although he did not think that being a clergyman would lessen his effectiveness, he was prepared to abandon his clerical clothing if necessary. This must have seemed peculiar to Mr. White. Barr had said in his first letter that he had just received a licence from the Archbishop of Canterbury to preach in England and was about to do deputation work with the Colonial and Continental Church Society (cccs).

The cccs was the most rigorously evangelical of the several missionary arms of the Church of England. The society had just hired another clergyman with an interest in immigration and much more recent Canadian experience. Though the Reverend George Exton Lloyd was a native Londoner, he had received his theological training in Canada and had been ordained as an Anglican minister there. This tall, spare man had an impressive record as an educator and missionary, and it was only a serious lung ailment that had cut short his Canadian career and brought him back, after convalescing for two years, to work in London.

Like Barr, Lloyd had spent a brief time on the Canadian prairies as a young man, but his exploits were far more glorious than Barr's. Interrupting his studies, he had joined the University of Toronto company of the Queen's Own Rifles when they were sent to the Northwest Territories in 1885 to quell the second Riel rebellion. During the Battle of Cut Knife Hill, he was shot in the back while trying to save two men who had been left behind. The dramatic account of the attempted rescue—the doctor probing for the round lead bullet with no anaesthetic to ease the pain, the seventy-mile ride to the hospital tent on a springless cart, being left for dead outside and a friend's insistence that he was still alive—was the stuff of legend. Here was a genuine hero who now set out to spread the word all over the British Isles about the opportunities available on the Canadian prairies.

Lloyd's official responsibility was to arrange for the ministrations of the Church of England to be available to colonists in their new homes. As he spoke to large gatherings of prospective emigrants, he often was asked questions about Canada, and for this reason he decided to write what became a fateful letter to the editor of the *London Times*.

The heading in the September 22, 1902, edition was innocuous enough. It read, "The Canadian Wheat Belt." But Lloyd's words were compelling as he revealed his strong conviction that the Canadian prairies must be filled with people of British stock.

> Millions of acres of the finest agricultural land in the world are being offered by the Canadian government (160 acres a head free) to all *bona fide* settlers and yet English people are looking on while Americans (who generally know a good thing when they see it) are rushing over the border by thousands to seize the opportunity and, of course, the future reward.

He offered to do what he could to help people form themselves into groups for the purposes of emigrating. "Why not make up parties of, say, 100 each and go out and settle in townships in company together? Why not a large party for next March?" he suggested.

Newspapers from all over the British Isles reprinted Lloyd's letter. It was read by thousands of interested people, including Isaac Barr, who was finishing a six-month appointment as Curate in Charge of St. Saviour's Church in a suburb of London. He had not been devoting himself full time to his parishioners, however. Since the Canadian government had rebuffed him, he had been swept up in the great surge of patriotism occasioned by the coronation of Edward VII.

The king, who had spent his long apprenticeship as the Prince of Wales developing a reputation as a lovable rogue, was finally to be crowned. The people of Great Britain were in dire need of something to celebrate. The economy was precarious, and processions of unemployed ex-soldiers could be seen on the streets. The delirious atmosphere created in London by the forthcoming coronation was enough to make the most reluctant patriot celebrate, and Isaac Barr was by no means reluctant.

Canada was full of patriots as well, but in the senior dominion of King Edward's Empire, imperialism was a controversial topic. Prime Minister Laurier's decision to send Canadian troops to South Africa had not been universally popular. But there was more agreement on the need for increased immigration, and Laurier gave it top priority by appointing Clifford Sifton minister of the interior, a ministry that included the Department of Immigration. When the Liberals assumed power in 1896 after almost two decades of Conservative rule, they found the Department of Immigration moribund. It was obvious to Sifton that new blood was needed. New employees must work hard to keep their jobs. Immigration must increase. The organized Northwest Territories—Saskatchewan, Assiniboia, Alberta and Athabasca—must be filled with farmers.

But not just any farmers. Sifton had very strong ideas about the suitability of various nationalities. Even though many American farmers were experienced in the conditions they would meet on the Canadian prairies, they might encourage their government's imperialistic interest in the Canadian West. Farmers from eastern Europe had demonstrated their ability to work hard and live frugally, but they were "foreign." They did not speak English nor did they understand British ways. A Slavic majority, some of whom were "Catholic," seemed even more threatening than American annexation to many Canadians of British origin, especially those in Ontario.

But Sifton wanted farmers. He judged Blacks, southern Europeans, Jews and Orientals to be poor agriculturalists by their very ethnic origin. If allowed to emigrate, they would settle in the cities where their presence would add to Canada's growing urban problems. And to his list of undesirable groups he added one other—the English city dweller.

The ideal immigrant, according to Sifton's criteria, would have been a farmer from Scotland or the north of England. The call went out for "men of good muscle who were willing to hustle" through specially edited publications sent to every agriculturalist in Great Britain. Local agents were appointed on a commission basis in every city and town throughout the agricultural districts. But few British farmers came forward.

Settling for second best, Sifton decreed that Americans were to be encouraged because of their experience in farming, but the campaign must be continued in Britain. Because the Canadian high commissioner, Lord Strathcona, was disinterested in the promotion of settlement, Sifton established separate offices in London and placed Mr. W. T. R. Preston in charge as commissioner of immigration.

And so it was to Preston that Isaac Barr wrote on August 5, 1902, amid the imperial hysteria of the coronation, to propose that he gather together twenty-five families who were familiar with agriculture and help them emigrate. They would establish the core of a British colony on the Canadian prairies that would attract many more of those most desirable of all immigrants. Barr had written to the press outlining his plan and received inquiries as a result, he said. Having dangled this carrot before Preston, Barr got straight to the practical considerations. Because he would have to devote his full time to the organization and since he did not have private means, he requested that Preston arrange for Barr's activities to be conducted under the supervision of Preston's office while (if Preston considered it wise) appearing to be independent of it. Barr graciously announced that he was prepared to accept a very moderate salary. If Preston could assign him desk room in his offices, so much the better.

Here was a man offering to provide just the kind of immigrant that the department desired, but almost nothing was known about him. Preston showed the letter to his assistant, Mr. C. F. Just, who said that he knew only what Barr himself had told him, but that Barr seemed to be a masterful kind of a man with experience of settlement in the United States.

The fact that Barr was a Church of England clergyman was a point in his favour as well. These men enjoyed great influence in turn-of-the-century England. Because public schools employed many of them as masters, most of the future leaders of the country had been instructed by Anglican priests. It was Church of England missionaries who had spread the word about God and the Empire into Asia and Africa. The Empire felt truly indebted to these men and showed them great respect.

Barr's earlier letters to W. J. White illustrated how pragmatic he was about his clerical status. When it was useful to his cause to be a clergyman he mentioned it, when it was not he did not. In a letter to Preston, he speculated on the publicity value of his resignation from St. Saviour's. "The announcement in the papers that I had given up my clerical work to further the Colonization movement could attract attention." Over the course of the next few months he used the prefix "Reverend" less and less, and he had dropped it entirely by the following summer. His clerical collar suffered a similar fate.

Much more important to Barr than his Church of England affiliation was his sense of being "British." His choice of the slogan "Canada for the British" showed that he knew his audience well. On several occasions, both in the press and later in his pamphlets, he reassured potential colonists that their Britishness would be inviolate. No European immigrants would be allowed passage on the special steamer that would transport the colonists. Experienced farmers would be asked to join them in Canada, but "these farmers . . . shall be of British descent."

Many people thought Barr was doing the right thing. A group of industrialists told him he would be "rendering an imperial service, helping to bind Canada more closely to the Empire." An article in the *Belfast Evening Telegraph* said, "Blood is thicker than water, and the present great loyalty of the Dominion to the mother country would be augmented by the advent on a large scale of fellow British subjects." And it was their common interest in British emigration that would bring Barr and Lloyd together and make them allies in their insistence that the Canadian government grant them an exclusive reservation where only British people could homestead. It was, Lloyd would say, "the foundation of their whole scheme."

But Barr's meeting with Lloyd was still a month away when the Canadian government found itself, almost by accident, supporting Barr's plan. When Commissioner Preston agreed to pay for the production of a pamphlet that Barr had written, he inadvertently legitimized the movement. Barr's subsequent letters to the press said that the Canadian government favoured the plan and that officials of the "Canadian Emigration [sic] Department will lend most willing help." In a letter dated August 23, he encouraged applicants to pay their money as a show of good faith to the Canadian Commissioner of Emigration [sic]. All this had been done without Preston's permission, but to anyone reading the newspapers, the Canadian government appeared to be endorsing Barr's scheme.

In the last weeks of August 1902, Barr's pamphlet, entitled *British Settlements in North Western Canada in Free Grant Lands*, was ready to send to all interested parties. In words that seemed to have flowed out of his pen unchallenged and unedited, it described in detail Barr's colonization dream. It was directed to "people of the right kind—English, Scotch and Irish," and it promised free land in Canada, 160 acres of it, for only the payment of the ten-dollar homestead fee.

The main body of the pamphlet went into minute detail regarding the time of departure, the amount of luggage to be allowed, what to take in the way of household effects and clothing, the types of accommodation available on board ship and on the Canadian train, and advice on ploughing, planting, and building a house and stable. It was these details that appealed most to his readers. Here was a man who knew everything they needed to know. He could make it easier for them and safer. Barr was not sure where the colony would be yet, but this seemed not to disturb any of the hundreds who replied. Since most of them had only a vague idea of Canadian geography anyway, they were content to wait for the precise location to be revealed.

Barr summed up the general advantages of his wonderful scheme as follows:

Good climate, conducive to vigorous health, notwithstanding the occasional extremes of heat and cold; fertile soil suitable for ranching and mixed farming; an abundant rainfall, with good water everywhere easily obtained; some timber for building, fencing and fuel; excellent hay and pasturage; railway facilities either provided or certain in the near future; good markets for all a farmer can produce; a school system that cannot be surpassed; perfect religious freedom; and the British law and order which all know and love so well in their native land.

The source of Barr's information about the prairie west is unknown, but there was plenty available, much of it excessively optimistic and even dangerously misleading. Some of his promises were true. The climate was conducive to vigorous health; there certainly were extremes of heat and cold; the soil was fertile in most places; there was some timber for fuel and fencing, and the pasturage was indeed excellent. But how Barr knew this for sure is open to question. When he made his choice of land in the ensuing months, its location would make mockery of his promises of railway facilities, markets and a school system. The Barr colonists would have to wait through several hard years in their remote location for these promises to be kept.

The date of embarkation was set for mid-March 1903. The mode of travel was to be a steamship to Saint John, New Brunswick, a train to Saskatoon, and a two-hundred-mile wagon journey to the north and west. The time of sailing would be set so that the colonists would reach their destination "when warm spring weather has set in, permitting life in tents by women and children without the slightest inconvenience or danger, and, indeed, with only pleasureable experiences."

While Preston and Just speculated on Barr's ability to engineer the scheme, Barr launched a barrage of speeches and advertisements. By August 30, 1902, Mr. Just observed to his superior,

Mr. Barr evidently intends to work pretty hard for his scheme, and I suppose you will make enquiries about him as I have suggested as no doubt we would like to help him if he is all right. He is a Canadian Church of England clergyman and quite a hustler.

Although the term "hustler" had a less negative connotation in

1902 than it does today, Barr had indeed hustled the commissioner's office into providing much more support and legitimacy than they had intended. Any effort on the part of the Canadian government to investigate Barr's credentials was swept aside in the sheer speed and energy of Barr's commitment to his wonderful idea. In the following months, Barr's letterhead would bear the words "(Under the sanction of the Canadian Government)," and even by early September 1902 things had gone too far for anyone to dispute it.

The response to his advertisements and speeches was overwhelming. By September 6, fifty people had decided to go; by September 8, two hundred inquiries had been received. And by September 22, when Lloyd's letter appeared in the *Times*, Barr had received so many replies that he was planning to leave immediately to reconnoitre the Canadian prairies.

One of Barr's many letters to the editor appeared on September 22 as well—this one in the *Belfast Evening Telegraph*. Like other national groups emigrating, he wrote, Anglo-Saxons must go in groups and create separate settlements. "British people flourish most vigourously, feel most at home, and are happier when surrounded by their own countrymen in the overseas colonies." His movement, he went on, would organize the first really homogeneous British settlement in the West.

With ambitions so similar, it is hard to believe that Barr and Lloyd were unaware of each other's existence. Not only were the two men interested in the same sort of emigration scheme, but they were employed by the same agency of the Church of England. Nonetheless, when Barr requested an interview with Lloyd after reading his letter, Lloyd professed great surprise.

In the last days of September, George Lloyd and Isaac Barr came face to face for the first time. Barr was fifty-five years old, short and thick-set. The tall, lithe Lloyd was fourteen years his junior. And although the two men shared a common vision, their methods and personalities were very different. No record exists of their meeting beyond what Lloyd would recount almost forty years later, but by the time it ended, Barr had explained his scheme and Lloyd had agreed to give him the names of all the people who had written to him.

Unlike the commissioner's office, Lloyd had made a real attempt to check Barr's credentials. He had asked his superior, Canon Hurst, if he knew of Barr. As it happened, Barr had served with Hurst as a summer student in Windsor, Ontario, thirty years before. As far as Hurst could remember, "everything was satisfactory." Lloyd also knew that the Archbishop of Canterbury would have checked with the bishop of Barr's former parish before granting him a licence to preach in England. In checking further, Lloyd found that the Bishop of Spokane had described Barr ambiguously as "a clergyman of unusual ability and power."

Although the bishop may have been hedging when he used the term "unusual," Isaac Barr was certainly a powerful preacher. But his oratorical abilities could lead him astray, as his biographer Helen Evans Reid later asserted. "As the words flowed forth with thundering conviction he too would be carried away by his own persuasiveness until sometimes the mere telling appeared to make it so."

Between the two vague endorsements from Canon Hurst and the Bishop of Spokane were thirty years of Barr's life, at least the first thirteen of which were controversial. He left his post in Prince Albert shortly after arriving there because he was worried about his family and was "unable to sustain the burden of his remote station." Subsequent postings were terminated due to his unorthodoxy, his quarrels with congregations over money and finally his preaching of the theory of evolution at a time when it was heresy even to mention it. Had the archbishop contacted the Bishop of Huron, Barr's superior for much of this time, he would have received a much different report on Barr's suitability for the ministry.

But Lloyd's inquiry into Barr's credentials had produced nothing untoward, and so he agreed to give Barr his list of potential emigrants. The response to Lloyd's letter had been overwhelming. His small sitting room in the London suburb of Wood Green was overflowing with letters. Taking three days off work, he opened every one and noted the questions asked. He determined that there were forty-two questions that required answers and arranged for them to be printed in the form of a circular letter. The printer agreed to provide the letter at cost because it was for patriotic purposes; Lloyd's wife, Marion, and one of his daughters stuffed envelopes and saw to the mailing.

The circular informed the reader that Lloyd was neither an emigration agent nor a government official but the secretary for a church society. He did, however, wish to draw their attention to a "very good scheme" being organized by a curate. Lloyd said he had gone into the plan carefully in consultation with Canadian government officials. "I am satisfied it is the very thing that I want to see carried out," he wrote.

Another ally had been added to Barr's cause, another ally who was swept up in the promise of the scheme and failed to see its weaknesses. The government and Lloyd, both interested in encouraging immigration of the right sort of people, lent credence to the scheme that so recently had existed only in Barr's mind. Later, Lloyd would say that he considered his part in the affair finished when he mailed out his circular letter, but that he checked in on Barr whenever he had an opportunity and "sometimes suggested changes." In truth, from the first day he and Barr met, he allowed himself to be drawn into the scheme more and more deeply.

Lloyd's letter had struck a chord with a particular group of prospective emigrants. These were people dissatisfied with their lives in Britain but unprepared to face the challenge of emigration on their own. They were the same sort of people who were responding to Isaac Barr's letters in the press.

Barr assured the Canadian government that most of the potential colonists were experienced in farming. In his enthusiastic reports to Mr. Just, he described his correspondents as

> generally men of sufficient means to give them a good start [and] a large percentage are either practical farmers or else sons of farmers. Nearly all those living in cities or towns spent some years of their lives on farms and desire to return to farm life.

The government wanted to believe that this was true, and so they accepted Barr's word. It may have been that the first people to respond were mostly agricultural workers, but when the final list was assembled, the proportion of people experienced in farm work came to about 20 per cent, including gardeners and milkmen. The success of the proposed colony was dependent on many things, but farming experience was crucial, and when all was said and done, most of the Barr colonists had no farming experience at all.

In the following year, when the near failure of the scheme caused months of recrimination and re-examination, many bureaucrats looked back at the summer and fall of 1902 and wondered how events had come about. The efficient and well-organized Department of Immigration had got itself involved with an unknown Anglican priest in a scheme to establish two thousand people, most of whom had no farming experience, in an isolated section of the Northwest Territories, and no one could remember how it had happened. No one in government had tried to find out who this man Barr was, and no one had challenged Barr on the practicality of his plans. When Sifton was examined by the Opposition in the House of Commons the following summer, he would say that the department would have preferred to deal directly with the settlers but that they preferred to have Barr as their intermediary. Sifton could only say that the presence of his deputy minister in London in the fall of 1902 had inadvertently sealed the bargain.

Deputy Minister of the Interior James Allen Smart was an experienced politican, a political crony of Sifton's and a fellow Manitoban. Some even called him Sifton's alter ego. His September visit to London and his decision to co-operate with Barr rather than risk losing the potential immigrants made it possible for Barr to convert a vague and untested scheme into reality. Smart took over from Preston in the departmental dealings with Barr. The only knowledge that anyone in the department had of Barr, his past, his abilities and his honesty, was from Barr himself and from the confidence of hundreds of people who knew nothing of him either.

On October 1, 1902, Barr's engagement at St. Saviour's Church ended. The parishioners can hardly have noticed his going, so little time had he devoted to pastoral matters. By the time his leavetaking was officially announced, he had already sailed for Canada.

He was off on his mission, his fare paid by the Canadian Pacific Railway (CPR) and the Elder Dempster shipping line, both of which stood to benefit from a large colonization plan. He would talk to officials in Ottawa, view the proposed settlement area and, in the words of his pamphlet, "select land for the first British Settlement." The phrase had such an established ring to it. It sounded orderly; it sounded controlled; it sounded as though the settlement was already there waiting for the British to claim it.

Great and Multifarious Schemes

ON OCTOBER 16, 1902, STANLEY RACKHAM BROKE HIS FAST WITH ROLLS, BUTTER and French chocolate. He left the Lisieux Hotel on Rue de la Savonnerie in Rouen and walked three blocks to the cathedral to observe the Butter Tower and climb the new central spire. There were, he observed in his diary, no other English people present, but a good number of French—nearly all gentlemen.

Stanley was a gentleman, an English gentleman, but he was a gentleman without a job. This holiday in France was a respite from months of anxious waiting as he attempted, so far unsuccessfully, to find a niche for himself within the British Board of Agriculture. Surely a man from a distinguished family, a man with a degree in agriculture from Cambridge, a man who had lived abroad in Canada, surely such a man could find a position for himself in his homeland. He had passed the time earlier that fall visiting friends, taking constitutional walks and catching glimpses of the king and queen in military processions or at St. Paul's Cathedral.

On a trip to his alma mater to see an "amusing play," he took tea at Christ's College, where someone suggested he try for a post in Nigeria. As soon as a doctor had pronounced him fit, Stanley embarked on a flurry of visits to the Colonial Office, the London School of Tropical Medicine and a museum exhibiting a special display of malarial mosquitoes and West Indies eruptions. Stanley's parents were against "this Northern Nigeria business," but he was twenty-five years old and ready to be of some use. He applied for the post.

Dressed in top hat and tails, Stanley Rackham attended the Colonial Office for an interview. He came away discouraged. Most of the applicants were veterans of the recently concluded South African war and would undoubtedly be considered more desirable candidates for Nigeria.

E. J. (Jim) Ashton was a veteran of the war in South Africa who had entertained thoughts of returning there to work for the Bechuanaland police, but he thought the prospects in South Africa were poor for a "white man with little cash in a country where there was an abundance of native labour." Besides, he had promised his father he would return to England when the army was through with him. By October of 1902, he had been home for three months and, aside from some vague talk about going to Canada with an army friend, had little idea what to do with the rest of his life.

He had sailed from England in January of 1901, an inadequately trained recruit in the Sherwood Rangers Yeomanry. His motives were less than illustrious. Joining up had been "at least as much owing to dissatisfaction with life as a bank clerk, as from patriotic motives."

Although he had completed his education at the age of sixteen, his academic record was spotty. A last-minute burst of zeal had earned him top marks but had not guaranteed him an illustrious career. Instead, he found himself employed, somewhat reluctantly, as a bank clerk in the Stamford Spalding and Boston Bank in Boston, Lincolnshire.

As an elderly man looking back, Jim Ashton would say, "Outside interests appealed to me more than banking and though perforce doing a fair day's work, I was not a star member of the staff." Outside interests he pursued with a vengeance. "Gentlemanly pursuits" like regatta club dinners and tennis played on private lawns were balanced with deep-sea fishing weekends well supplied with beer and gin. But always he remained aware of how limited were his means. His choice of reading material—Adam Smith, Darwin and Huxley—showed his reflective side.

Though rowing and cycling kept him fit, his looks were somewhat marred by a crooked nose, the result of an incident in the boxing ring. A crooked nose can be interesting on a man, but it did not improve his chances of an advantageous marriage. Socially minded mothers regarded bank clerks as "more or less detrimentals," owing to their small salaries. But this well-read, athletic young man would likely have gone on to find himself a wife had not he locked the second cashier in the bank vault following an altercation. The second cashier happened to be the nephew of the chairman of the board, and Ashton began to think that a career change might be wise. Since the Boers were causing some trouble in South Africa, the logical choice was to become a soldier.

Ashton's father did not approve. British policy in South Africa was wrong, according to the older man, and the colonial secretary was too aggressive. But Ashton's father may have seen that the boy would become a man fighting the Boers. On the night before Ashton sailed, his father brought him a gift, a Mauser pistol, which combined in its cold steel a father's concern and a father's blessing.

Eighteen months in South Africa transformed a callow lad into an experienced fighting man. He learned to live in the open and survive on a monotonous diet. He became seasoned by months of hard riding and by the ever-present danger from the elusive Boers, who had adopted guerilla tactics in this last year of the war. And he found out that he had been taught a rather narrow view of the world.

> History as taught in England at that time helped to give the boys the idea that they were members of a definitely superior race. . . . Our history books emphasized English victories. . . . As a result we formed a vague idea that an Englishman was the equal of about a couple of Frenchmen, or a similar number of Yankees . . . and could take on an even larger number of almost any other nation with a fair chance of success.

Besides an altered world view, Ashton returned from South Africa with a grudging admiration for the Boer farmer. Here was a man whose ownership of a large expanse of land gave him dignity and an air of authority. It spawned in Ashton an interest in farming, an interest he shared with his new friend, a Scot named Alex Nicol whose parents farmed in the Midlands. The two men spent the fortnight-long voyage home making vague plans to farm somewhere in the Empire.

In another part of that empire, Isaac Barr was meeting with the Canadian deputy minister of the interior, James Smart. Barr was anxious to set out for the prairies, and the two men agreed to meet again upon his return, when he would have more detailed knowledge of his plans.

Full of excitement, Barr boarded the train for the Promised Land. He travelled through bustling Winnipeg and upstart Regina and, leaving the main line of the CPR, proceeded by branch line to the failed temperance colony of Saskatoon. The regular stagecoach to Battleford took him along an old wagon trail used mostly by Metis men who worked as freighters; the trail led north and west through prairie still furrowed by the tracks of buffalo and strewn with their bones, through gullies and over rudimentary bridges. On his return to Britain, he would describe the road as "excellent, all streams bridged and bad spots turnpiked and graded." In truth, the road consisted of a path for single horses bracketed by two paths for wagon wheels, reasonably passable in dry weather or when the ground was frozen solid and the bridges in repair, but an entirely different matter during the spring melt and runoff.

By prairie standards, Battleford was a venerable little town. Its population was made up of Indians, Metis, cowboys and retired mounted police. Founded at a crucial crossroads of the fur trade, it had become an important Northwest Mounted Police (NWMP) post and had received national attention during the Riel Rebellion of 1885. It had been the capital of the Northwest Territories until Regina, an instant town created by the CPR, usurped its position in 1882. Although shifting patterns of commerce had played havoc with the economy of Battleford on several occasions in the past, the advance of settlement seemed to foretell renewed prosperity. With no other supply point between it and Edmonton 225 miles farther west, Battleford stood at the leading edge of the huge wave of immigration that was sweeping through the territories. That and the promised new railroad, which even now was being surveyed, augured well for the town's future.

Between Battleford and Edmonton lay an almost empty land. The occasional trapper, a few Indians and Metis, the odd American or Canadian homesteader, these were the only people who chose to live in such isolation. Soon, the boosters said, the new railroad would change all that, and Isaac Barr knew that they spoke the truth. No less a personage than the third vice-president of the Canadian Northern Railway (CNR) had assured Barr that a line would be built to Edmonton by 1903.

Barr was received enthusiastically in Battleford, in particular by the local Anglican clergyman, the Reverend Julius Foster Dyke Parker, who came away from having met Barr with several misleading impressions. The proposed colony would, Parker reported, be nondenominational, have a large proportion of farmers among its members and be delighted to include Canadians and Americans. Barr was especially misleading in his comments about Canadians and Americans. Until the Department of Immigration insisted later that he allow room for experienced settlers, Barr was determined that pushy Yankees and crude Canadians would not mar the purity of his British colony despite their experience as settlers. Barr recognized an ally in Parker and kept him informed of his activities even after he returned to Britain.

The crusty editor of Battleford's local paper was a harder man to woo. Patrick Gammie Laurie had made the *Saskatchewan Herald* a success by being nobody's fool. While he reported Barr's comings and goings with the lack of accuracy usual in small, poorly funded operations, he was gathering ammunition that he would use in the spring to launch an attack—an attack against Barr in particular and all perpetrators of group settlement schemes in general. "Big reservations have been the curse of this country," he would write, "and now that the country has become known and is attracting settlers on its merits it is time to give them a chance by leaving the land open to the first comer."

Barr did not stay long in Battleford. James Smart had recommended some land to the west, and everyone Barr talked to agreed that he should see it. In the company of a land guide and an American farmer named Owen, he followed the railway survey stakes in a westward direction through the triangle of almost empty land that began at Battleford and fanned out between the Battle and North Saskatchewan rivers to the Fourth Meridian.

The Fourth Meridian was a line of longitude, 110° west, established in 1878 as part of the square mile survey, a system new to Canadians when it was proposed in 1869 and modified to coordinate with the American survey. It was a good system. It mapped road allowances and laid the prairies out in townships six miles square, each divided into thirty-six sections. The survey was accurate and provided heretofore unknown information about the vegetation and soil in each area, including the revelation that the amount of arable land was much larger than expected.

But accurate and informative though the survey was, it had suffered the ravages of time. Most of the wooden posts that marked the corners of the sections and quarter sections had disappeared. Cracked by summer sun, bleached by winter frosts, charred by prairie fires in the twenty years since they had been driven into the ground, they had fallen over and rotted in the damp grass. Only the iron posts remained, marking the six-mile intervals between the corners of townships.

The deterioration of the survey did not diminish Barr's excitement. He had found his "promised land," his "far-flung, fenceless prairie," to quote Kipling as he did on occasion. His description of what he and Mr. Owen saw as they examined it in detail may have been enhanced by his enthusiasm.

> We went most carefully over the townships, digging into the soil at many points, investigating the water and fuel supply, and we both concluded that the reality far surpassed the most glowing descriptions we had had of the country. We found scarcely any variation in the character of the soil and no waste land. As Mr. Owen said, 'One could sit down blindfolded anywhere, and decide to homestead and he would make no mistake.'

The soil *was* generally good—the surveyors had discovered that twenty years before—but the quality of the land was not as uniform as Mr. Owen speculated. Nor was there a good supply of water. The sloughs and streams of the fall and spring dried up in the summer. Barr's promised fuel supply consisted of crowded clumps of small, gnarled poplar trees that dotted the rolling prairie here and there. Barr wasn't worried, however. When all the trees had been used, he was sure there would be coal available from outcrops along the banks of streams just as there were farther west at Edmonton.

The weather was wonderful. When Barr returned to Britain he would write:

> There are but few cloudy days; the sky is generally wonderfully clear, and the effect of this upon the spirits is most enlivening and stimulating. Every stranger travelling through the country notices the cheerful mien and wonderful alertness of the people. . . . Old residents will tell you it is largely due to the climate.

How unfortunate for the colonists that Barr happened to see the Promised Land during that period known on the prairies as "Indian summer," when day after day of sunshine makes it possible to believe that winter will never come.

Barr claimed to know this land intimately from his sojourn on the prairies in 1875, but it is doubtful that he had spent time this far west. He had been posted by the church to Prince Albert but had been there only a few weeks when the illness of his wife and child, whom he had left behind in Ontario, caused him to leave his position. Yet in the ensuing years he would refer often to his familiarity with the area. He informed Commissioner Preston that he knew the country very well from Prince Albert to Fort Pitt, a former Hudson's Bay Company (HBC) fort due north of colony site. In 1903 he would tell a reporter for the *Manitoba Free Press* that he had hunted buffalo over the lands he had chosen for the colony and been deeply impressed with Saskatchewan soil and climate.

All this seems very unlikely. If, during the few weeks he was stationed in Prince Albert, Barr did manage to fit in a buffalo hunt in an area 175 miles to the west, there was no one else who could confirm it. And even if he had seen the area, it would have been in autumn. Any knowledge he had of the winter, spring and summer was not based on personal experience.

After leaving the Promised Land, Barr pressed on to Edmonton. The former fur trading post was poised on the edge of a boom occasioned by the completion that year of a bridge over the North Saskatchewan River that connected Edmonton to Strathcona, the terminus of a CPR branch line from Calgary. Now Edmonton could receive supplies via the CPR and send them by barge down the North Saskatchewan River to the very area Barr had chosen for his settlement.

Barr arrived in Edmonton on November 10 in the company of his brother Jack, a horse trader with a reputation for driving a hard bargain. In contrast to his stocky Anglophile brother, Jack was slim and hard and spoke like an American. Inexperienced colonists were no match for wily Jack Barr.

Isaac Barr met with several suppliers, then retraced his steps through Battleford, Saskatoon and Regina to arrive in Ottawa around the middle of November. He presented his case to Smart for a reservation at the Fourth Meridian on the proposed CNR line.

Smart had received some interesting correspondence in Barr's absence. The first letter was from Mr. T. G. Pearce, a resident of the small Alberta town of Agricola. Besides farming on an extensive scale, Pearce had a reputation as an organizer of colonies, based primarily on his experience ten years before of leading a migration of settlers from

Parry Sound, Ontario, to Alberta. He and his settlers had endured many hardships on their journey. Wishing to let others benefit from these experiences, the commissioner of immigration in London had asked Pearce to correspond with prospective immigrants, and it was through some of them that Pearce heard of Isaac Barr's plans.

In great alarm, he wrote to Deputy Minister of the Interior James Smart on October 27, 1902, to say that "the intentions of this gentleman [Barr] betray inexperience in matters relating to life in Alberta." Not only would this be dangerous for the colonists Barr would be leading, but the results "would be disastrous to future immigration." What most alarmed Pearce was Barr's plan to have his colonists arrive on the prairies so early in the spring. Pearce had made the same mistake in 1892, and his charges had spent a stormy, wet week under canvas, developing influenza and lung ailments as a result. Pearce insisted that Smart put him in contact with Barr.

Smart had also heard from the Reverend George Exton Lloyd. While Barr was wooing Canadian bureaucrats and rhapsodizing over perfect climate and fertile soil, Lloyd was very involved in maintaining the London end of the operation. In memoirs written in the last year of his life, Lloyd would say that he had "washed his hands of the whole thing," but time and circumstance had distorted his recollections. Lloyd was receiving fifty letters a day from prospective colonists and harassing Commissioner Preston regarding the establishment of an exclusive reservation.

On November 14, just before Barr was due to arrive back in Ottawa from the West, Lloyd wrote to Smart to tell the deputy minister that the ten townships proposed for the new colony would not be enough. Lloyd already had the names of five hundred interested emigrants. Smart replied that nothing would be decided until Barr met again with immigration officials in Ottawa. Lloyd was "very much crestfallen." In his letters back to London, Barr had given Lloyd the impression that the reservation was a foregone conclusion.

But Barr had returned to Ottawa with his persuasive powers at their height. Smith was apprehensive, but he had to admit that Barr's scheme was attracting more settlers than the deputy minister had dreamed possible. Barr said they were mostly farmers, and Smart knew they were all British. Barr's enthusiasm for his scheme and for the land that he had just seen was impossible for the deputy minister to resist.

By November 25, Smart had agreed to reserve sixteen townships until February 15, 1903. By that date Barr was to have collected a ten-dollar homestead fee from each of the people applying for land and forwarded a list of their names to the immigration office in London, which would record the homestead entries. If there were not enough names, a corresponding portion of the lands would be removed from the reservation. The remaining land would be held for persons entered until April 15. Barr was cautioned that he must levy no extra charges beyond the homestead fee. He agreed to the conditions.

Smart informed Barr of T. G. Pearce's concerns about the colony, and accordingly Barr wrote the man a long letter full of his plans, asking for advice and criticism. The contents of the letter alarmed Pearce further. When he next wrote to Smart in early December, he said,

> I am inclined to think that my criticism would not be acceptable to him. I also find statements which would lead me to the conclusion that he is not a practical man to undertake such a responsibility.

But Barr had wooed James Smart and won him over. He had laid out his scheme in his eloquent style, his enthusiasm and charm blinding Smart to more practical considerations. As the deputy minister said to Pearce in a letter written December 12,

> I have met Mr. Barr and formed a fairly good opinion of him, although I really had not much opportunity of looking into the class of work he had been doing. He is most enthusiastic and also very clever, and I am inclined to think that he probably stands a good chance of making a success of his work.

But Smart took Pearce's comments to heart when it came to Barr's timing of the colonists' arrival. In a letter written the same day to Preston, the commissioner of immigration in London, Smart said,

> I have been considering the question of Mr. Barr's colony, and I am a little afraid that in bringing these people out in March he would be making a mistake, as they might get a very bad impression of the country.

Preston, for his part, had been talking to W. J. White, the immigration official who had met Barr almost a year before. White had been watching the scheme develop with some alarm. He reminded his colleague that Barr was a man of considerable force and could exert influence through his rhetoric. It was White's opinion, however, that they need not worry because Barr's scheme would never come to fruition.

> On the whole Mr. Barr's propaganda ha[s] assumed such magnitude and the many schemes he has in connection with it are so great and multifarious, I'm afraid very little will come of it.

But Barr had left Canada more determined than ever that his plans would succeed. He had two and a half months to fill the reservation with people committed enough and trusting enough to send him ten dollars each for the free homesteads. Barr believed in the scheme. Lloyd believed in the scheme. Smart believed. Five hundred prospective colonists believed. He must now convince many more.

Sixteen townships encompassed 576 miles of free land. Even allowing for the alienated land in each township—the one and three-quarter sections for the HBC, the two sections to endow schools and the odd-numbered sections reserved to reward the railways—there was still a lot of free land reserved exclusively for the British. And Barr had plans for the railway land, too.

The setting aside of railway lands was an important element in Dominion government land policy, which sought to promote both railway building and permanent settlement in the huge land tract it acquired when the HBC surrendered Rupert's Land in 1870. The contract signed between the government and the CPR ten years later granted the railway, among other considerations, 25 million acres of that land.

Selling the land would help to finance the railway, and it would assist homesteaders by providing additional acreage for them to buy adjacent to their free quarter sections, thus increasing their chances of being successful farmers. Successful farmers would provide business for the CPR. In order to promote the prosperity of their future customers and, of course, give a greater financial return, the CPR specified that the grant must be on land "fairly fit for settlement."

Accordingly, the CPR sought out the arable land wherever it lay. One of those areas was between the North Saskatchewan and Battle rivers—Barr's Promised Land. The odd-numbered sections in each township of the colony reserve were CPR lands. Barr was anxious that his people be able to buy as much of this land as possible from the railway, and he just happened to be the agent for the CPR. He would urge the colonists to act quickly to prevent Americans and Canadians from buying in the colony reserve.

William Henry Holtby was a carpenter, and although he had no extra money to invest in railway lands, he had heard about the free lands available in Canada. His third wife, Agnes, had produced three sons, and it made a man think about what the future held for boys in England. Willie, as his family called him, went to a meeting near his home in Hull where a "Canadian salesman" told him, among other things, that the climate in Canada was very invigorating and that there was lots of fresh air. For a man who had lost two wives to tuberculosis, fresh air had special appeal.

Willie's brother Robert was a commercial traveller living in nearby Leeds, and Willie knew that he would be interested in fresh air too. Both Robert and his son Oliver suffered from asthma, and both had recently been ill. Oliver had just returned to work and his father was still convalescing when Willie told them about Barr's scheme.

Years later, the descendants of the two brothers would be told that the family had emigrated because of Oliver's weak chest. Oliver painted dishes in the Coalport China Works, where the dust from grinding the pigments bothered his lungs. Because the doctor was afraid tuberculosis would develop, Oliver's chest became the family's official reason for leaving. It had a noble ring to it, but the real reasons were a little more complicated.

Robert Holtby had another son who was his namesake. Bob Holtby was a healthy specimen, and he regarded his father's concern about Oliver's chest with some cynicism. He knew that his father "wanted to get away from the worry and fuss of a commercial traveller's life." When the elder Holtby arrived home one night with a bundle of information about the Barr Colony, Bob could tell he was very interested.

Bob's mother, Kate, was not. She pointed out the disadvantages of leaving Leeds. There had been Holtbys in the north of England for hundreds of years; they had a very nice house that was completely paid for; their family and friends were close by; their eldest daughter, Kitty, had just found a job; their sons were established—Oliver in the china works, Bob in the same firm as his father. In another three years eighteen-year-old Bob would be eligible to become a travelling salesman, and he did not want to go to Canada either.

Kate was furious with her sister-in-law, Agnes, for supporting Willie's silly idea. Agnes was hardly the emigrating type, with her precious jewellery and her insistence on putting on airs. The woman was so rigid she would not even bend down to pick up her infant son's toys. Kate could not imagine how Agnes could think of encouraging Willie.

Kate's husband, Robert, could talk of nothing else. When wife and son voiced their misgivings, Robert "got wild and said we were trying to damp him and said it had always been the way, whenever he wanted to do anything his family were all against him." His perception of his family's attitude was probably accurate. It was not a happy household. The marriage had been a mistake—a classic case of marrying on the rebound. Robert never forgot that Kate had been in love with someone else until shortly before she agreed to marry him. When her first son was born, he had taunted her with accusations that the child, despite physical evidence to the contrary, was not his.

Kate had stuck with the marriage. That was what a woman did. The strained atmosphere that existed from the beginning was enhanced by the fact that both she and Robert were reserved people and did not show affection easily. Robert used the whip on his sons to discipline them. Dreamy, delicate Oliver fell into line quickly, but Bob was a "robust, bubbly soul." He stood up to his father and suffered the whip many times for his trouble.

Ironically, it was Bob whose change of heart sealed the family's fate. The more he heard about Barr's scheme, the more he came to like it. He finally decided it would be a good idea for all of them (or almost all—his diary makes no mention of how the move would benefit his mother). His father and Oliver would have improved health; each of the three men would be eligible for a quarter section of free land; his two younger sisters, Bessie, fifteen, and Dodie, nine, would be happy wherever the family was; and Kitty could stay in England and come out later if that was what she wanted. The decision was made. When the doctor was told of their plans, he said it would either kill Oliver or cure him. In his diary, Bob recorded that "the music started as it were [and there has been] scarcely a moments peace since then."

Kate remained very much opposed to emigrating, but she knew her duty and she reluctantly began to make ready. There were household goods to sell, boxes to pack, passages to book, tickets to buy. Plans were gone over with Willie and Agnes, whose son William, Jr., would remember vividly the long sessions in the kitchen–sitting room discussing the forthcoming adventure. The two families were bombarded with information from Barr and with requests for money. "Be sure to send your homestead fees immediately. Have you any money laid by? How much will you have in hand by March? Can you borrow a loan (if necessary) to help you start? Would you like to invest in the store syndicate? the Canadian Co-operative Home farm training plan? the Transport Syndicate? the Hospital Insurance plan? Railway lands will go fast, be sure and invest. Have you bought your steamship tickets yet? your train tickets? Do you wish to buy a tent before you leave, rubber ground sheets? army blankets? leather kit bags? folding lanterns? Send cash with order."

The date of departure was set for March 21, 1903. The Holtbys had three months to wind up their lives in England and be ready to start new ones. And there were hundreds more like them all over England, Ireland, Scotland and Wales who were doing exactly the same thing. One man was in control of this huge undertaking, and he had only a short period of time in which to plan the emigration of the "largest body composed entirely of British subjects which has ever left Britain for the Canadian Northwest."

Barr put out a second pamphlet in the final days of 1902. It overflowed with information presented with a large measure of early Edwardian hyperbole. His trip to Canada was described in detail; personages with illustrious-sounding names were introduced and quoted as saying that the land was a good choice. Over and over Barr returned to the theme that the West was filling up and soon there would be no free land left. "It is estimated that before the end of June, 1903, not a single homestead will be open through to Edmonton on both sides of the CPR for many a mile."

To the neophyte, the pamphlet seemed to be full of practical information, but an experienced hand would have seen that much was missing. No mention was made of the long winters, the late springs, the early frosts, the tormenting mosquitoes or the tenacious sloughs. But there were sins of commission, too. Barr gave the impression that preparations in Saskatchewan were already underway, when in reality there was but one advance man who was compiling a list of prices in Battleford. And his attempt to inject a little harsh reality into the pamphlet only fueled the heroic dreams of the would-be emigrants.

> I do not desire to present a picture that is highly rose-col-
> oured. There are difficulties and drawbacks to be encoun-
> tered, but for the brave man obstacles are something to be
> overcome, stepping stones to victory and success. Britons
> have ever been the great colonizers. Let it not be said that
> we are the degenerate sons of brave and masterful sires. . . .
> If you are afraid, stay at home—don't come to Canada. It is
> a land of brave and conquering men. But if you are honest
> and brave, and intend to work hard, if you propose to lead
> the temperate and strenuous life, then come and cast in
> your lot with us, and we will stand together and win.

This haphazard publication became a precious document to many of the colonists. One woman said her father quoted it as though it were sent down from God. Phrases from the pamphlet were repeated verbatim in the diaries and letters of the colonists. Even after the pamphlet and its author proved untrustworthy, many kept the thin six-by-nine-inch paper booklet as though it embodied in its few ragged pages the hope with which they had embarked on their great adventure.

Barr had been told by James Smart that he was to levy no charges beyond the ten-dollar homestead fee. But he needed money, a large amount of money, to finance this huge undertaking and to support himself while he organized it. Ever resourceful, Barr had several possibilities in mind, all of them a result of the efforts within the Ministry of Interior to encourage immigration.

One possibility lay in the fact that Canadian immigration agents in the United States were paid three dollars for every man, two dollars for every woman and one dollar for every child who actually settled in Canada. Perhaps that could be extended to cover British immigrants. Another possibility lay in the bonuses being paid to organizations sending settlers in groups. Or maybe there was something for Barr in the bonuses the department was offering to steamship agents to pro-mote Canada. He would have been wise to wait until some sort of funding had been secured. But this was not a scheme founded on wise action. If he or the department had paused to look at it carefully, there would never have been a Barr Colony.

Barr would continue to lobby for government bonuses until long after he had severed all connections with the colony. But as early as November 1902, at the same time Barr was in Ottawa coaxing Smart to grant the reservation of land, Smart informed Preston that Barr was not entitled to any government bonuses because he was not bringing out any domestics. Preston informed Barr of this early in January 1903. Barr wrote to Smart in great alarm.

> I have informed Mr. Preston that unless I am allowed to do so I shall be compelled to throw up the whole thing because a large amount of money, at least 20 or 30 thousand dollars will be necessary in order for me to outfit this party properly and to provide for it on arrival in Canada. . . . I beg to say here most emphatically that I am not 'on the make' in this matter.

The Elder Dempster steamship line and the CPR had paid for Barr's trip to Canada in the fall of 1902. In addition, he would receive a commission for every boat ticket bought by his colonists and for any railway lands he sold. Small wonder that he insisted that everyone sail on the same steamship line or that he promoted the sale of railway lands so heavily. These commissions were his only source of income.

No government money was forthcoming, so Barr looked for other ways to ensure a ready cash flow. He had recognized that some people would not be free to join his colony until later, and he offered to file for their homesteads in their absence. All they had to do was send a small fee. He knew that some of the younger men without capital would want to work elsewhere in Canada, thus delaying their arrival in the colony. He would file for their homesteads. All they had to do was send a small fee. Colonists who could not afford to buy a team of horses and a plough could arrange with Barr to have their land broken. All they had to do was send a small fee.

A medical practitioner from Wales wrote to say that he could not emigrate until August and asked Barr to enter for a homestead for himself and his brother. He also paid a deposit on 160 acres of CPR land. Barr agreed to further the doctor's interests in the colony in return for help with the hospital. In addition, the doctor was assured that his homestead would adjoin his railway land, that the railway land would be adjacent to where the town would be built and that his brother's homestead would be next to his. Barr promised to have a house erected on the railway land by the time the doctor's party arrived in late August. The man agreed to write later telling Barr approximately what preparations he would require for the arrival of

himself, his wife, his child and a maid. Barr promised that all this
would be done for him. All he had to do was send a small fee.

Barr also actively looked for new ways to make his colony function
well. That the syndicates would be the instruments of his undoing
would not have seemed possible in January 1903 when several men of
capital met in his office. The turnout was gratifying. Obviously these
men shared his enthusiasm. By February he could announce that the
British Canadian Settlement Stores Syndicate in the Saskatchewan
Valley, Northwestern Canada, had allotted all one hundred of its
founders shares at fifty pounds each and was offering ten thousand ordinary shares at one pound each. An advance party consisting of five
founding members would precede the main group to Canada and arrange for the setting up of a co-operative general store, a lumber yard
and a sawmill.

The Saskatoon and Saskatchewan Transport Company was formed
for the conveyance of goods, mail, express packages and passengers.
Two of the four founders were Barr and his brother Jack. Jack's reputation may have reached Britain, because the shares in this enterprise
did not sell well despite Barr's repeated reminders to his correspondents.

In the preparation of these syndicates, Barr was like a child invent-
ing an imaginary world. His pamphlets laid out his plans down to the
smallest detail. One scheme was so far-fetched that it existed only in
the detailed brochure. The title read, "The Canadian Co-operative
Home Farm No. 1; A Practical School for Training in Agriculture and
Stock Raising; Canada for the British." The detailed plan for a training facility was a tacit recognition that most of his colonists were un-
skilled in farming. The plans included such details as how big the
houses would be and whether single members would be allowed to
marry. It all sounded a little communistic, a concept that frightened
many and that Barr assured them was the furthest thing from his
mind.

His best idea was more practical, but it foundered on unsound eco-
nomics. The circular describing the Hospital Insurance scheme was issued in March just before embarkation and as such was probably a
last-minute idea. For the bargain price of one pound per person per
annum, a family would receive hospital care for all illnesses except
communicable ones and maternity, for which extra fees would be
charged. Doctors and nurses would accompany the colonists and set
up a field hospital at the site. The Department of Immigration liked

the idea and judged that sufficient preparations had been made solely on the existence of the four-page circular.

True to form, Barr concentrated his efforts on the minute trappings of the scheme. The tickets that were issued upon payment of the fee even named the mythical hospital. St. Luke's was to have Barr as its proprietor and the Reverend G. E. Lloyd, M.A., as its Visitor.

Upon his return to London, Barr had rented office space on Fleet Street at Number 14, Serjeant's Inn, the same building where George Lloyd worked for the CCCS at Number 9. Lloyd was very much in evidence at Number 14. The avalanche of letters addressed to him had continued, making it necessary for him to reassure his employer that in the matter of the colony he was acting on his own responsibility. Although he passed all correspondence on to Barr, he was surprised by the number of questions regarding religion and told the CCCS that money must be raised to provide a minister for the colony.

The society agreed to support a clergyman with Canadian experience for three years and, accordingly, advertisements to that effect were placed in the newspapers. Lloyd wrote another letter to the editor of the *Times* explaining that the chaplain, whoever he was, would need a large tent, a small harmonium and some immediate help towards building four wooden school churches for the 576-square-mile colony. "Are there any Englishmen at home who will give this colony a good send-off?" he asked.

None of those who responded to the advertisement for a clergyman had any experience in Canada, and in fact Lloyd was committed to filling the vacancy himself. Barr had announced in the Christmas pamphlet that Lloyd had been in charge while he was away and had finally decided to come with the party. Even earlier in the fall, when Barr had asked Lloyd to join him, Lloyd had said, "It is much more than probably [sic] . . . that I shall go with the party in March." And so, the colony that had been characterized in the pamphlets as "non-denominational" had a Church of England chaplain.

How reassuring this must have been to Belfast resident Isabel De Vere Hole Crossley, a widow with seven children and a great admirer of Church of England clergymen. Since her husband, a wealthy linen manufacturer, had died at the age of thirty-nine in an attempt to stop a runaway horse, she had been living in a state of genteel poverty. This necessitated a great deal of resourcefulness when it came to placing each of her seven children in a suitable career. Her third son,

Frederick Ivan, posed a special problem. When this tall, exuberant lad graduated from the Belfast Institute at the age of fourteen, he refused to continue on to university. Since he was not interested in banking, his mother sent him to live with his aunt and uncle, who owned a peach plantation near Jacksonville, Florida. In the four years since then the boy had reached manhood, learned about peach growing and contracted malaria. A doctor had advised returning to a colder climate.

In January 1903, Ivan Crossley was living at home. He was nineteen and restless. He talked about going to South Africa or Australia. When a cousin mentioned the colony that was being "put together by an English clergyman," Ivan's mother was delighted. She encouraged him to go to London and meet with Barr immediately.

The scene at the Fleet Street office of the British Colony for the Saskatchewan Valley was chaotic. Secretaries and assistants attempted to handle as many as one thousand letters a day; syndicate organizers lined up to talk to Barr; Lloyd made suggestions; steamship agents arrived with changes in plans; government clerks brought messages; advance men attempted to solidify arrangements; suppliers of blankets, tents, groundsheets and lanterns touted their wares. The number of employees increased until there were forty of them vying for desk space and Barr's attention.

In the vortex was Barr, adding to the chaos with yet another wonderful idea, fretting over changes in plans by outside agencies, exalting over the popularity of his scheme, answering each letter from prospective colonists with a personal reply, and at the end of the day stuffing money into his pockets to take home for safekeeping, until Lloyd suggested that the commissioner of immigration in London send a clerk each evening for the homestead fees. Throughout January Barr worked twenty hours a day, and he reported to Deputy Minister Smart that he was nearly overcome. The addition of more staff, in particular of a twenty-one-year-old woman named Christina Helberg, made his days less frantic. He even managed to find time to take Christina to dinner and the theatre in the evenings.

Prospective colonists were drawn to the Fleet Street office and the excitement it exuded. Alex Nicol and his army friend Jim Ashton met Lloyd there and were persuaded by him to change their plans from ranching in Calgary to farming with Barr. Stanley Rackham heard about the colony on February 4, went to the Fleet Street office on February 5 (where he met Bernard Smith, who would become his partner in the venture) and registered for free land on February 6.

From then on he was a frequent visitor. He was especially interested in the cinematograph, which was to be taken along to record the expedition in moving pictures.

Ivan Crossley went home to Belfast full of enthusiasm. His mother agreed to pay his passage and give him a little money to get started. Barr's pamphlet had said, "Young unmarried men may venture with but little over travelling expenses, as there will be plenty of work in the country at good wages." Could this really be true? Ivan wrote to Barr asking for confirmation. The reply did not come until March 16, but it was most reassuring.

> The more capital a man has the better but a young man like yourself should be able to succeed in the Colony on the principle of co-operation with others on a comparatively limited capital. As you have been in Florida and had experience there I should judge that any man who can successfully farm in Florida can do so in my colony.

Crossley signed on immediately. Another "farmer" was added to Barr's list.

CHAPTER III

Is Anyone in Charge?

IN THE TINY SETTLEMENT OF BATTLEFORD, NORTHWEST TERRITORIES, ON A DAY in late February 1903, Patrick Gammie Laurie, editor and chief factotum of the *Saskatchewan Herald*, pored over a telegram sent by a reporter from the *Tribune* in Winnipeg. The wire said that Mr. Barr had asked the government to reserve an additional forty townships; he had offered to pay the entry fees at once and to locate the homesteaders within six months. Barr said he had secured strong financial support and had $2.5 million at his immediate disposal.

For Mr. Laurie, the issue at stake was not the accuracy of the telegram, although he might well have questioned it, but the fact that the government had apparently agreed to increase the size of the parcel of land to be reserved exclusively for Barr's colony. He had stated his opposition to this method of land allocation in print on more than one occasion. Big reservations were the curse of the country. In the following weeks Laurie received information that Barr had requested even more townships to be set aside. He was puzzled. If so many people were coming, surely some preparation would have been made for their arrival. He decided to investigate.

Everyone in town knew that Barr's advance man, Charlie May, had been in Battleford since November but, lacking money, had made no preparations. Jack Barr was said to have gone to Montana to select horses, and there were rumours that the government was going to fix up the agricultural hall for the new immigrants, but there was no evidence that Barr himself had done anything.

In London, Commissioner Preston had been uneasy for some time. He informed William Scott, his counterpart in Ottawa, that the response to Barr's plan was so overwhelming that it would be necessary for the department to "take hold of this end of it." In Preston's judgement, Barr was incapable of organizing and carrying through an undertaking of the size to which this one had grown.

Deputy Minister Smart travelled to Britain for a meeting with Barr, who assured him that he had shipped tents, purchased horses, wagons, stoves and supplies, sent his representative forward to Battleford, and was making all his own arrangements. Reassured, Smart cabled Sifton to that effect. But the minister, a safe distance away from Barr's charm and eloquence, was not fooled. Commissioner Scott confirmed what Laurie had reported in the *Herald*—no preparations had been made by Barr's agents to receive his people. Charlie May had come to Winnipeg expecting funds from Barr, but he had found no money waiting and no clear instructions. He was told only that another agent with access to money would soon arrive.

In the first few days of March, messages coursed back and forth across the Atlantic. In the spare language of the cable, Sifton demanded that Smart find out who this unknown agent was.

> We must know who he is so as to find out what he is doing. Cannot afford to take chances. Do not allow Barr to put off with vague statements, must have details.

When questioned, Barr stated that he had a large number of men at both Winnipeg and Saskatoon who were making all necessary arrangements. Sifton was not appeased, reiterating that "We cannot locate any proper preparations by Barr."

In the strictest sense of the word, Barr was not lying. He did have people in the Northwest, but they had insufficient money (or no money at all) and so were unable to accomplish their designated tasks. In addition to Charlie May, there were five men who had paid fifty pounds each for a seat on the board of the British Canadian Settlement Stores Syndicate. It appeared that the qualifications for membership on the board of directors, besides the possession of sufficient funds to purchase shares, were enough gullibility to have faith in the movement and enough flexibility to be able to travel on short notice. Led by one George Douglas, they had boarded the S.S. *Pretorian* in early February in such haste that it was necessary for Barr to wire them their instructions after they sailed.

Barr's cable revealed the state of chaos in his organization. He did not know who was travelling with Douglas, and he had not yet obtained articles of incorporation for the stores syndicate. He asked Douglas to draw these up and to register them. He also told Douglas to order stoves from Winnipeg's McClary Stove Manufacturers and to arrange for the company to forego payment until the money could be collected from the colonists.

Expecting to find some money to purchase supplies waiting for them in Winnipeg, Douglas's party found only a letter of instruction from Barr. A meeting with J. Obed Smith, commissioner of immigration for the prairies, revealed that none of the five had experience in the work they proposed to do. Douglas and another one of the directors decided to leave Barr and branch out on their own.

Barr's mystery agent, a clerk named W. S. Bromhead, was even then en route from London. Barr had given him the task of preparing the camp where the colonists would stay in Saskatoon. As soon as Bromhead's ship docked in Saint John, he hastened to Ottawa to introduce himself to immigration officials. The only pieces of equipment he had brought with him were twenty-five marquee tents. He had no money, no knowledge of Canada or of how to conduct business there, and very little authority. The department was more convinced than ever that it must intervene.

Bromhead proceeded to Winnipeg, where he attempted to persuade the dissident members of the stores syndicate to rejoin the colony. He cabled Barr requesting money and received instead an order to proceed to Saskatoon and supervise erection of the tents. The agent could not know what was happening in London, where Barr was intimating that Bromhead had squandered the money he had been given. Barr had cabled George Douglas, whom he mistakenly assumed had rejoined the stores syndicate, to tell him that Bromhead's authority had been cancelled.

Barr's irrational behaviour was a measure of his desperation. He was trying to finance his huge undertaking with borrowed money in the hope that funds received from the Canadian government in the future would cover his debts. As borrowing charges mounted, he had to think of ways to provide necessary supplies but avoid paying for them until he had sold them to the colonists.

Each new development further alarmed immigration officials and strengthened their belief that they were correct to intervene. It was very important to the department that the colony succeed. In the correspondence and conversations of these men charged with filling Canada's prairies with worthy immigrants, this sentiment was repeated many times:

The greatest care will have to be taken in handling this large company of English people in a reverent manner that they will be fully protected and reach their district in safety.

The writer of this particular passage was C. W. Speers, who had been appointed chief nursemaid to this most precious group of immigrants. His official title was Colonization Agent, but his ministrations on behalf of the Barr colonists, and the detailed reports he submitted chronicling their experiences, made him seem to be much more. He was the man on the scene, the man who would become the arbitrator of quarrels, the obtainer of supplies, the facilitator of events. He would be lauded and vilified many times before he saw his charges settled.

By the end of March Speers had assessed the situation thoroughly and reported,

I am more than ever persuaded that the greatest care should be exercised in the manner in which these people are permanently established to ensure prosperity. Practical methods should be adopted, first class teams used in transport, competent freighters who will be able to grapple with the conditions, such as fording streams, avoiding muskegs, and encountering successfully any freshets, and by carefully protecting the people against disaster.

The commitment was made. The Canadian government would not let these people fail. Sir Alfred Jones, chairman of the board of the Elder Dempster Line, the shipping company that would transport the colonists across the ocean, was equally convinced of the importance of the undertaking. "The success of Canada as a place of the future for settlers really depends upon the prosperous issue of this venture."

But Canada's stake in the colony's success was of little concern to Barr as the date of sailing approached. He wished fervently that Canada would leave him alone to deal with the thousands of details filling his mind. The Department of Immigration interfered at every turn by asking that he demonstrate his preparedness, refusing to provide funding, reminding him to pay the homestead fees and demanding a substantial deposit to demonstrate good faith.

The department also had been worrying away at him for weeks

about his choice of a departure date. First they told him it was important to get the people on the land early in the year so they could get some ploughing done and plant a crop. Then Mr. Pearce from Alberta convinced Smart that the immigrants must not come out too early, and this was communicated to the harried Barr.

Barr kept the department at bay for some time. In his second pamphlet he had stressed the importance of having the colonists go as early in the spring as possible. But just before the new year, he allowed the department to think that he had been persuaded to delay his departure until March 28. A few days later, Barr announced that his group would leave England on March 21, and Lloyd used that date in a January 15 letter to the *Times*. Then the date was changed to March 25.

This uncertainty was difficult for the shipping line. And the number of passengers kept fluctuating as well. In mid-February, Barr told Elder Dempster that more than one ship would be needed because he would have between four and five thousand people. By early March, he had revised the number to fifteen hundred. Colonists who had booked themselves on other ships were advised to change their reservations to the S.S. *Lake Manitoba*. Finally, Sir Alfred Jones intervened. On March 6 he cabled Deputy Minister Smart to say that

> slight repairs justify us detaining Lake Manitoba until Wednesday April 1 will do this if you think emigrants are going out too early.

Barr notified his colonists of the new date, making it very clear that the delay was the responsibility of the shipping company. The shipping company shifted the blame by announcing that they were responding to a special request from Dominion government emigration officials.

Stanley Rackham noted the new date in his diary. Being a single man, he was not greatly inconvenienced by the change. Signing up with Barr had been just what he needed. He had been feeling "unemployed," an unacceptable emotion for one who regarded many of the unemployed as "loafers." Now he had a purpose in life, and he busied himself making preparations. He investigated different varieties of grass seed, met with his new partner Bernard Smith, had yet another medical examination and a dental one as well, and checked in at the Colonial Office, the Board of Agriculture, the civil service, and the

Army and Navy stores. He visited friends and relatives and attended a biograph show depicting logrolling and lumber work in Canada. He packed books, purchased supplies, received gifts of aluminum plates and a medical outfit, and faithfully recorded each detail in his journal.

Jim Ashton purchased a cabin class ticket for £8.10.0 Liverpool to Saskatoon, congratulating himself on his foresight to buy early and at such a reasonable price. Postwar Britain was full of bargains. There was an abundance of secondhand bell tents, for example. Ashton had lived in them in South Africa and knew them to be ideal "for providing bare shelter economically." He also knew that they left much to be desired if lived in for an extended period of time, but since Barr said the colonists would be in houses soon after they arrived, a bell tent would do perfectly well. Living in East Anglia with its frigid North Sea winds had taught Ashton what kind of clothing to buy—heavy corduroy trousers, jackets with wide collars, woollen underwear and socks, and flannel shirts. With the purchase of grey wool blankets and mattress ticking, and a shotgun and saddle from home, he was ready to concentrate on the task of turning himself into a farmer. To this end he arranged with a man who owned land near his lodgings in Stamford to allow him to practice ploughing and "to learn something of the idiocincracies [sic] of farm implements."

Alex Carlyle-Bell's experience was quite different. At the age of thirty-four, he was unaccustomed to work and unused to dealing with the practical side of life. However, he had been left financially independent following the death of his father in January. Perhaps now he could make a new beginning. His bride of six months was not strong, but the climate in the New World was said to do wonders for a person's constitution. Wealthy friends in England persuaded him to give Canada a try. They advised him to take plenty of money with him and to leave some in a bank in London. By simply sending a bank draft from Canada he could get more whenever he needed it. The rest of his fortune he would invest in something solid and long-term.

Mr. and Mrs. William Salt Topott did not have to worry about long-term investment of money. As a butcher, William had never made enough to put away any extra. That was why 160 acres looked so good to them, and "all for ten dollars." Topott had seen the vastness of the land in South Africa and was sure that the Canadian prairies would be just like that.

The delay in departure troubled Martha Topott a little. When the boat sailed she would be seven and a half months pregnant. By the time she reached Saskatoon she would be in her final month. She could always wait and come later—lots of other women were doing that—but Martha Topott wanted to travel with her husband, and Barr's "Hospital Circular" helped her decide to do so. Barr promised that a doctor, two nurses and a hospital tent would travel with the party. Surely a delivery in a hospital tent supervised by a doctor could be no more dangerous than one at home.

Elizabeth Jones was past the age of childbearing. Her four sons were in their twenties, and she was forty-eight. A lot of people thought forty-eight was old, but she did not feel old. Neither did her husband, Nathaniel. He still went about his business in the same energetic way, always interested in doing new things. Though he had started out as a linen draper, it had not taken him long to better himself. For the past twelve and a half years he had been the manager of the Milner's Safe Company in Manchester. Nathaniel believed strongly in the correctness of things and in taking responsibility.

Nathaniel wanted to go with Barr's group. He and Elizabeth agreed that it was a sensible thing for a family with four sons to do. With 160 acres each of free land, the future looked much brighter than it did in England. With his usual gusto, Nathaniel plunged into arranging their journey. He even had some suggestions for Barr regarding the boat trip, the train journey and the trek from Saskatoon to the colony. But Barr was not interested in advice; he needed money. His reply to Nathaniel dealt with the buying of tents and the joining of syndicates.

Their plans were proceeding apace and cabin class accommodation on the S.S. *Lake Manitoba* was reserved when Elizabeth decided to stay at home. Let the men go out ahead and endure the hardships. Men always enjoyed that sort of thing. She would join them when they were ready for her. It would be good for her sons to fend for themselves without their mother to look after them.

In Belfast, Isabel Crossley prepared herself for a second separation from her son. She arranged for a family picture to be taken. With Ivan lounging in the carving chair and her two daughters and four other sons grouped around her, she gazed sombrely out at the camera. Ivan would have something to take with him to remind him of home. She would have a picture to remind her of Ivan just in case she did not see him again.

It was a sad country that could not provide for its sons. That was what Great Britain had become by the turn of the century. Barr had touched a chord in many when, in one of his press letters, he referred to people "who were at their wit's end to know how to settle their sons."

An article that appeared in several British papers spoke of the people who found the struggle for existence in the densely populated country "a constant and wearing anxiety." Men in middle age were vulnerable too. With the shortage of jobs and the slowness of promotion, they worried that they would lose their positions to younger men. Joseph Hill was a middle-aged butcher with three sons.

> When I lived in Woolwich, what with low wages and slack work it was no light matter feeding so many and keeping a roof over their heads; and there was always a nasty feeling about what would happen when I got too old to work.

Free land was what drew most of the Barr colonists. Sarah and Walter Pinder left England because they could not afford to buy the land they farmed. The parcels of land were so small in any case that Walter could not justify owning a rake or a hay wagon. Nor could he hunt for food or for pleasure, since the wealthy men who owned the land hired gamekeepers to prevent others from hunting on it.

And it was not just the small farmer who found land in Britain too expensive. The Rendell family had worked an estate in Devonshire for two hundred years. Alice and William Rendell, the most recent tenants, had sufficient money to own shares in the Canadian Pacific Railway, but they could not afford to own the land they farmed.

Before the middle of the nineteenth century, convicts and the hopeless constituted a large percentage of those who emigrated permanently. But attitudes had changed since then, and the post–Boer War revolt of the young against the narrow conventions of late Victorian England had made emigration respectable.

The colonies of the Empire also provided a place for wealthy families to send sons who could not find a niche at home or who had failed to live up to expectations. These young men were shipped off with the promise of a generous allowance provided in regular remittances. Some of these remittance men, as they were called, were an embarrassment to their families. One writer referred to them as "the kind of man that did so much to bring the Englishman into disrepute in Canada." Isaac Barr was thinking of them when he wrote in his Home Farm pamphlet,

> There have been causes for the occasional failure of young
> men of British birth in Canada, among them a too great re-
> liance on too many remittances from home.

The colony would have a few men who fell into this category, but
fortunately another species of young man, the returned soldier, would
join in much larger numbers and with a great deal more enthusiasm.
Service in the Boer War had opened young men's eyes to a larger
worldview and given many of them a taste for adventure that could not
be satisfied by a return to their old lives in Britain. They had been
tested in the war and discovered that they could survive; they had become accustomed to hardtack and bully beef cooked over cow dung
fires; they had fallen under the spell of the sparsely settled, untreed
veldt. And when an English fighting man saw himself in a mirror re-
splendent in his uniform, his body hard from months of lean living
and his skin bronze from the sun, it made him feel good, and it made
him want to seek out a place where he could feel that good about himself for the rest of his life.

There was little opportunity in Edwardian England for a woman to
experience such a transformation. Women, especially middle- and
upper-class women, were meant to be married and were trained solely
for that goal. But Britain had been oversupplied with women since
Napoleonic times, when a succession of wars had decreased the proportion of men in the population. Since that time, many more men
than women had emigrated, thus perpetuating the imbalance. Without
enough men to go around, there were women who were left unchosen
and without a proper place in the order of things.

Middle-class women found that spinsterhood had little to recom-
mend it. Genteel spinsterhood often equalled genteel poverty. Work-
ing-class women, single or married, had been employed outside the
home for generations, but not until recently had it been considered respectable for a middle-class woman to have a job. Even then, working
outside the home was acceptable only if the woman was single and
poverty was her alternative.

On the Canadian prairies the imbalance between males and females
would be reversed, with an oversupply of bachelors and a grievous un-
dersupply of unmarried women. A spinster who emigrated would very
likely find herself a husband; at the very least she would have broad-
ened her horizons.

Barr welcomed such women, although he cautioned that they have sufficient means. The Canadian homestead laws did not allow a woman to stake a claim. It was necessary, therefore, that unattached women have jobs or inheritances in order to support themselves. Barr thought some might find employment in the settlement, and this was encouragement enough for at least twenty women who signed up to come by themselves. They were nurses, saleswomen and dressmakers, and at least one of them was an heiress.

Laura Sisley had not inherited a huge fortune from her banker father, but she had enough money to do something worthwhile. In her spare time after work as a saleswoman, she directed a Church of England Boys Club in the middle of London. She decided to take a group of these underprivileged teenaged boys to Canada and pay their expenses until they had established themselves.

Widows were the one exception to the rule against women filing for homesteads. It was not surprising, therefore, that there were several widows included in Barr's group. Lucy Budden was a fifty-four-year-old widow with a ten-year-old daughter and five sons ranging in age from fourteen to twenty. Free land offered her and others like her one of the few opportunities available to provide security for her children.

The number of single women who signed up for Barr's expedition was less than a hundred. The majority of them planned to be housekeepers for their brothers or widowed fathers. Some came reluctantly, knowing that they would have to work harder than they had ever worked before, but knowing too that staying behind was even less attractive.

Staying behind was what many of the married women would have preferred to do. To their way of thinking, emigrating was folly. Why leave the town where they had been born, where nearby relatives could help during childbirth and or in sickness, where neighbours lived so close that they could call to them from the doorway? Such a network of help and friendship was hard to abandon.

Yet despite their reluctance, over two hundred married women, including several who were pregnant, consented to go to Canada with the Barr Colony. They knew that it was their duty to accompany their husbands. They knew that there would be more opportunity for their children. They saw the excitement in their husbands' eyes and the lightness of step at the thought of land and freedom, and so they sorted through their special things, selected the most precious, said their good-byes and followed along.

When Bernard Boden asked his darling Madeleine to marry him during a blissful holiday at Chudleigh Glen in Devon, she promised to become his wife as soon as he could support her. Bernard was a sensible young man of twenty-three with an unsentimental approach to life. He planned to go to Canada with Barr, make his fortune and then send for Madeleine. He thought it would take about three years, and in the meantime she could continue at her job. He promised to write often and hoped she would do the same.

Accompanying Bernard to Canada was his brother Percy, who was two years his junior. Percy's fiancée, Madge, had promised to wait for him as well. Although they may not have realized it, both couples would have little to fear from competitors while they were separated. With the abundance of unmarried women in England and the abundance of unmarried men on the prairies, neither the women nor the men were likely to find someone new.

The Bodens were anxious to get to Canada as soon as possible to get a head start on farming. Accordingly, they sailed from Liverpool in early March aboard the S.S. *Lake Erie*. But they were not the first group of Barr's colonists to leave Britain. Already on the high seas and bound for Canada by way of New York on the S.S. *Celtic* was yet another of Barr's advance agents, the Reverend Dr. John Robbins, with 120 people in his entourage.

Robbins was Barr's official agent, leader of the so-called "Pioneer Party." This was the man who was rumoured to have Barr's money with him, who would finally make good on all Barr's advance plans. A Canadian by birth, the reverend doctor was said to be travelling in distinguished company—no less a personage than the son of Sir John A. Macdonald's postmaster general. Reporters anxiously awaited Robbins's arrival.

As the train pulled into the Winnipeg station on April 2, the portly cleric stepped down onto the platform, but he did not make himself immediately available to the government officials who were keen to talk to him. By the time they found him, several days later, they had learned that not only was he carrying insufficient funds but he was making "inexcuseable purchases" with the money he did have. Robbins bought $1500 worth of groceries, which he proposed to sell to the colonists in Saskatoon, a town whose stores were already well stocked. By the time Robbins left Winnipeg for Saskatoon, government officials had dismissed him as a man of questionable ability.

Newspaper reporters looked forward to the next "advance party."

Approximately sixty men, women and children had sailed on the *Lake Megantic* on March 18, and they arrived in Winnipeg by special coach on April 7. The *Manitoba Free Press* was ecstatic. Here at last was a proper vanguard of the long-promised British settlers. They were "strong, manly, clean, well dressed, [and] intelligent." Some had left ranches in Australia when a five-year drought killed thousands of sheep; some had been in India and South America; nearly all were experienced farmers; none were "lackadaisical lounges"; the children were wonderful; the ladies were refined. All the advance publicity from Barr must be correct. These fine-looking specimens would set the prairies right.

In Ottawa to meet with his superiors, Obed Smith joined the fine-looking specimens as their train passed through. They told him they had scarcely heard of Canada before this year, and they had a thousand questions to ask him. Paramount in their minds was the necessity of getting onto the land early. To this end they hurried on to Saskatoon. There they were greeted by the group that had come on the *Lake Erie* and told that no one could go any farther because the wagons they had been promised had not yet arrived.

While a growing number of stalwarts camped in Saskatoon waiting for Barr's organization to catch up with them, the main body of colonists made their final preparations to leave Britain. There had been so much to do. Lectures sponsored by the Canadian government took up several evenings, and shopping expeditions occupied many of their days. No one lacked for advice on what to buy. Relatives who had not crossed even the English Channel suddenly became experts on what was needed to survive on the Canadian prairies. Neighbours who knew someone who had emigrated had their opinions too. But by far the most prolific advice-giver was Isaac Barr.

In his first pamphlet, Barr had advised that feather beds, old china, garden vegetable seeds and a good English saddle were essential parts of a colonist's equipage. Do not, he advised, take hobnailed boots, farm implements or a revolver; do take a heavy overcoat, strong boots, carpentry tools and a shotgun. After his return from Canada he had modified his list of necessities somewhat. A sewing machine, composite candles, a small candle lantern, waterproof sheeting—these items were essential. It was obvious that Barr had sought practical advice from the people he met on the prairies.

Barr had also announced restrictions on the amount of luggage that could be taken. Third-class passengers would be allowed fifteen cubic feet of luggage free of charge, cabin-class would be allowed twenty. Children could take half those amounts. Luggage required during the voyage should be labelled "Wanted." Luggage needed on the railway coach in Canada should be packed separately so that it could be obtained easily in Saint John. Any extra luggage could be sent ahead to Liverpool on a goods train. Heavy goods could be marked "Settler's Effects" and shipped in advance via depots throughout the British Isles.

It was the settler's effects that caused a lot of the trouble. In his first pamphlet, Barr had cautioned against bringing bulky or unnecessary articles of furniture, but he had said that musical instruments would be conveyed free of charge. By the time he had written his second pamphlet, he had come to regret his generosity. There seemed to be an untoward number of people who wanted to bring pianos.

The chairman of Elder Dempster thought pianos were a fine idea and agreed to transport them free on the steamer. Barr tried dissuasion. Pianos would have to be specially packed; they were awkward to transport by rail and would have to come by slow freight; they would be difficult to store in Saskatoon and even more awkward on the trek; at the settlement they would be white elephants.

Six-year-old Madeline Edwards was disconsolate. Her parents said her most prized possession, a doll her own size, was too large to bring. All over Britain such choices had to be made. Favourite possessions were left behind, household goods were sold, clothing was given away. More remarkable than the items left behind, however, were the ones that simply had to come. Agnes Holtby brought all her jewellery and a tin trunk full of cherished (and breakable) possessions. Bernard Boden brought his camera and photographic developing equipment. Laura Sisley brought a portable organ. Persian carpets, large pieces of furniture and entire settings of expensive china were deemed essential to a new life on the prairies.

To supply more immediate needs, a little planning was advised. Families wishing to cook on the trains were told to pack a basket with enough utensils for a week. Those saving money by travelling on colonist cars instead of the more comfortable tourist cars would need pillows, blankets, drop curtains with safety pins, soap and towels.

And it was necessary to bring money. Barr's advice in this regard was to prove dangerously inaccurate. "The more money the better of course," he wrote, but he advised that a family could get by with one hundred pounds after they had paid travelling expenses. Single men could band together and pool their resources. Young men willing to work could get by with five pounds. Young men with no money at all should arrange to travel on the first train, get off in Winnipeg and work in Manitoba for a year to acquire some savings. Barr would hold their homesteads for them if they sent him the ten-dollar fee.

Ivan Crossley was going straight to the colony as fast as he could get there. On March 30, his mother and his six brothers and sisters accompanied him to the Belfast wharf. As the steamer pulled away, he could hear his family singing "God Be with You Till We Meet Again." The hymn was sad and sentimental.

> When life's perils thick confound you,
> Put his loving arms around you;
> God be with you till we meet again!

The young are invincible. They do not anticipate life's perils. All Ivan could see ahead was adventure and new opportunity. He watched his family as they receded from view and then turned to investigate his fellow passengers. By the time he reached Liverpool early the next morning, he had made friends with three other young Irishmen all bound for Barr's colony.

The Holtby family arrived in Liverpool the day before the sailing, took a cab to Jackson's boarding house at 17 Earle Street, and arranged with an agent to place their luggage safely on board the ship. Having changed their sterling into dollars, they visited an art gallery before returning to the boarding house for "a rare good tea." Bob's reluctance to emigrate had vanished completely. He was keen to see what the future had in store, and he felt wonderful. That night he slept soundly.

The majority of Barr's colonists would spend the night aboard one of three special boat trains bound for Liverpool from London. Thousands of passengers and well-wishers had converged on Euston Station from points all over London. Feeder trains brought more travellers from the south and east. Brightly coloured shipping labels plastered on hundreds of pieces of luggage soon transformed the drab platforms. Women's hats, fashionably large, floated here and there on a sea of humanity. The metallic sound of concertinas wove in and out, a carnival background for the chatter of a thousand voices. High-spirited young men animated the whole crowd, which burst into cheers whenever more people arrived. Around family groups children darted, their random activity a response to the charged atmosphere as their elders prepared to say good-bye. The occasional lone man with no one to see him off stood quietly smoking a pipe.

As midnight approached, the crowd grew more subdued. Then, quietly at first and raggedly, "Auld Lang Syne" was heard. More voices joined in until the sentimental song filled the far reaches of the cavernous station. Then someone began to sing "Old Folks at Home," and the crowd joined in again. Now the crowd became more festive, and the strains of the latest popular song took over. "We've made up our minds to sail away," the voices sang, and the porters called out, "Take your seats." Families hugged each other, grandmothers wept and young women bestowed chaste kisses on freshly shaven cheeks and promised to come when they were sent for. From a throng of waving handkerchiefs and hats, each train chuffed out of the station.

A reporter watching the scene was surprised. He had seen thousands of emigrants leave for Liverpool in his time, but these people were different.

> They were no common emigrants these. All of them were of a fairly well-to-do appearance, as if they had not found it impossible to exist in England, but had decided they might do better in the fertile land out west.

The reporter could have been describing Stanley Rackham. Stanley's leave-taking had been as measured and polite as one might expect. On the Sunday just past he had attended chapel and then returned to his parents' home for tea. His health being one of his major concerns, he was "generally cheered up" by a visit to a doctor who lectured him at length on "medicine and surgery." After a visit from a friend, he brought his diary up to date and went to bed "feeling pretty cheerful." The following morning he took his leave from his family in the garden and walked with a friend to the bus—his last moment of quiet for some time to come.

The uncommon emigrants settled in for the journey by rail to Liverpool. That night, as the trains made their way north and west, picking up more of Barr's people at Watford, Bletchley, Northhampton, Rugby, Nuneaton, Stafford and Crewe, few slept. The starting and stopping, the murmur of voices as new passengers found seats and settled hand luggage, the mounting excitement, the upright seats—all conspired to prevent sleeping. It was a rumpled, cranky lot that left the trains in Liverpool in the morning and made their way to the Beaver House Hotel on St. George Square where the Elder Dempster shipping company provided breakfast.

At the boarding house on Earle Street, the Holtby family breakfasted royally and with an appetite—a good sign to be sure. When the boat from Belfast docked at seven o'clock, Ivan Crossley and his fellow Irishmen did not linger over their food. This was a morning to be outside, as hundreds of colonists made their way to the docks. The crowded streets and the excitement made Ivan think of a summer fair.

They came on foot and by cab. They advanced on the Princes landing stage, descending the broad, covered gangways to the long floating dock. Steerage passengers were expected to board the ship at 9:00, cabin-class passengers at noon, but most people came early just to see the ship.

The S.S. *Lake Manitoba* of the Elder Dempster line lay at anchor out in the Mersey River. Bob Holtby thought she was good-looking with her black-and-white paint job and her funnel striped with two white bands. A little black-and-white tugboat hugged her side as though instructed to complete the scene in a picturesque fashion. The early spring sun highlighted the ship. The river flowed sedately by, heading upstream. Looming in the background on the New Brighton side was the tower, its amusement grounds deserted until summer.

Sir Alfred Jones of the Elder Dempster line had written to James Smart three weeks before to say that he had provided Barr's people with a magnificent ship. In truth, despite the impression she made at a distance, the *Manitoba* was rather ordinary. Although she was less than two years old, she had been fitted out first to transport large numbers of soldiers who had little choice in their style of accommodation. After this voyage she would be transferred to the ownership of the CPR and be used for transporting freight. She had been built to carry 700 passengers and her Board of Trade rating was for 800; 1960 Barr colonists now stood on the landing stage waiting to board her.

Nine o'clock came and went. It was rumoured that the *Manitoba* must wait until the tide changed at 10:00. Ten o'clock came and went. The Holtbys had been there since 8:20 with hundreds of others. Eleven o'clock, and still the *Manitoba* stayed in midstream. The crowd grew noisier, tongues loosened by a sense of common grievance. Ivan Crossley could see people of all ages and from all walks of life. He

could see dogs of every description, parrots and canaries. He could see
a great variety of guns and revolvers. "One would have thought we
were going to invade Canada," he observed, "instead of entering it
peacefully."

The youthful Crossley, unencumbered by family or many possessions, was able to be detached.

> You never saw such a conglomeration of different people
> with their carts and their guns and food and all kinds of
> baggage and poor old grandmothers crying because their
> daughters were going away and of course we were young
> and didn't care much what links we were severing but we
> got a great kick out of it.

The docks became more and more crowded. Bob Holtby found a
vantage point from which to survey the crowd. Betraying his urban
biases, he tried in vain to pick out the farmers. Instead, the sounds of
the city-bred were heard on every side as East-end Londoners called
to each other in a Cockney twang.

Finally, at 11:30, the *Manitoba* came alongside. The crowd pressed
towards one of the ship's gangways, unaware that the luggage would
be loaded first. Liverpool lorries, the largest wagons Bob Holtby had
ever seen, were wheeled to the dock's edge, laden with wicker crates,
suitcases, sea chests, tin boxes, large wooden cases bound with iron
hoops and trunks, all bearing the red and blue labels of the steamship
company and all designated "Saint John, New Brunswick" and
"Wanted" or "Not Wanted" or "Hold." Many bore old labels from
India, South Africa and Australia. There was so much luggage it was
staggering. It looked as if everybody had exceeded the limit for luggage carried free of charge.

At 12:30, Stanley Rackham came through the barrier with his bags.
There to meet him were his new partner Bernard Smith and Smith's
father. Hands shaken all round and farewells said, at 1:30 the two
young men answered the call for cabin passengers, climbed the gangway and positioned themselves at the railing to watch a steady stream
of their fellow travellers come on board.

The long wait had frayed tempers. Some people were shoving and
even fighting to secure a place in the line-up to board. The Holtby
men sought to protect Kate and Agnes and the children from the
crush of impatient passengers. Unlike the broad gangways leading

down from the street to the landing stage, the one up to the ship was narrow. Bob could feel his camera being pushed hard into his shoulder. Gaining the deck was a relief. The Holtby men settled the women into their cabin and then went below to the third-class accommodation.

Misty rain had replaced the sunshine of the early morning. A raw, cold wind blew. The Band of the First Liverpool Volunteers played, first on the dock and later on the ship. Women cried, some hysterically. The third-class passengers were given the signal to board. Once on deck, they fought their way through fellow colonists and piles of luggage for a place at the rail. Some passengers climbed the rigging for a better view. The band played "Good-bye Dolly I Must Leave You," and the crowd on shore replied with hymns and tears and fluttering handkerchiefs.

At three o'clock the *Manitoba* moved away from the dock and into the Mersey. As Isaac Barr watched from his cabin high on the boat deck surrounded by his closest followers, he was a man fulfilled. In his last letter to the hundreds of people who now stood below him, he had sounded the rallying cry. "Let us take possession of Canada. Let our cry be CANADA FOR THE BRITISH."

CHAPTER
IV

Hardtack and Salty Tea

IN THE STERN HOLD OF THE S.S. *LAKE MANITOBA*, A SMALL BOY TEETERED PRECARI-
ously on top of an enormous pile of luggage. Then his foot slipped,
dislodging a bag and sending it bouncing and crashing to the deck. An
ominous fizzing sound was followed by the smell of smoke as
someone's entire supply of matches ignited.

Things were not going well on the *Manitoba*. The amount of luggage had overwhelmed the ship's crew. As more and more trunks and
boxes came on board, they threw them haphazardly onto piles, paying
no attention to the labels specifying which pieces were "Wanted" on
the voyage. Some boxes broke open, spilling their contents to mix
with the personal belongings of others. Some passengers did not find
their luggage until they reached Canada and spent the entire voyage
without a change of clothing.

Stanley Rackham passed the first evening taking stock of his surroundings as he searched for his trunks. There seemed to be far too
many people on board. "The steamer," he observed, "is more like an
excursion steamer to Clacton than an Atlantic liner." He counted himself fortunate to have a cabin. There were many in steerage who could
have afforded cabin accommodation if it had been available, but an entire cabin deck had been sacrificed when the ship was converted to
carry troops. When Jim Ashton and Alex Nicol saw their cabin, a four-
berth affair "directly over the screw," they wondered if the extra expense had been worth it. Still, they were travelling in luxury compared
to those in the cheaper accommodation.

All but three hundred of the passengers were lodged in the steerage
section of the ship in three large dormitories. The aft dormitory held
older single men and married men whose wives and children were in

cabins. Amidships were the quarters for married couples with young children and for women travelling alone. Women and men sleeping in the same dormitory was upsetting to many. The lack of privacy was an additional concern. For a woman of gentle sensibilities to be required to dress and attend to her toilet behind rudimentary curtains within the sound of male voices and the smell of pipe smoke was an unforeseen tribulation of the worst kind.

The forward hold dormitory was at once the most lively and the most fetid, for it was there that the younger single men shared a space forty feet square with no more than ten feet of head room. Open bunks built of plain deal boards ranked side by side, eight deep, head to head all around the hold. Each bunk had a hay-filled mattress and nothing else, leaving those who had brought no blankets to sleep in their clothes. The only sanitary facilities for steerage passengers were the makeshift latrines on deck. Ivan Crossley had never seen anything like it but decided if everyone else could take it, so could he.

The first night passed peacefully, with the ship steady, the sea calm and the lighthouses on the Isle of Man just visible off the starboard bow. The morning light revealed Scotland to starboard and Ireland to port, the sight of the latter inspiring Bob Holtby to address his diary in a lyrical manner until sea sickness laid him low.

Though mal de mer began for some passengers even before they reached the open ocean, sickness became the general rule when the roll of the Atlantic caught the crowded ship. Bob Holtby lay suffering in his bunk, trying to ignore the smell of food wafting down from the galley and seeping through the close dormitory air. His diary for that day contained one terse sentence: "Sickness and nowt to eat."

The next day, reasoning that he might feel better if he stood up, he rose from bed and struggled into his trousers. The effort forced him to lie down again. Then, having gathered his strength, he sat up and put on his shirt. Again he felt the need to lie down. His prostrate position restoring him somewhat, he rose a third time and was able to put on his stockings and shoes, but the effort necessitated a return to the prone position. Thus, gradually, he dressed himself and, having finished the demanding task, sought out a pillar upon which to lean. As he told his diary later,

> [I was] too jolly ill for anything. This sea sickness beats any-
> thing I have ever had. It takes all the life out of you and

makes you wish they would come round and pitch you
overboard.

At suppertime, Bob took refuge up on deck. It was not only the
smell of soup, potatoes and sawdust and the faint residual aroma of
army horses that drove him topside. It was the monotonous slop, slop
of the bilge water echoing the ship's side-to-side roll that had begun
to play on his nerves. On deck the fresh air helped him, but even there
his fellow passengers heaved and retched over the rail.

In the cabin assigned to the Holtby women, Kate lay stricken like
her son. The rolling of the ship was bad enough, but when she tried to
eat in the married quarters dining room, "the noise and the rabble"
were too much to bear. The ship's doctor arranged for food to be sent
to her cabin. She remained there for the rest of the voyage, ruminat-
ing on the lunacy of the family's decision to leave England.

Paradoxically, the *Manitoba* was enjoying a calmer than usual crossing, encountering no rough water throughout the entire voyage. It was
a lack of proper ballast, which even the mountain of luggage and the
overabundance of passengers could not remedy, that left the ship riding high and vulnerable to the movement of the swells. Gradually, all
but the most severely affected grew accustomed to the ship's rolling
motion and began to regain their appetites. Soon hunger and boredom
had become more pressing problems.

Barr's pamphlets had promised that dining would be civilized even
in third class. Menus would be sent to each person before embarkation; all meals would be served on tablecloths laid with cutlery; third-
class passengers would not be required to cook or serve their own
food. But when the *Manitoba*'s stewards heard in Liverpool that the
ship was to carry emigrants, several of them deserted. Barr hired passengers to serve in their place, but he could not improve the quality of
the food and service quite so easily.

In the centre of each dormitory, surrounded by tiers of bunks, were
long, rough tables. For a passenger to be sure of getting a place at
mealtime, it was necessary to be there thirty minutes ahead. The
plates and cups that lay before the hungry passengers had been dipped
in hot water and returned to the table still coated with a watery version of the previous meal. Accordingly, it was necessary for each passenger to clean his cup and plate with a piece of bread—a disagreeable
task to be sure, but it helped to pass the time until the stewards appeared with the food.

People with nothing to do all day but look forward to the next meal showed their impatience by banging the table with their knives and forks, often accompanied by someone playing on a tin whistle. A loud cheer greeted the appearance of the food at the top of the stairs. One morning, in response to the cheers, the steward tripped, spilling a whole tray of porridge. Howls of dismay went up. While the steward retreated to the galley for more porridge, some of the hungriest fellows scooped up the spilt mush from the floor onto their plates and ate it in its natural state.

In addition to porridge served without milk, there was corned beef, bread, buns and tea for breakfast. Dinner was usually codfish, potatoes, bread and coffee; tea was boiled eggs and bread. The eggs were rolled down the middle of the table from a large basket at the end. According to Ivan Crossley, "Some eggs were hard-boiled, some soft and some had chickens all ready to hatch." Supper was less grand—a bag of ship's biscuits passed around among the passengers.

Not surprisingly, opinion regarding the meals seemed to be mostly negative. The bread was only partly baked; the food was badly served; the knives and forks were dirty and rusted; the meat was inedible. Many swore the drinking water was salty and the crew did admit to running out of fresh water two days before the end of the voyage, leaving only tea and coffee with a pronounced briny flavour to quench people's thirst. The British are especially fastidious about their tea. This salty liquid, ladled out of a soup pot, was beneath contempt.

Human beings are nothing if not inconsistent. Ivan Crossley thought the food was terrible but complained that there was not enough of it. Loud grumbling was usual following the meals, but a small crowd soon gathered around the bill of fare that was posted to announce the next menu.

It was the poor quality of the food that brought Barr his first taste of passenger unrest. On the first night, a group of men from the forward dormitory insisted that Barr come down and see how they were fed. Accompanied by some of his entourage, Barr descended the stairs to be greeted by a large crowd, which muttered ominously as he climbed onto a box where he could be seen. His explanation that he was doing his best satisfied very few, least of all the man who threw a biscuit. It hit Barr in the mouth and knocked him off his platform. Regaining his feet if not his dignity, Barr disappeared up the stairs, shouting, "I'll never come down here again. I'm through with you people—you're a lot of savages."

The missile hurled at Barr was the size of a saucer, about half an inch thick and coloured a delicate brown. But hardtack was anything but delicate in texture. Someone called it "dog biscuits." Mary Pinder remembered that it could not be softened even by dunking it in tea.

Mary and her family slept in one of the second-class cabins and ate in the married quarters dining room, which was painted white and made brighter by a skylight. Cabin-class passengers had little to complain about. Their quarters were small but private, and their beds were made up for them by a stewardess.

Isaac Barr's entourage slept in cabin class too. Included in this select group were Barr's secretary, George Flamanck, and Mr. Lloyd, his wife, Marion, and their five children. Mrs. Lloyd spent the first days of the voyage nursing sick women and children in a makeshift infirmary set up in the ship's smoking room. Less noticeable among Barr's group was the young clerk-typist Christina Helberg, who had been wooed by Barr in London and would marry him later in the year.

Barr's crowded cabin was like a miniature version of the office at Serjeant's Inn, but here all activity was directed towards the allocation of homesteads. This was an exercise of prime importance to Barr, since he had hoped to have everyone assigned to their land before the party left England. Failing that, he was determined that he would complete this task on board ship.

The cornerstone of Barr's wonderful scheme was that it would be "All-British." This had been the driving force in his negotiations for a reservation and his insistence that the reservation be located on empty land beyond the vanguard of settlement. Only then could he ensure that no land had already been claimed by "unsuitable" settlers.

Included in his definition of "unsuitability" were Canadians and Americans. In his prejudice against Americans, he was not alone. Minister of the Interior Clifford Sifton was wary of them too. But some of the Americans coming to the West at that time were experienced dry land farmers, and Sifton was prepared to swallow his objections in the interest of filling up the prairies. Barr was not prepared to be so flexible. Americans, despite the fact that they spoke a version of English, would dilute the British flavour of his colony.

Barr did recognize the value of experienced farmers, however, and when pressed had agreed to having a few Americans scattered throughout the colony to provide expert advice. Canadians were another matter. If the English were forced to, they would take advice from Americans, wrote a newspaperman, but they were loath to listen to Canadians.

> The deep seated sense of superiority to a "colonial", almost inherent in every Englishman, is not offended by being advised by an American, whom they recognize as the representative of national equality.

Barr's lack of enthusiasm for his hosts was shared by many British immigrants. An Englishman who settled in Assiniboia wrote in 1904 that an all-British colony would be preferable to what he had experienced.

> What a paradise a town would be that was free from 'dead' uns', 'burns', 'sharks', etc. In my short experience in the country I have seen emigrants by the score fleeced by these scoundrels.

The animosity of the English towards their colonial cousins was returned wholeheartedly. Stories had reached England of the shop windows in Canada that bore the sign "Help Wanted. Englishmen need not apply." English settlers were made the butt of practical jokes by Canadians who thought their manner of speaking and their Old World customs were hilarious.

But despite the hostility on both sides, the Canadian government and Barr saw eye to eye in their desire to bring British settlers to the Canadian prairies. In their enthusiasm for British settlers, officials of the Department of Immigration had been most accommodating, but on one matter they drew the line. Knowing the dangers the prairies held for the inexperienced, they insisted that non-British settlers be allowed to homestead on 25 per cent of the available quarter sections within the colony. In return for Barr's agreement to this stipulation, the government would limit outsiders to those who could speak English, that is to say Canadians and Americans. In catering to Barr's desire to exclude "foreigners," the government was able to ensure that experienced settlers would be interspersed with the British, an alarming number of whom, it was becoming apparent, had no farming experience at all.

Whether the Barr colonists would take the advice of experienced North American farmers was another matter entirely. As they eagerly crowded into Barr's cabin on board ship to be assigned their land, they were heartened by Barr's suggestion that groups of four homesteaders join forces and claim a whole section together. They could then benefit from each other's mistakes and avoid having to seek advice from anyone who was not British.

Barr was also interested in grouping people on homesteads according to where they came from in Britain. He pictured ready-made neighbourhoods populated by people who already knew each other from back home. "For women especially, whose life is to be spent on a farm," he had written in his second pamphlet, "the certainty of friends and neighbours is of vast importance."

But even before the S.S. *Lake Manitoba* sailed, a Dominion land agent in Battleford had complicated matters. R. F. Chisholm's duties normally included assigning homesteads to the settlers who came to his office, but Barr's much-maligned advance man, Mr. Bromhead, insisted that Barr had been given exclusive right to allocate every homestead within the reservation. Chisholm pointed out that Canadians and Americans would be coming into his office to register homesteads long before the Barr colonists arrived. Because he had no way of knowing which homesteads Barr had assigned, Chisholm disputed Barr's right to do so.

Just before the *Manitoba* left Liverpool, immigration officials had informed the colonists that it would be impossible to ensure that the land would be vacant. This was a denial of the promise that had been made to Barr. Added to that was the new decree that 25 per cent of the reservation be made available to outsiders. It became imperative to Barr that he have as much land as possible claimed in advance to force the government's hand.

Jim Ashton thought that assigning the land ahead of time was a good idea. He joined the crowd of people standing around the maps Barr had laid out in his cabin. Barr said it would save time and avoid confusion later. He said the land was very uniform, so no one would be treated unfairly. He reminded them of what Mr. Owen had said when the American farmer saw the land with Barr—"One could sit down blindfolded anywhere, and decide to homestead and he would make no mistake."

And so they lined up clutching the receipts that proved they had paid their homestead fees before they left Britain, and they were assigned the free land that would make them masters of their own fates. Barr had been most accommodating. Friends were assigned next to friends, relatives near relatives. It seemed as though no request was impossible to grant. One man, a stonemason, wanted enough rocks on his homestead to build a house. Pointing to a map, Barr proceeded to select a quarter section that he said would have an abundance of rocks.

Having resolved the location of their homesteads, the passengers returned to the more immediate concern of the quality of the food on board ship. On Sunday, the food took a sudden turn for the better. The pea soup, roast beef, peas, plum pudding and sauce tasted so good that it was possible to ignore the fact that all the courses were served on the same plate. Bob Holtby noted,

> The complaints about the food have been completely knocked on the head today for I'll be bound that today's dinner has been a good deal better than at least half the people on board are used to.

The weather had been better than usual that Sunday. The sea was calm, and although the blue sky was periodically obscured by banks of fog, the ship emerged from the damp and chill each time to brilliant sunshine and displays of porpoises and flying fish. Lloyd conducted a church service in the saloon to a standing-room-only crowd accompanied by Miss Sisley on her portable organ. She played again for a second service held on deck in the fog. That evening Lloyd led a third group of worshippers in the single men's quarters aft. Accompanied by three violins, the congregation sang hymns, their efforts enhanced by some of their number who had attended choir practice during the week. The church of the mid-Atlantic, as someone called it, was intimate and cosy. Dressed in shirtsleeves, the parishioners smoked pipes as they lounged on the bunks and rails of the dormitory, their coats, hats and kit bags hanging from nails, their gun cases, trunks and bundles of bedding stacked randomly on the floor.

The Reverend Isaac Barr was nowhere to be seen. The biscuit-throwing incident on the first night and the subsequent demands from disgruntled passengers had driven Barr to the sanctuary of his cabin. By contrast, Lloyd was an inspiration. In addition to maintaining the spiritual welfare of the colonists, he could be seen every morning on the cabin-class deck and every afternoon on the steerage deck, standing on a box surrounded by passengers, lecturing on "Canadian Life and Problems."

But Lloyd's informative lectures did not fill the day by any means. The only passengers with something important to occupy their time were the mothers of young children. Everyone else was open to suggestion. Five musicians strove to blend their diverse talents into one harmonious sound; a woman told fortunes; cardsharpers dealt clandestine "three card tricks" with a wary eye out for the authorities, and everyone wrote letters home.

The single men, who made up the majority of the passengers, began their day at 5:30 A.M. with a long wait in line for a chance to wash, followed by breakfast. Then the balance of the day loomed ahead. Aside from the occasional organized boxing match, the most popular occupation was card playing. Bob Holtby had never seen anything like it.

> Now and then you hear the chink of money changing hands but it is done very quietly and they are dead nuts on gambling here. Some of the South African soldiers on board are very keen card players and gamblers which shows what it must have been like out there during the war.

Attracted by neither alcohol nor gambling, Holtby was hard pressed to amuse himself. He was sick of having nothing to do. He spent more and more time on his bunk. So accustomed did he become to the noise of the crowded dormitory that he could sleep through anything. He had adapted quickly to the squealing and yelping of the two retriever pups his next door neighbour kept in a basket near his bed. By the time the ship had been at sea for a week, nothing bothered him. One night there was a fight in the dormitory. The loser "dropped down in a fit" and had to be seen by the doctor. When the doctor left, a man who had been drinking rolled from the top of the stairs to the bottom. Bob Holtby slept through it all.

On the ninth day the sky was clear, and although the sun was hot at noon, the evening was very cold, presided over by a radiant moon that illuminated an immense iceberg half a mile off. The following day, French sailing vessels were seen cutting across the path of the *Manitoba* bound for the Grand Banks of Newfoundland. The sight brought many people up on deck with their opera glasses and telescopes. As the cold air bit into their thin English clothes, they kept warm by marching around the deck, whistling and singing. Periodically, fog wrapped the ship in a moist gray shroud as air warmed by the Gulf Stream moved over water chilled by the Labrador Current. The coast of Canada was drawing near.

Preparations in Canada for the arrival of the colonists were not going as they should have been. The Department of Immigration had been dithering for several weeks about whether to intervene and to what extent. J. Obed Smith, in his capacity as commissioner of immigration for the prairies, was the man with whom the immediate responsibility lay. Although he was well qualified in experience and intelligence for the job at hand, he could see a disaster brewing, and he was impatient with his superiors, who seemed unable to make the final commitment to assume control. Almost two weeks before the *Manitoba* sailed, Smith had sent a plea to Ottawa, saying,

> It certainly seems to me that we are only wasting time in discussing the housing and care of the people any longer with Mr. Barr or his alleged representative.

Not a single dollar had been spent in Canada on any of Barr's subsidiary companies; one agent after another had arrived only to have his authority cancelled. "As the matter looks at present everything is simply at a standstill," Smith wrote. He asked to be given authority to make arrangements and ignore altogether any made by Barr.

Finally the politicians and bureaucrats began to act. Sifton instructed the minister of agriculture for the Territories to hire two farm instructors for six months. Two land guides were hired as well, and they were given instructions to prepare campsites at intervals along the trail between Saskatoon and the colony site. The *Manitoba Free Press* soon caught wind of the preparations and reported, "The Dominion government intends to see Mr. Barr's undertaking successfully accomplished."

Poor Mr. Bromhead, to give him credit, was trying still to accomplish the impossible. With no money and no authority, with Dr. Robbins making himself scarce in Winnipeg, with the seventy-five colonists from the *Lake Megantic* due to arrive any day and the main group already on the high seas, he was valiantly attempting to prepare the Saskatoon camp.

An urgent telegram on April 1 from Bromhead to the department office in Winnipeg implored someone to explain why the goods that were to have been sent on March 20 still had not arrived in Saskatoon.

The land guides were waiting for a shipment of stoves so they could take some out to the campsites they were setting up.

Speers, the department's man in Saskatoon, was anxious that he be well prepared for the arrival of his charges. His initial responsibility was to ensure that the first group to leave Saskatoon be properly out-fitted so that the rest of the colonists could see how it should be done. To this end, Speers had asked Doukhobor settlers to provide oxen and horses "of the right kind," and he had arranged for cordwood and hay to be provided in Saskatoon and along the trail.

The department ordered ox teams and wagons with drivers from Duck Lake and Batoche to provide transport for hire at three dollars per day. The Canadian Pacific Railway agreed to furnish a limited number of teams of horses and oxen provided that these were later re-sold at reasonable prices to avoid any financial loss to the railway. A fast freight carrying military tents hurtled westward towards Saska-toon. Seven cars of cordwood had already arrived, and more was ex-pected. Large marquee tents were erected in Saskatoon and at each campsite along the trail; at each marquee, lumber floors were laid, cook stoves installed, hay and firewood stockpiled and fireguards ploughed. Forty tons of hay were stacked at Battleford. An operation of large proportions had swung into action.

The department's official position was that Barr's colonists would get the same treatment as all other immigrants. The only difference, the department said, was that "the long distance to be travelled will necessitate more arrangements than in ordinary cases." In fact, when challenged by the Opposition in the House of Commons the following summer, Clifford Sifton admitted that Barr's people had been treated with lavish care.

> We did what never was done before for any immigrant —
> sent out people to set up tents with stoves and caretakers;
> other settlers have to sleep under their wagons.

Government agents, one for each section of the Immigrant Special Train, left Ottawa for Saint John to await the arrival of the *Manitoba*. Superintendent of Immigration William Scott, accompanied by the Member of Parliament for Saskatchewan, T. O. Davis, was also en route to Saint John. They were determined to talk in earnest to Mr. Barr about his plans for transportation from Saskatoon to the colony.

Almost two thousand British colonists were about to arrive. To the dismay of the Canadian government, the international press chose that moment to become interested in the whole undertaking. Up until then, bureaucrats and politicians had been able to regard the occasional carping editorial in the Battleford or Winnipeg newspapers with all the seriousness that a horse reserves for troublesome flies. But now that American and English papers were taking notice, Ottawa was concerned.

Ignored by almost everyone, the Winnipeg newspapers had reported the movements of Barr's agents from the time they arrived in the West empty-handed. Reporters knew that the Department of Immigration had effectively but gingerly taken over the preparations being made in Saskatoon and beyond. They had seen people shake their heads over the isolation of the reservation and had heard the conflicting reports about the farming experience of Barr's people. The Winnipeg newspapers sent reporters to Saint John, where they observed that Scott and Davis were waiting too. The presence of the two men told the reporters that things were not going according to plan. Now the Winnipeg papers had something that would interest the big boys.

Within three days of the arrival of the ship in Saint John, Commissioner Preston in London cabled Deputy Minister Smart in Ottawa. A Reuters dispatch from Winnipeg had appeared in London papers, claiming that Barr's project had practically failed. And it appeared that the colonists who had arrived in advance had been communicating with their relatives in Britain. Telegrams from families and friends demanding an explanation rained down on the commissioner's office in London, where Preston was trying without success to prevent their publication.

On the *Manitoba*, Barr proceeded with plans for disembarkation. In his second pamphlet, which was the colonists' only real source of written information, Barr had described the procedure.

> At Saint John the party shall step from the steamer onto the train and shall not be compelled to seek shelter in an emigration shed or in hotels. If the train is not quite ready when the steamer arrives, we shall remain on her until it is. There will, however, be no delay.

Mr. Barr had been wrong before, and the colonists were on the lookout for another mistake. Although most of what happened on the final two days of the voyage was beyond Barr's control, people had a great deal to complain about.

April 10 was Good Friday, but the requirements of the shipping company precluded any religious observance that might normally have occurred. The first order of the day was a count of passengers by the ship's purser in an effort to detect stowaways. All passengers were required to report on deck, then all the doors were locked except for one through which everyone was required to pass. The count was 1960, and no stowaways were found. The passengers were then addressed by Mr. Barr, who told them that, in preparation for the train journey ahead, he had arranged to have eight thousand loaves of bread baked on board and would sell them at cost the next day.

Amid suspicious muttering about what an old rogue Barr was to make money by selling to captive consumers, the colonists prepared for bed, confident that this would be their last night on board the ship. As Bob Holtby left the ship's rail, he noticed the beacon of the Cape Sable Light and was heartened by this evidence that their voyage had almost ended. He fell asleep to the sounds of "two cockneys in the middle of the floor fighting and blaspheming furiously."

The passengers awoke on Saturday, April 11 to find the ship lying at anchor in the Bay of Fundy with Nova Scotia on one side and New Brunswick on the other. The *Manitoba* was expected to dock that afternoon, as soon as a few formalities had been observed. Last-minute packing of night things and blankets occupied everyone until 9:00 A.M., when Barr began to sell bread.

It was not the first time Barr had been accused of making money from the colonists, nor would it be the last. Diarists writing at the time said Barr made a small profit on the bread. Remembering the incident thirty-seven years later, Lloyd said Barr sold the bread for ten cents a loaf when the same bread would have been available in Saint John for five cents. Lloyd had spoken to Barr about lowering the price, he said, but the damage had already been done.

Considering that the captain had been unable to predict the exact time of arrival in Saint John, and considering the demand that would have been placed on the bakeries of that city if 1960 people had required bread all at once, especially on Easter weekend, Barr's provision of bread made sense. His profit, if he sold every loaf and did not have to pay the ship for baking a special order, would have been only a few dollars, hardly enough to make it financially worth his while. But in the years that followed, his detractors would add "the bread incident" to his list of crimes.

All day long, official visitors arrived at the ship by tender, their activities observed by two reporters who met with Barr and Lloyd over lunch. A pair of bank officials boarded, carrying satchels of Canadian money to enable passengers to exchange their British currency. The reporters observed that the bankers ran out of money before their business was completed and presented this to their readers as evidence of the wealth of the new immigrants.

Another set of visitors arrived to speak with Barr. Superintendent Scott and Member of Parliament Davis came bearing messages from the Department of Immigration. They were most insistent that Barr accompany them to Ottawa for a discussion with the deputy minister.

The final visitor that afternoon was a doctor who came on board to check that everyone had been vaccinated against smallpox. Although the passengers had been reminded before they left Britain of the stringent laws in Canada regarding the admission of diseased persons, some had not taken the law seriously. Passing singly before the doctor, they were required to bare their upper arms to show their vaccination scars. Ivan Crossley remembered that several passed inspection by pressing a shilling hard against their skin just before their arms were examined.

Fifteen people did not appear for inspection. The doctor was adamant. The yellow quarantine flag would not be lowered until the fifteen had been checked. By the time the doctor was satisfied, the tide was too low for the ship to proceed to the dock. It would be high again at midnight, but because the captain refused to risk the troublesome currents in the dark, the ship remained at anchor in the bay. The passengers would have to spend another night on board.

Their leader was not among them. Whether it was to avoid the anger of the colonists or because he had important business to do in Saint John, Barr had disappeared. His absence was noticed first when officials from the CPR came on board to meet with him. They returned twice more that evening to no avail. Lloyd refused to become involved, pleading lack of authority. By now the CPR officials were desperate. The delay in docking the ship was costing them increasing amounts of money in demurrage fees.

Frustrated passengers leaned on the rail to watch as the setting sun silhouetted the houses of Saint John against the coloured sky. The occasional lamp flickered here and there in the descending darkness.

Soon more and more appeared, until the whole bay was dotted with twinkling lights. In the streets of that city, policemen, firemen and railway officials searched in vain for Isaac Barr.

Easter Sunday dawned, giving fresh hope to the people on board ship. The sound of church bells filled the morning. Oliver Holtby took a deep breath of "New World" air and thought how thin and fresh it seemed. In Barr's continuing absence, Lloyd agreed to take charge temporarily. He called everyone up on deck and told them the procedure for boarding the train. A delegation representing five hundred of the passengers surprised him with a gift of $300, which they had collected in gratitude for his shipboard ministrations. Lloyd was becoming a very popular man.

The *Manitoba* had come alongside the wharf at 5:00 A.M. Observing that the gangways had already been lowered, the passengers were optimistic that their maritime confinement would soon be at an end. Alas, they were informed that the luggage had to be unloaded first. As they remembered the disordered piles of bags and boxes in the hold of the ship, many despaired of ever setting foot on dry land again.

All night they had listened as the crew brought the luggage up on deck. Now they watched as box after bag after dilapidated trunk slid down wooden shutes to the landing stage. Each hoped that the suitcases with clothes hanging out the sides did not belong to him or her. Workers on the dock attempted to arrange the luggage in alphabetical order, but the sheer quantity threatened to defeat them as the piles mounted higher and higher and the passageways between grew more and more narrow.

Several hours later the passengers were given permission to disembark according to which train section they had been assigned. The first people down the gangway were single men bound for jobs in Manitoba. Customs officials inspected their hand luggage and released them. They wandered up and down between the mounds of luggage in an attempt to find their heavy gear and arrange for it to be loaded aboard the first section of the train.

As passengers for the second and third sections were allowed to disembark, stories started to spread. Someone heard there was so much baggage on shore that there was no room for people. Someone else heard that there had never been an immigrant ship with so much luggage. A barely suppressed air of panic permeated the landing stage as people searched among the towering piles of boxes and trunks unable to find their own belongings.

The Holtby family was lucky. Their luggage was intact and easily located. It was not until they realized that their train was a quarter of a mile from the boat and there were no porters or trucks available that they started to worry. Obviously the luggage had to be moved piece by piece to the train, but food and stamps had to be bought and more money exchanged. Bessie Holtby, her fifteen-year-old chin quivering slightly, was plunked on top of the pile and told to guard it until the men finished their errands and could carry their belongings to the train.

Bessie's undignified perch turned out to be a perfect vantage point from which to observe the chaotic scene around her. The citizens of Saint John had come to inspect the new arrivals. It was obvious from their Easter Sunday finery that many of the Canadians had come straight from church. Bob Holtby was impressed by how healthy they looked and observed that they had "a pleasant expression that you don't see on every English face." He found them to be very kind and most polite when answering questions. He also found them to be exotic—"mostly dark haired and dark skinned"—and surmised that this was due to having French blood in their veins.

Colonist William Hutchinson, an amateur reporter, had an even keener eye for the unusual. He espied "Indians, negroes, Jews, half-castes and many Chinese with pigtails," but he was reassured by the air of prosperity that seemed to surround everyone and by the fact that they all seemed to be well dressed.

Ivan Crossley tried to see his fellow colonists through the eyes of the Canadians. Did the British people look odd coming down the gangway with their queer walking sticks and umbrellas, their hunting togs and other "curious get-ups"? "Where are the Indians?" someone wanted to know. "Are they dangerous?" "Where are the Northwest Mounted Police?"

There was no platform at the Saint John railway station, just tracks running down the middle of Union Street, which could accommodate only one section of the train at a time. The first section of the Immigrant Special Train had fourteen cars: eleven for passengers, two for baggage and a separate car for thirty-one dogs.

The dogs had been a special problem ever since the group left Liverpool. Considered essential members of the family by some and essential to survival in the wilds by others, they ranged from huge Newfoundlands to tiny lap dogs. They had roamed at will about the ship and slept and defecated anywhere they chose. Complaints were made to the captain, the crew rebelled and dark threats were heard, but the story that troublesome animals were thrown overboard during the night was probably not true. Had such an event taken place, there would have been mutiny among the passengers and no need for the special dog cars that were part of each section of the immigrant train.

So great was the confusion that no one could be sure when the first section actually pulled out of Saint John, but it was sometime in the early evening. The second section steamed into the landing area and began to take on young families and single men bound for the colony. Twenty-year-old Betsy Lee leaned on the arm of her husband. She was nine months pregnant and found it difficult to manoeuvre on her own.

Section Number Three had one baggage car, one dog car with 130 inhabitants and twelve coaches. As it pulled up for boarding, 450 people made a dash for seats. In the shove and scramble of getting children, hand luggage, picnic baskets, bedding and food on board, the Holtby men scored a minor triumph when they obtained seats in a tourist car for the women and children, and a major triumph when they found similar seats for themselves in the less comfortable colonist cars.

Stanley Rackham waited until the pushing and shoving ended. He had stayed on board ship for dinner and tea, passed through customs at a leisurely pace and deposited his hand luggage where he knew the train would draw up. The car he chose was not overcrowded, and he was able to find a suitable seat with no trouble.

But there was trouble in the third section when several families heard that their blankets and tents were still on board the ship. A promise from officials that a fifth section of the train would follow with all the settlers' effects did not satisfy them. The blankets at least were needed for the train journey.

Barr had not been seen since the afternoon before. Pressed again to take charge, Lloyd was able to locate the trunks full of brown blankets that Barr had intended to sell in Saskatoon. With the assistance of Ivan Crossley and one or two other men, Lloyd went through the cars of the third section issuing blankets and noting names on the understanding that the blankets would be returned when the train got to Saskatoon.

According to Lloyd's memoirs, he and his assistants were two-thirds of the way through the train when he heard a voice behind him say, "What are you doing with my blankets?" He turned to see Barr, his face very white and his eyes very fierce, looking "for all the world like a spirit drunk man." But Lloyd did not say outright that Barr *was* drunk. Ivan Crossley remembered that Barr had been, and that he was funny to watch as he took over the operation, attempting to make change and count blankets.

But both Lloyd and Crossley were recalling the incident through a curtain of years and old age. By the time Lloyd wrote his memoirs, he had reason to dislike Barr intensely. And Lloyd's memoirs shaped the recollections of many of the colonists. Crossley wrote his memoirs twenty years after Lloyd's account was published, and he may have been influenced by what Lloyd had written. The passage of time had blurred Crossley's memory for a number of other details about the departure from Saint John as well.

Barr left no record at all. It is possible that he had disappeared from the *Manitoba* the day before frustrated by events on board ship, isolated by the anger of the colonists and envious of Lloyd's popularity. It is not impossible to believe that he sought solace in drink and returned in a drunken state just as the third train was preparing to leave. It is, however, much more likely that he left the ship to meet further with Messrs. Davis and Scott and to attend to business in Saint John. His angry confrontation with Lloyd could well have resulted from a perception on his part that Lloyd was giving away the blankets Barr hoped would be a source of much-needed income. And it seems that, had Barr actually smelled of liquor, Lloyd would have reacted with the intolerance of a man who opposed the consumption of any amount of alcohol.

Lloyd also wrote that Barr had been removed from the train by CPR officials on that Sunday evening and locked in his cabin on the ship until after the fourth section had left Saint John. There is no other evidence to confirm or deny this final detail of the events of Sunday night, but Barr was in Ottawa by Tuesday morning, and no mention was made of any such confinement in the department files.

If the bread and blanket incidents were the beginning of Lloyd's disenchantment with Barr, as he implies in his memoirs, he did a foolish thing when he entrusted to Barr the money he and his wife had been given by the grateful passengers on the previous day. Sometime in the following week, Lloyd gave the $300 to Barr with the request that he find him a good team and buckboard.

Barr would soon give Lloyd sufficient reasons to mistrust him, but on that Sunday night in Saint John the important thing was to get the trains moving. At 11:00 P.M., the third section of the Immigrant Special Train pulled out of the station, leaving only one more section to be loaded and sent on its way.

The *Toronto Star* described the passengers on the fourth section as "the bathtub, piano carrying fellows," the ones with money, the ones who took on superior airs. Lloyd remembered that they all seemed to be women and children, but there were actually many young men on board as well. The train, extra long to accommodate all the remaining passengers, finally pulled out at midnight.

In the darkness of the first hours of Monday morning, the landing stage in Saint John, littered with unclaimed luggage, was a forlorn sight. Faced with mounting demurrage fees, the CPR was desperate to load the trains and clear the station, and they promised that the unclaimed luggage would be put aboard a fifth train and sorted in Saskatoon.

Two days later, the S.S. *Lake Simcoe* arrived in Saint John, setting a record for speed of crossing. Included among the passengers were Barr colonists Alice and William Rendell and two of their three children. Alice was six months pregnant with their fourth child. Forced to sail on the later vessel because of business in London, the family had endured a distressing voyage marked by several mishaps—a man broke his leg, someone cut the throat of a steerage passenger and the purser discovered twenty stowaways. Although the ship docked late in the day, the passengers were not allowed to stay on board overnight and were instead hustled off "in a most disgraceful way" into the teeth of a sleet storm. The sleet covered everything on the landing stage, including all the unclaimed luggage from the *Manitoba*, still sitting there after two days.

The Rendell family sought refuge in a café nearby. It was long past midnight when suddenly an alarm sounded. A fire in the immediate vicinity filled the landing stage with black smoke. The tired family was "literally thrown" on board the train as it hurriedly left the station to escape the fire. The fate of their luggage, which included a piano, and the fate of the luggage from the *Manitoba* was entirely unknown to them.

Chapter
V

Doing the Gentleman

THE TOWN OF BROWNSVILLE WAS A MEAGRE COLLECTION OF LOG CABINS THAT clustered around a railway station in a clearing in the dense forest of northern Maine. On Monday, April 13, 1903, the entire male population gathered to watch hundreds of Barr colonists pour off the Immigrant Special Train, Section Three. Lean, muscular Yankees in red woollen shirts and Indians with long braided hair scrutinized top-hatted clerks and tweed-jacketed farmers, who in turn marvelled at their first sight of real lumberjacks and real "Red Indians."

The tracks that bisected Brownsville had been built across the State of Maine by the CPR to provide a direct connection between Saint John and Montreal. Brownsville was a short stop, offering passengers little more than a chance to stretch their legs and observe some local colour. The local colour in turn stood with its hands in its pockets, working wads of tobacco between cheek and tongue and hawking the occasional stream of brown juice in the vicinity of the newcomers' fine leather boots.

Fifteen minutes after arriving, the train began to pull out of the station, and the passengers still standing on the platform scrambled to get aboard. In Britain one stepped easily into a moving train through individual doors at platform level. In Canada one leapt from a platform lower than the train itself and separated by a considerable gap to reach the doors located at either end of the coach. Much agility and fleetness of foot were required.

The male passengers in the first section had practiced jumping off and on a moving Canadian train at every station. As they approached each new town, there was a rush down the aisles to the doors. An observer standing on any of the platforms would have been astounded at the sight of hundreds of young men pouring out of the space between each coach as the train gradually came to a halt.

This behaviour was not without its dangers. When the first section of the train eased its way into the station at Chapleau, Ontario, a small community near Lake Superior, a young man named Blekler tripped as he jumped from the train, trapping his leg under a wheel. As he sank into a sitting position, he smiled foolishly up at the crowd and protested that he felt no pain. The leg was badly crushed. CPR officials arranged for him to be taken back to a hospital in Sudbury.

The four sections of the immigrant train were connected by a string of rumours. As each section pulled into a new station, the local people had stories to tell about the trains that had been there before. The story of poor young Blekler travelled back from section to section along with a collection of money that soon amounted to almost $400, more than enough to provide him with a proper funeral when he succumbed to his injuries a few days later.

Other news passed from train to train, too. Newspapers from Canada, the United States and Great Britain were printing stories about the Barr Colony that were most unreassuring. "An influential section of the British press is watching distrustfully the Barr movement," wrote the *Manitoba Free Press*, "for it has but little confidence in Mr. Barr's executive ability." The *Minneapolis Journal* compared the new venture to the ill-fated Jamestown colony in seventeenth-century Virginia and then compounded the foolishness by reporting that there were ten thousand colonists headed for Barr's All-British Colony. The newspaper had its facts straight, however, when it reported that Barr had agreed only under pressure to include a few experienced Canadians and Americans.

> It will be bad enough even with the admixture of one-fourth Canadians and Americans, to turn these raw Englishmen loose on the great plains of the Canadian west. The mosquitos alone will be enough to rout them.

Two days later the same newspaper ran the headline "Failure of Barr Colony." "A piece of fine appearing patriotism has come to naught," it tut-tutted.

> Compare this class of settlers with those Americans who quietly and individually make their way to their new homes

without any assistance of any kind. . . . This is the kind Canada is now getting in large numbers, and though they were earnestly urged to come, there is quite a disposition to make less of them than of the impractical tenderfeet from Britain.

In Winnipeg, the *Telegram* reflected a sentiment expressed by so-called "disinterested parties" in other prairie communities when it advised the Barr colonists to "withdraw from the colony and take up land within reach of neighbours, civilization and supplies." The other communities were hardly disinterested. Two thousand new immigrants said to comprise the wealthiest group ever to come to Canada would have made a welcome addition to Winnipeg, Regina, Saskatoon or even Battleford. "Stay with us," the boosters of each town would say. "Spend your money with us."

The newshounds were on the trail of a big story. In addition to the *Manitoba Free Press*, three Toronto papers, the *Globe*, the *News* and the *Star*, assigned reporters to hasten to Saskatoon and to accompany the All-British Colony all the way to its destination.

While the newspapers prophesied the early demise of the grand plan, Bob and Oliver Holtby had more pressing problems. Like most of the men, they were travelling in third-class colonist coaches, the more comfortable second-class tourist coaches having been reserved for the women and children. The workings of the seats fascinated Bob with their cleverness. His father and uncle seemed to sleep well on the lower seat, which drew out to make a bed for two. Above them, attached by chains to the ceiling, was a bunk that could be pulled down at night to accommodate two more people, or so the railway said.

It may have been that the two brothers could not have slept together in even the most comfortable of beds, but the combination of the narrowness of the bunk and its closeness to the ceiling made sleep virtually impossible. Added to that was the fact that, unlike the bunks in tourist class, which had pillows, bedding and drop curtains for privacy, the bunks in colonist class were bare. Unless they rented straw mattresses from the CPR and had brought their own blankets, pillows and curtains as Barr had suggested they do, third-class passengers slept on bare boards with their overcoats for cover and their boots for a pillow.

In his first pamphlet, Barr had promised them all comfortable sleeping accommodation. In addition, "both tourist and colonist cars provide absolute privacy," he assured them, "and objectionable persons are strictly excluded." Some of the men might well have accepted the occasional objectionable person if they could have been comfortable as well. The description in Barr's second pamphlet was more accurate. The colonist cars were not all that comfortable, he admitted, but "single men should be prepared to rough it a little. It is better to begin at once."

Barr had no intention of roughing it himself. He had instructed Mr. Bromhead to arrange that "a pullman car be attached to the train for himself and some of the more well-to-do people." Barr's arrangements were altered, however, by the government's insistence that he come immediately to Ottawa.

Undaunted by this change in his plans, Barr continued to issue instructions even as he was hustled to the capital city to explain himself. His first task was to replace the two English doctors who had failed to appear in Liverpool. From the ship, Lloyd had sent a cable to a minister he knew in Montreal, introducing Barr, stating their need for two doctors and specifying that they wished to have Anglicans. "We did not want French Canadians for an English party," Lloyd explained later.

Dr. Keating, a visiting physician at a small city hospital, was prepared to join the colony if he could bring his new bride. Barr agreed. Keating then contacted Dr. W. W. Amos, a graduate of Queen's University who was working as a house surgeon in Montreal. He agreed to join Keating on the strength of Barr's promise of a monthly salary, expenses and transportation to Saskatoon, where formal contracts would be signed. They were urged to come as soon as possible.

Barr was needed in Ottawa to discuss transportation. Both he and the department had arranged for teams and wagons to be waiting in Saskatoon for purchase by the colonists, but despite protestations to the contrary, Barr had made no arrangements to provide freighting services for those who could not afford such a large investment. Under some duress, Barr agreed to telegraph the Indian agent in Battleford: "Hire me 25 teams to transport goods and people Saskatoon to colony $3 per day and found."

Barr filled his spare time in Ottawa sending telegrams, most of them paid for by the Department of the Interior. Among the several wires addressed to Dr. Robbins was one instructing him to charge a dollar extra for the tents to cover the cost of freight.

Barr ignored a telegram from Bromhead warning him that all was not ready in Saskatoon and requesting that the colonists be held in Winnipeg. Instead, Barr boarded a train heading west. A similar request by Bromhead to the department was ignored as well.

Bromhead could not get enough supplies. Saskatoon was too small to provide for two thousand extra people. But Bromhead's fellow organizer, Dr. Robbins, denied there was a problem. In an interview with the *Manitoba Free Press*, Robbins said that he, Charles May and the officers of the transportation and trading syndicates had everything well in hand. "Ample tent accommodation will be ready," he said, "fires will be burning and kettles boiling when the colonists arrive." When Robbins made his foolish boast, the first train was due in Saskatoon in just two days.

Unaware of the lack of readiness in Saskatoon, the colonists aboard the trains sped across a country that seemed to have no end. Mile after endless mile, the coaches lurched and swayed along the track. Canadian trains travelled fast, sometimes reaching speeds of thirty-five miles per hour, pulled by engines larger and more powerful than British ones. Because the CPR had been built in haste to span a vast, underpopulated country, the roadbeds were of marginal quality. Passengers were jolted constantly in their seats and literally thrown from side to side as the train careened around the curves. Some women cried out in terror, fearing that the train would be thrown off the track and "hurled down some of the deep and dreadful canyons and gullies."

Each train had skirted Montreal, stopped in Ottawa and then followed the Ottawa River north through well-settled farming country. At Mattawa the tracks swung west to North Bay and Sudbury and then struck out through the bush towards the shores of Lake Superior. Pine and hemlock gave way to spruce and balsam fir. Following the curving shore of the giant lake, the train sliced through rock bluffs and slid through dark tunnels. Caught between the lives they had left behind and the lives they had yet to begin, the passengers stared out the windows at a cold and rocky landscape where the only signs of life were the stunted evergreens and scrawny aspens struggling to survive.

Although the country they travelled through was barren, silent and cold, the coaches they travelled in were crowded, noisy and warm, very warm. Seeking cool fresh air, passengers opened windows, but the engine smoke blew in. They fled to the open spaces on the platforms between the cars, but the cold air drove them back inside to endure the chaos, the overcrowding and the heat from the cooking stoves.

The tourist coaches were at once the most comfortable and the most chaotic as mothers attempted to feed and amuse children in surroundings that were short on playing room and long on dirt. Cinder grit lay on everything—the seats, the floor, the food. The aisles were filled with children and stove tops covered with cooking pots. At first, every mother was determined to cook her family proper meals. Impatient women argued over how long they had been waiting for a turn at the stove or how many pots they were entitled to use at once. When it became apparent that there was not enough space for everyone to cook a whole meal, it was agreed that kettles should have precedence. For the rest of the journey, families ate cold food washed down with hot tea.

Most of the single men were unequipped to cook their own meals and, for that matter, unable as well. They resigned themselves to eating bread and bologna or whatever could be purchased in a headlong dash to the closest store at stations along the way. The smaller towns had no bakeries, and the bakeries in the larger towns could accommodate only the first few customers who came charging breathlessly into the shop.

Stanley Rackham had retained a gentlemanly mien by planning his food purchases in advance, and although he said that some of the tinned goods he had bought on board the *Manitoba* tasted as if they had been to South Africa and back, he managed well with the addition of some of Barr's bread. William Hutchinson had brought tea, coffee, bread, butter and cheese, sardines, salmon, potted meat, Swiss milk, sugar and biscuits. With those savoury tidbits and the occasional hot meal bought from the station restaurant at a longer than usual stop, he was more than satisfied.

Barr had promised that food could be bought cheaply at all the stations along the way, but he had not allowed for avarice. As the four sections of the Immigrant Special Train moved westward, prices at the restaurants and grocery stores near the stations rose higher and higher. Bob Holtby said that the prices were 100 per cent higher than those in England. That may have explained the behaviour he observed as the passengers shopped at a big Hudson's Bay Company (HBC) store in Fort William.

[The] goods were arranged so conveniently that a good

many of our party went in with the crowds, filled their pockets with all sorts of things and came out again without going through the formality of paying.

This may have been why William Hutchinson described the Fort William HBC store as "the cheapest and best place we had yet found."

Snow and ice still lay on the ground at Fort William, but it was warm enough for William Hutchinson to sit by an open window in his shirtsleeves. The platform was crowded. In addition to the usual shoppers racing to buy food and dog owners anxiously encouraging their pets to drink, eat, walk and heed nature's call, there were women and children taking advantage of the longer stop to stretch their legs. At a similar long stop in Ottawa, a large number of local citizens had assembled to meet them. Hutchinson was pleased to be able to report that "we created a favourable impression, being described as the finest body of settlers yet seen in the Dominion."

The impression made on the citizens of Ottawa was enhanced by the information Barr gave to the reporters there. As he told the *Toronto News*,

> Most of those you see are men of large means and all of them have money. About £500,000 sterling is represented aboard. . . . We have in this party five earls' nephews, several capitalists, many clergymen, lawyers, doctors and whatnot.

There was no shortage of sources for this kind of information. The *Manitoba Free Press* enhanced this impressive list by reporting that a large portion of the colonists were practical and experienced farmers. One month before, the paper had quoted George Douglas, then the head of the stores syndicate, as saying that everyone in the colony came from the well-to-do middle class, his criterion being the possession of £100 sterling. In a dispatch to his hometown newspaper, William Hutchinson reckoned that most individuals were worth between £200 and £300. The party was composed of British subjects from all over the world, he reported, reservists and yeomen who had served in South Africa, gold miners from Western Australia, tea planters from India and Ceylon, and men from Hong Kong, Brazil, Egypt and Central and Northern Africa. On the day before the S.S. *Lake Manitoba* sailed, the *Free Press* in Winnipeg had assured its readers,

> There is no need for undue apprehension about the ability
> of these colonists to look after themselves. These settlers
> are all of a very desirable class, largely composed of experi-
> enced agriculturalists and all have sufficient means for their
> own sustenance for the next two or three years.

Just in case the image of wealthy aristocratic farmers had been over-
done, Dr. Robbins took it upon himself to reassure the newspaper
readers of Winnipeg. "It is a mistake," he said, "to confound these
hard-working colonists with the sons of rich men reared in the lap of
luxury, who have failed in the past in Canada."

This grand advance billing grew out of Barr's efforts to convince
first the Canadian government and then the Canadian people that his
colonists were exceptional and deserved special consideration. Living
up to all this misinformation would be very difficult. The stage was set
for even greater notoriety when it began to look as though the scheme
would fail. Newspaper reporters sniffed the air for a whiff of failure
and gathered their forces to deliver news of that failure to readers on
both sides of the Atlantic—to Canadians who were hostile to repre-
sentatives of the colonial power; to Americans who resented the special consideration being given to inexperienced settlers; to families in
Britain who feared for the survival of their loved ones, and now to Europeans who wondered at Canada's special treatment of English immigrants when so many non-English speaking people were receiving
scant assistance.

As a former soldier and bank clerk, Jim Ashton illustrated both the
strengths and weaknesses of a typical Barr colonist. Of yeoman stock,
Ashton's family had farmed Lincolnshire land for generations, em-
ploying several servants and farm labourers. The sons of the family
had been educated at fine public schools. But his family had not owned
the land they farmed, and when his father could no longer make agriculture pay, he had gone into banking. Ashton's only knowledge of
farming was some distant childhood memories of living in a large
house surrounded by tenants' cottages, but his experiences as a bank
clerk had made him sure that his future lay in farming land of his own.

Ashton was not rich, nor was he titled. He hoped to parlay a decent
education, his military experience and his youth into a successful life in
Canada. But he missed England. As the train bells clanged to announce departure from Fort William, he longed for the whistles of
English trains, and he guessed it would be some time before he would

grow accustomed to all the new things this huge country had in store for him.

Four hundred Barr colonists knew that their dreams of future independence would be postponed for a year while they earned enough money in Manitoba for a grubstake in the colony. They were all young, and almost all of them were men. They had joined Barr's party knowing that they did not have enough money or enough farming experience to succeed in the Northwest Territories. At the insistence of the Department of Immigration the four hundred, all of whom were on the first train, planned to disembark in Winnipeg and spend a year working for others. And there were people on the other three trains who should have followed their example.

The prospects were good in Manitoba for anyone who was prepared to work hard and who had no qualms about living outside the city. A man could expect about thirty-five dollars a month and free board and lodging if he worked for a farmer. Most farm jobs ended as soon as the cold weather came, however, making it imperative that the workers save money to get them through the winter. After a year, if they had been sufficiently frugal and if, as sometimes happened, their employers had not reneged on their wages, they could join the colony, where Barr would have registered their homesteads for them in their absence.

There were a few women among the four hundred. It was easy for them to get work as domestic servants, work that lasted through the winter. A careful woman with an employer who did not try to exploit her could save enough money to set herself up in the colony until she found a suitable husband.

Special Train Number One steamed into Winnipeg, "the great centre of the Northwest Territories," at 4:30 A.M. on April 16. The passengers from all but two of the cars climbed down onto the platform to be greeted by members of the Society of the Sons of England, who were distributing pamphlets full of useful information.

The passengers in the remaining two cars, which would continue on to Saskatoon, peered out at the darkened city. One man had a thirst big enough to make him defy an edict that they remain on board. He left the train in search of strong drink and soon espied the Occidental Hotel. As he approached the establishment in some haste, he fell prey to a gang of toughs who relieved him of his "loose cash." The incident was reported in the local newspapers, not, it would seem, to decry the lack of hospitality shown by Winnipeg's denizens of the night, but to point out the folly of wandering about a strange city in the dark with pockets full of money.

The second train arrived, added the engine and two remaining coaches of the first train and left for Saskatoon double-headed. Train Number Three chuffed into Winnipeg in time for breakfast. In the pale light of early morning, the city looked splendid to colonists bored by the monotony of the Canadian Shield. They marvelled at the grandeur of the brick and stone town hall, at the width of Main Street and the modernity of the electric trains that ran down its centre.

In the full light of day, the colonists saw the frontier city through Old World eyes. Carts bumped "horribly" when crossing the electric train rails, which had not been sunk properly into the ground. Side by side with the fine buildings of brick and stone were wooden ones, some in a state of decay, patched with new wood in a manner that made Bob Holtby think of how his trousers had looked when he was a boy. The streets were dusty and the day was hot.

It was a city all the same. William Hutchinson noted that a bath could be had for twenty-five cents and a *table d'hôte* lunch for the same amount, and he set out to obtain both. Stanley Rackham travelled by the electric train as he systematically tended to his errands—a trip to the bank for money, a quick look at some horses, then on to the post office, where he found no mail but only disquieting rumours of what lay ahead.

Winnipeg was abuzz over the arrival of the Barr colonists. Reporters were allowed to board the coaches to observe the exotic new breed of settler in its temporary habitat. The colonists had not tidied up for their inquisitive guests. For its readers' information, the *Free Press* noted that the coaches were littered with "magazines, newspapers, cards, cameras, good toilet sets, hammocks, books, chessboards and 'a score of English luxuries.'" Each passenger who consented to be interviewed received a free subscription to the newspaper for one year.

The ordinary citizens of Winnipeg arrived at the station in a constant stream to have a look for themselves. In contrast to the thousands of immigrants who had come through Winnipeg in the last few years, these newcomers were obviously people of quality, the women so well dressed, the men so dashing. Their luggage alone marked them as a cut above the rest.

By the time the fourth train arrived, a huge crowd had assembled. This was the train that was rumoured to carry the most affluent members of the party. The crowd looked for signs of great wealth and saw some of the younger men dressed as though for a weekend at some fine country estate, attired in breeches and top boots and well armed with guns, revolvers and, in deference to the frontier, sheath knives. And this was the train that was supposed to carry the aristocrats. The crowd strained to see if an earl's nephew or some other equally important personage would make himself apparent. And this was also the train with the largest number of women and children. Female members of the crowd made careful note of the broad-brimmed hats and the trainless suits in the style of la belle époque. And, finally, this was the train that carried the Reverend George Exton Lloyd, and there he was, a tall man in a black Inverness cape, his broad-brimmed clerical "shovel" hat marking him easily.

Lloyd's reputation had grown as the group crossed the country. Now, as he walked up and down the platform, the crowd surged after him to ask questions to which he gave reassuring answers. Yes, the entire party had been carefully selected; yes, careful plans had been made to provide transportation of goods and people to the colony; and, oh yes, the government of Canada had been most helpful and most accommodating.

Obed Smith met each train in Winnipeg. At his request, each section appointed a committee to meet with him, and at each meeting he was assailed with complaints about the overcrowded steamship and with expressions of doubt about Barr's arrangements. The commissioner told each committee that the government had everything well in hand. Sufficient food would be loaded onto each train to last until two days after their arrival in Saskatoon, and the government agents who had accompanied the colonists from Saint John would continue on with them. Reassured by his promises, the committees cheered loudly for the government and for the railway, whose crowded coaches, cinders and soot seemed to have been forgotten in the flush of high spirits engendered by Smith's adroit handling of the situation.

With just as much at stake as the government, the cpr was determined to rectify any problems. The railway company bought food in Winnipeg and sold it on the train at low prices. When the last section pulled out of the Winnipeg station and it became apparent that several passengers had been left behind, the cpr loaded them onto a coach and supplied an engine to chase and catch Train Number Four.

It was enough to put everyone in a good mood. Someone said that it was because the grumblers had been left behind in Winnipeg.

Someone else said that it was because of the perfect weather. Whatever the cause, a few people always wanted to wander around outside
whenever the train made an unscheduled stop. The crew tried to prevent this. It took so long to get everyone back on, and then there was
always someone who was left behind, and he would be running down
the tracks after the train, yelling for it to stop, and someone on the
train would pull the communication cord and the train would stop and
that would delay them some more. Not fifty miles out of Winnipeg,
near Portage la Prairie, the forces of nature took a turn at slowing
their progress, as five thousand antelope held civilization at bay while
they crossed the tracks at a slow and graceful pace.

The train had to make a lot of predictable stops, too. Regular trains
took precedence over special trains on the single track line. In addition, the trains frequently had to take on water for the steam engine
and for the use of the passengers. During one stop in the middle of the
prairie, someone saw a gopher, and then there were many more. Out
came all manner of firearms—.22s, shotguns, rifles, pistols, revolvers—and the hunting instinct, suppressed in most of the colonists for
generations, found an outlet. Men who had watched at home while the
privileged classes hunted for game on private land, men who had been
chased by gamekeepers, were now free to hunt all they wanted. These
strange little creatures perched on their hind legs looked like easy
marks. The gophers, more curious than afraid, watched as the gun-
slingers fired inaccurately on all sides. Finally prudence overcame
their curiosity, and they disappeared down their holes lest a bullet inadvertently find its mark.

Jim Ashton belonged to the class in the Old Country that was able
to hunt. His family had attended fall shooting parties at which beaters
flushed out hundreds of game birds to be ceremoniously slaughtered
by the assembled guests. He thought of the Mauser pistol his father
had given him when he left for South Africa. He had been on his way
to a war where the enemy refused to fight by the rules, where guns
were in order. He was not so sure that they were in order here. As the
train slowly began to move again, he shook his head at his fellow passengers, who, having regained their seats, leaned out the open windows and continued to fire at the innocuous little rodents.

It was probably the sight of the legendary Canadian prairies that
had cheered everyone the most. After the barren landscape of the
shield and the disquieting rumours in Winnipeg of the colony's failure, the open miles of grass offered encouragement. Bob Holtby noted

that the early spring plains looked like "a great brown sea" inhabited by herds of deer and flocks of geese, ducks and prairie hens. Stanley Rackham talked with some old-timers on the platform at Brandon and got back on the train feeling encouraged. The old settlers had "seen rough times and had come through all right and said we ought to stick to it and do the same thing."

It took only one day for Bob Holtby to become bored by the unchanging scene outside his window. He woke to see "the same old prairie" with only the telegraph lines to break the monotony of the view. He was annoyed that the telegraph lines followed the terrain up and down instead of being level, as they were in England. Stanley Rackham was in a similar frame of mind as he stared out the window between Indian Head and Regina. Even more herds of antelope failed to relieve the dreariness of the barren prairies untouched as yet by even a hint of green.

As they neared Regina, they passed several trainloads of settlers' effects belonging to Americans who had arrived in large numbers over the past year to settle land between Regina and Saskatoon. This influx of experienced farmers had done very little to enhance Regina, however, which seemed insignificant to a stranger's eyes. There were almost as many people on Barr's special trains as there were resident in the territorial capital.

William Hutchinson congratulated himself for remembering to set his watch back one hour. Many of the passengers had forgotten about the time changes, which may explain why some of them had missed the train in Winnipeg and probably accounts for the discrepancy in times of arrival and departure that were recorded in their diaries.

At Regina the Immigrant Special Trains switched from the main line of the CPR to the Qu'Appelle, Long Lake and Saskatchewan Railway. A German-Canadian company had built this line in 1891 and leased it to the CPR, neither company allowing for the increased volume of settlers now headed for Saskatoon and the free land beyond. The train carrying the Barr colonists on the final miles of their railway journey rocked and lurched over thin tracks of rusting iron laid upon a roadbed pocked with badger holes.

Stories of trains running westward with no provisions were creating a stir in London. According to the Reuters News Agency, there were problems too with the provision of shelter, supplies and transport. Concerned families sent a flood of telegrams to the office of Commissioner Preston, who demanded an explanation from Reuters. The agency's Winnipeg correspondent provided corroborating details, adding that the government was now acting to save the colonists from further hardships. Ottawa told Preston that Barr's private enterprise had indeed failed, but that there was no cause for alarm because the government had taken over.

Seeking to repair the damage done by the Reuters dispatch, the immigration office in London asked Ottawa to supply a brief cablegram from a member of the colony who could express satisfaction with the way things were going and sign the cable with his former English address to give it credibility. Preston promised that he would meet again with Reuters to convince them that their correspondent in Winnipeg had "other ends to serve than furnishing reliable information." In the meantime, however, Reuters had sent the dispatch to the continent, and the resulting editorials in German newspapers advised possible emigrants that they should reconsider in view of the Canadian government's inability "to handle those who are in fear of starvation."

So far, the government had failed to counteract the bad publicity, nor were its bureaucrats able, on short notice, to find a settler who would furnish them with the desired testimonial. German emigrants would continue to be discouraged and English relatives would continue to fret, but for the men, women and children on board the Immigrant Special Train, there was only a sense of relief that their journey was almost at an end.

In Saskatoon, approximately two hundred colonists waited to greet the first train. Bernard and Percy Boden had been there for ten days, having sailed earlier on the S.S. *Lake Erie* in order to arrive in the colony well in advance of the main party. But their sea chests and boxes and the stove, tools and household crockery they had bought in Winnipeg had not yet caught up with them.

The Bodens' train trip had been an exceedingly unpleasant one and may have been the source of the negative reports reaching Britain. There had been no sleeping accommodation and few facilities for cooking. In Montreal, the passengers had refused to change trains until sleeping cars were provided for the women and children. The men had sat up all the way to Saskatoon. Now they could go no further because their luggage was missing. Bernard filled his days venting his frustration in letters to his fiancée, Madeleine.

> What is the most annoying thing we have had to put up
> with since our arrival here, is the humbugging and waiting

that one has to suffer from the railway company. We have already found out that it is not all 'beer and skittles' in such an undertaking as ours, we have had to rough it pretty much up till now and expect to for some time.

It was Bernard's fervent desire to leave Saskatoon as soon as possible. When he learned that he could get to the colony without Barr's assistance, he was even more anxious to be on his way.

There is bound to be trouble when the party arrives I am sure. I have heard very poor opinions expressed of Barr. Anyhow it is a case of looking after number one out here and Mr. Barr will not trouble me much.

Although there were no wagons available yet for sale, Boden bought three two-year-old oxen on the advice of some old-timers. He kept them just outside his tent and, when he was not writing to Madeleine, spent long hours carrying hay from town. "It is a very fagging job I can tell you."

Despite Bernard's misgivings, preparations for the main party had been proceeding, albeit behind schedule. While Dr. Robbins gave press conferences to assure reporters that all was well, Mr. Bromhead scurried about attempting to procure supplies and trying by telegraph, to no avail, to persuade Barr or the department to delay the arrival of the colonists.

The problem was not that Barr had failed to provide the equipment he had promised; some of it had arrived in Saskatoon by now. Bromhead had brought twenty-five marquee tents along with him. In addition, wood, hay, livestock and half of the stoves were in place. The problem was that only eight of the marquees had been erected, the remaining stoves had not yet come and there were no wagons to be seen. The army surplus bell tents, blankets and groundsheets that had been purchased in Britain by the settlers were still on the trains.

The people on board the trains that lurched and swayed towards their final destination had begun to regard "Saskatoon" as the answer to all their problems. Barr had promised in his pamphlet that the camp would be ready for them. He had promised that marquees would be waiting for the single men and bell tents for the families. He had promised that a baker would be engaged to provide all the bread they needed and a butcher would be there to slaughter cattle for fresh meat. Many of Barr's promises had proven to be empty ones, but the fine weather and the prospect of the end of the train journey rekindled optimism.

Betsy Lee had climbed onto the train in Saint John with her mind focussed on her most pressing problem, her pregnancy. Within twenty-four hours, her labour had started, and her baby had been born in Ottawa, where the train was delayed for an hour and a half so that a doctor could attend the delivery. Mother and new babe had then continued on their journey. At each of the longer stops along the way, a doctor had come on board to check Mrs. Lee and her offspring, the first Barr colonist to be born in Canada. In Winnipeg the remnants of the first train had been added to theirs and they had proceeded with two engines towards Saskatoon.

On the morning of April 17, 1903, just before noon, the two engines tooted in unison as the double-headed train chuffed across the old wooden bridge that spanned the ice-choked South Saskatchewan River. Saskatonians made a rush for the depot. They peered down the tracks to see the uncoupling of the extra engine and cheered at the extravagant tooting of the remaining locomotive as it bore down on the station pulling its load of more than five hundred passengers.

The train came to a halt between a lone grain elevator and the tiny depot, and nothing happened for a moment. Then some of the more impatient colonists began to throw their hand luggage through the windows of the coaches and scramble out after it. Dr. Robbins was dismayed. Desirous of restoring order and some sense of occasion, he called to the colonists to line up and, to his amazement, many of them did, forming ranks on a roped-off section of the station platform. Colonization Agent Speers made a flowery welcoming speech on behalf of the Territories and informed the travellers of the plans made for their comfort. Three cheers were offered for the king, the government and even for Mr. Barr, the euphoria of the moment having restored the latter to the good graces of all assembled.

Betsy Lee left the train on a stretcher carried on the shoulders of four men who took her to the immigration hall, a spare-looking two-storey frame building that stood alone across the tracks from the town. Martha Annie Topott watched as Betsy was borne away. The two women had survived the ocean voyage in their pregnant state, and now Betsy had her baby. Martha had been unable to eat on the boat, the smells in steerage making food seem intolerable. She had made up for it on the train, though, eating everything in sight. Still the trip had seemed interminable. In her advanced state of pregnancy, everything seemed to last too long. Well, here she was in Saskatoon with a two-hundred-mile trek to look forward to and the baby due any day. Mr. Barr had promised a doctor, a hospital tent and two nurses. She hoped that this was one promise he meant to keep.

Chapter VI

Sharpies, Swindlers and Fast-talking Salesmen

ON SUNDAY, APRIL 19, A CELEBRATION OF MORNING PRAYER WAS HELD IN THE large dining tent of the colony camp at Saskatoon. The women present demonstrated with their choice of dress that, although they had slept the night before in a tent, and the six nights before that on a train, and the twelve nights before that on an overcrowded ship, they had maintained their standards. Two-piece tailored costumes, the train of the skirt fashionably abbreviated as if in anticipation of the primitive terrain, extravagant hats and dainty gloves left no doubt that the women knew how to outfit themselves appropriately.

The men, on the other hand, were not as faithful to proper standards. Some wore broadcloth suits, to be sure, the sombre colours complemented, when the men regained the outdoors, by a fedora or English stiff hat. But just as many wore their tweeds and top boots, as though they were about to go for a Sunday afternoon ramble instead of a Sunday morning service of worship, and though their linen appeared to be fresh, some had adopted a decidedly casual appearance. There was even the occasional man who, upon leaving the tent, donned a newly purchased broad-brimmed straw "harvester."

Brilliant spring sunshine greeted the worshippers as they strolled out of the large marquee after the service. The bright yellow light fell on hundreds of tents spread out around them. Here and there were other marquees, ninety feet long, flying flags from all five poles.

It had been the military precision of the camp that impressed the colonists who arrived on the first train. The tents were pitched in neat avenues and numbered in order. Alas, when the tents that had travelled with the immigrant trains were assembled by inexperienced settlers, the precise lines had been blurred. Each greenhorn was required to wrestle a large bag full of ropes, pegs and canvas to his assigned site and then raise the contents satisfactorily. Making sense of the canvas and ropes and then pounding the pegs into the frozen ground was difficult enough; lining the tent up exactly with its neighbours was asking too much.

Living under canvas was a new experience for many of the colonists. In his first pamphlet, Barr had felt obliged to assure them that tents were "perfectly safe and pleasant temporary abodes for women and children at the season when we shall reach our destination." There being no alternative to tents either in Saskatoon or on the trail (or even in the colony, at least for the first few weeks), it was an adjustment that had to be made.

Although the camp contained tents in a variety of styles, army surplus bell tents were by far the most numerous. The graceful roof swept down from a single central pole to form a round enclosure with low vertical sides. But while they may have been graceful, comfortable they were not. They had been designed for the spartan life of a military camp. With no waterproofing, they leaked if accidentally touched during a rainstorm; with no hole for a chimney, there could be no stove inside; with no stove there could be no heat; with no floor they were primitive indeed. In addition, because they were secondhand, many of them were badly worn. But they had the advantage of being inexpensive, both for Barr to purchase in large numbers and for the colonists to buy singly for five dollars. And if there had not been the unexpected dollar charged for transporting them from Saint John, many of the men, at least, would have been content.

The women were not so easily pleased. A "head-lowering, back-bending bell tent" was no place to keep house. The sides were too low to hang clothing or store dishes. The only place high enough to stand upright was in the very centre near the pole. When it rained, the wet tent ropes lengthened and the wet canvas stretched. The added weight sometimes broke the pole, causing the tent to fall down on whoever happened to be inside.

The government marquees were so much more civilized. People could stand upright inside them, and they walked and slept on wooden floors. Raised by expert hands and held firmly in place with iron pegs ordered specially to pierce the frozen ground, the marquees were in no danger of falling down.

Barr's quarters outshone even the marquees. Bromhead had ordered a tent made of duck, a lighter, better quality material than canvas, for the quarters of the leader of the colony. A curtain divided the interior, sixteen feet wide and twenty feet long, into sleeping quarters and office space. Over his tent flew the Red Ensign, whose British merchant marine origins and Union Jack paid obeisance to the Old Country, but whose Canadian coat of arms denoted the new one.

Only Barr's tent and the one for the press flew the Canadian colours. All the other flags in camp, and there were many flapping in the prairie wind, were British flags of various kinds. Few of the colonists seemed to be aware that they were now in a different country—not a backward colony of Britain, but a separate, albeit fledgling, nation. Barr had assured them they would feel at home in Canada, and to most of them that meant they would not be required to adjust much at all. This was illustrated in a minor, but telling, slip of the tongue when referring to immigration halls.

Every community in the Northwest Territories had an immigration hall where the Dominion government processed and housed transient newcomers. Sometimes a local building was used, sometimes a tent, but often, as in Saskatoon, immigration halls were permanent structures built according to a fixed design. Spare, two-storey, wooden-framed, they stood out among the impermanent sea of tents that usually surrounded them, no-nonsense reminders of the government's presence.

The people of the All-British Colony called them "emigration" halls. At first it could be dismissed as an understandable error, but as the name persisted through the weeks and months that followed, this seemingly insignificant mistake took on symbolic importance. To have recognized that they were "immigrants" would be for the colonists to admit that not only had they left Britain behind but they were now akin to the groups of "foreigners"—non-British immigrants—who crowded into the Territories in response to Clifford Sifton's aggressive immigration policies.

The "foreigners" were distinguishable by their dress, by their inability to speak English and by their large numbers. They represented a host of nationalities, but most numerous were Austro-Hungarians, Germans, Italians, Norwegians, Swedes, Russians and Poles. Unlike Barr's people, they had to fend for themselves. No government tents waited for them along the route to their homesteads; no farming instructors or land agents smoothed their way. Even other British immigrants would not receive the attention that the Barr colonists did. As Deputy Minister Smart later admitted to Obed Smith,

Here we have a colony of . . . people causing us really more concern and more expenditure of money in looking after them than all the other 20,000 or 25,000 British settlers who have come out this year.

But if the Barr colonists were aware that they were receiving extra attention, they did not acknowledge it. They gave a cheer for the government whenever asked and then went back to the business of preparing for the trek.

They had been told in Barr's first pamphlet that the climate would be "conducive to vigorous health, notwithstanding the occasional extremes of heat and cold." They had checked their atlases before leaving home and noted that the proposed site for the colony lay at almost exactly the same latitude as Liverpool. From this information they had deduced that they would experience no worse weather than they were used to at home and perhaps even somewhat better. As if to confirm that assumption, the weather was wonderful—far better than a late April day in England, or even a midsummer one, for that matter.

Nights were another thing entirely. As soon as the sun set, the temperature plunged. People disappeared into their tents to re-emerge in mufflers and greatcoats or, for the more affluent, bulky fur coats that made their wearers look like Arctic explorers. Many people complained that it was too cold to undress for bed. Instead, they put on all available clothing before they climbed beneath their blankets, then shivered themselves to sleep with nothing between them and the frozen ground but mattress ticking filled with straw.

The ice on the South Saskatchewan River had broken up just before the colonists arrived, huge blocks mounding up against the pilings of the bridge and along each bank. Men made daily trips to the river to hack off chunks of ice and carry them back to be melted and boiled for drinking water. Nights were so cold that the water in the buckets formed a layer of ice an inch thick, which melted as soon as the sun rose in the morning.

Bob Holtby's job for an hour before breakfast was to reduce some of the large logs supplied by the government into manageable lengths for the family stove. Although chopping and splitting wood were new to him and the axe an unfamiliar instrument, he learned quickly and, as he did in many things, saw the positive side of his work.

Chopping is grand for your arms and it is grand fun to see

some of the cockneys chopping as though they were afraid
they were going to hit their toes.

In fact, it was the sight of Englishmen learning how to chop wood that
gave rise to the first of many stories about how green the Barr colonists were. The story was told that one inexperienced woodsman stood
inside a wooden box to protect his legs and feet as he tried to use an
axe. Whether the story was true or not, the doctors' work at first consisted almost entirely of dressing axe wounds.

The greenness of the newcomers and the rumours of great wealth
that had preceded them attracted people interested in quick profits. In
the previous six months, the population of Saskatoon had mush-
roomed. Some were outsiders, lured to the former temperance colony
by the advance publicity and determined to exchange shoddy merchandise for as much money as possible. Jim Ashton called them
"sharpies, swindlers and fast-talking salesmen." Mail-order houses like
the T. Eaton Co. and Simpsons displayed catalogues full of an enticing
array of goods. Farmers from the neighbouring areas, short of cash,
foolishly offered their own farm machinery for sale at high prices, the
lure of solid currency blinding them to their own need of the equipment.

And then there were the people of Saskatoon. It has been said that
"the buying of provisions in town was the great gift the Barr Colonists
made to Saskatoon." Nothing very good had happened in the nineteen
years since a group of Toronto businessmen had bought the town site.
The CPR main line missed it by 160 miles. Few settlers had been attracted to the isolated community even after the Qu'Appelle, Long
Lake and Saskatchewan Railway connected it to civilization. A mod-
ern-day writer summed it up rhythmically when he wrote, "Settlers
did not come. Business did not boom. No one seemed interested in
Saskatoon."

Then came the news of the Barr Colony. Advance publicity supplied by the leader himself said that many of the newcomers were
wealthy. They had been told to wait until they got to Saskatoon before
they bought farming equipment and groceries. Rumour had it that
some of them were city-bred and knew little about farming. It would
be so easy to sell things to people like that. The merchants of Saskatoon rubbed their hands in anticipation.

Jim Ashton did not believe that the local merchants had set out to
swindle the colonists. He blamed outsiders for the high prices and

shoddy merchandise. But George Lloyd was not so charitable towards the local citizenry.

> Some of the so-called businessmen incidentally thought it was wise to do business according to the modern method of "making hay while the sun shines". Some straight "gouging" was going on and case after case of sharp practice came to light.

Saskatoon was not much of a place in 1903. First Avenue presented a broken-toothed face to the world, its wooden stores a jumble of peaked roofs and false fronts stretching in a single line opposite a rusty railway track, a single stone building hinting at a more prosperous future. A rudimentary wooden sidewalk was flanked on one side by an occasional hitching post and on the other by random pools of water, and it was anchored at either end by two roughly built hotels. Inside the street-level saloons, rowdy patrons drank, smoked cigars and chewed tobacco. Outside, across the street, railcar after railcar, as many as forty each day, brought more and more settlers, all of them with some purchase to make in Saskatoon.

First Avenue had a country fair atmosphere. People paraded up and down, the chatter of many voices occasionally punctuated by a loud burst of profanity as yet another Canadian revealed his lack of gentility. Local wits demanded that strange-talking newcomers repeat their requests and then burst into guffaws over English spoken with a Cockney twang or a Yorkshire lilt. Cowboys rode their horses carelessly in amongst the pedestrians, and here and there a splash of scarlet signalled the reassuring presence of a mounted policeman. Farm implements lay at random along the street, surrounded by small knots of prospective buyers hanging on some fast-talking salesman's every word. First-time wagon owners drove back and forth, anxious to display their newfound skills with a team of horses or oxen and discovering the gaps in their knowledge when a determined pair broke off in a direction of its own choosing or a balky animal refused to move at all.

Near the tracks, the "Bain" wagons, so long awaited, were on view in all their utilitarian splendour. Robert and Bob Holtby paid the equivalent of sixteen pounds for one, a "shocking price," Bob thought, for something that although "smart looking" was made of second-rate material. A rectangular, high-sided green box rode on wheels painted red. The lack of springs in the chassis could be offset by a spring-mounted, removeable seat, separately purchased. Canvas schooner tops and the hoops to hold them were extra too, but they were necessary to protect the load from the elements. Some tried to save money by buying only two hoops instead of four, a foolish economy that lowered the status of the wagon owner in the bargain.

Thomas Edwards was not concerned with status, and he had no money for hoops and canvas tops. In order to cover his belongings, he built a lumber and tarpaper house on top of his wagon. In a camp full of matching tents and matching wagons, it was very noticeable. Someone dubbed it "Noah's Ark."

The Bible was often evoked. Barr had called their destination "the land of milk and honey." The term "promised land" was popular. Newspaper reporters, increasingly aware of the lack of experience among the colonists, began to call them "Barr's lambs," the sacrificial overtones not being lost on the more apprehensive in camp.

Few of Barr's lambs were prepared to go willingly to the slaughter, however. Discontent had been brewing since they had been crammed onto the *Manitoba*. The train journey had given them long hours to ruminate. By the time they reached Saskatoon, there was much to be angry about, and it was easy to blame Barr for everything. The failure of the extra baggage train to arrive was the final blow.

The doors of the baggage cars that accompanied each section of the train had been sealed by American customs officers when the trains took the short cut across northern Maine. The cars could not be opened, someone said, until proper permits were obtained. The colonists on the first section were not impressed with official seals. With Barr standing impotently in their midst on the Saskatoon station platform, they stormed the coaches, opening the doors, taking what they thought was theirs and throwing what they could not claim outside. The platform was strewn with belongings. To prevent a repetition of this unseemly behaviour when the other sections arrived, Barr assigned guards.

Held back by a cordon of resolute men some called "Barr's henchmen," various people in the crowd shouted insults as the baggage cars were unloaded and the contents heaped on the ground in piles. Then someone pushed against a guard and someone else landed a punch; one person slipped through the line and then another; two men grabbed the same box and fisticuffs broke out on all sides.

But most of the luggage had not even arrived. It had been left behind in Saint John for the fifth section of the train, and it seemed to have disappeared. News of the platform fire in Saint John had reached Saskatoon. Despairing settlers learned that although nothing had been destroyed, they might have to wait a week before the baggage train appeared. When the end of the week failed to produce the missing train, people resigned themselves to going on without their belongings. Weeks later it was discovered that the entire train had been mistakenly routed through Boston.

On the evening of Tuesday, April 21, a mass meeting was called to discuss a new problem more serious even than the missing luggage. There were among the colonists people who had no money left. Plans had been made to provide transportation for those who could not afford to buy teams and wagons, but now there were people who could not afford to buy supplies. Barr's estimate of a minimum bankroll of five pounds had proven ludicrously inadequate in the inflationary atmosphere of Saskatoon. In addition, the forced delay while they waited for the arrival of the missing baggage train was eroding everyone's supply of cash.

Colonization Agent C. W. Speers told the assembled crowd that he would prepare a plan of assistance and explain it to them the following day. The crowd unanimously commended the Canadian government and adjourned for the night.

There are several versions of the dramatic meeting held in the restaurant tent the next morning. The newspaper accounts, written in the heat of the moment and dispatched immediately to be published in Winnipeg, Toronto and Minneapolis the very next day, highlighted the confrontations and the emotions. The daily bulletins sent to the Department of Immigration by Speers contained the bare facts, expressed in a somewhat self-congratulatory manner. George Lloyd's memoirs emphasized his own role in the events, but he agreed with the account that appeared in the *Manitoba Free Press* except concerning how the meeting ended. The version of events appearing in the book *Next Year*, a fictionalized rendering of the Barr Colony experience by colonist Harry Pick, was sardonic and at times verged on the outrageous. A careful perusal of all versions provides the following account.

It seemed to Speers that he could go nowhere in the camp without being accosted on all sides by colonists seeking his ear. It was obvious to him that a meeting must be called to deal with the discontent, but he knew that such a meeting must be arranged with great delicacy. Barr's feelings had still to be taken into consideration even though the government had effectively usurped his authority.

Speers had spent a large portion of the previous day with a group of teamsters from Duck Lake and Batoche, whom Barr had engaged by telegraphing the Indian agent in Battleford from Ottawa the previous week. In the wire Barr had agreed to pay three dollars per day and room and board. When the Metis drivers arrived in camp with their freight wagons and teams, Barr refused to honour his commitment and instead requested that they haul colonists' belongings on a per pound basis. In addition, he expected them to provide their own supplies. The teamsters refused his request and "vowed vengeance on the government," and although Speers was able to engineer a compromise eventually, Barr continued to insist that he had not authorized the initial deal with the teamsters.

While attempting to organize the mass meeting, Speers discovered that Barr did not wish to attend. But Speers had found an ally in Lloyd. No longer reluctant to assume leadership, Lloyd agreed to preside at the meeting and to persuade Barr to explain his financial problems to the colonists in person. After receiving a written request from Speers that he be in attendance, Barr finally agreed to come.

The latter half of the nineteenth century had produced a phenomenon called the indignation meeting, said to be a Yankee institution although it was common enough in Britain. A call went out in the camp for all to attend an indignation meeting to discuss the excessive prices being charged and their effect on the colonists' ability to proceed. But excessive prices alone would not have caused the anger that drove the people towards the restaurant tent that Wednesday morning. A rumour was rife that Barr was receiving commissions from the merchants who were overcharging them.

Someone hauled a black sea trunk to the front of the assembled crowd, and the reluctant Barr climbed up on it. Always at his best with an audience, he began to woo the men and women below him with words, but he refused to admit that he had received commissions from the Saskatoon shopkeepers. The boos and hisses that greeted his denial took him aback. "I beg and pray of you . . . that you will act like reasonable men and will not be led by senseless, silly and groundless reports," he pleaded. Then he became defensive. "If I have made money out of these supplies, I say it is none of your business."

From the back of the tent a man shouted out that Barr had bought potatoes from the Doukhobors for sixty cents and sold them for a dollar. Barr called him a liar. Another man waved a piece of paper and said loudly that he had a letter proving that Barr had arranged for commissions from the Saskatoon merchants. Barr demanded to see it. Refusing to relinquish it, the heckler read it aloud. The crowd roared in indignation. Barr denied authorship. It was passed to Lloyd, who protested that though he was no handwriting expert, the signature looked like Barr's. Pandemonium prevailed.

At this point, the *Free Press* said, Barr changed the subject and handed the meeting over to Speers, who quietly told the crowd what the department intended to do for them and denied that it wished to remove Barr as leader. He asked Lloyd to speak and then suggested the formation of a committee consisting of himself, Lloyd and Barr, which would work to obtain jobs for those in need. According to the *Free Press*, the mood changed so dramatically that the crowd offered a unanimous vote of thanks not only to Speers and the government but also to the CPR and the travelling baggage master, a man named Smith who had not yet been able to produce the missing baggage train. Then cheers were offered for Speers, Lloyd and Barr, the national anthem was sung and the people left the meeting to scurry through a spring rain shower to their tents.

The *Minneapolis Journal*, a rather more vociferous rag, provided additional details about the raucous behaviour of Barr and the crowd. Someone, the reporter said, charged Barr with being afraid of the colonists and being guarded by the Northwest Mounted Police. According to the *Journal*, Barr was told that the meeting had been called to "put the whole thing in the hands of the government and get rid of you. We want no more of you." The cheers at the end of the meeting were for Speers, Lloyd and the government, the *Journal* said. A similar call for Barr drew more hisses than cheers.

Harry Pick wrote that when Barr stood on the trunk, it was to ask the people to be patient about their luggage. The entire crowd responded, said the novelist, by singing all eighteen verses of a newly written song. Such a song does exist. It has been the subject of a scholarly article, was validated by a second scholar and is included in Barr's biography, although without introduction and citing Harry Pick as the source. The chorus is the part most often quoted:

> Barr, Barr, wily old Barr,
> He'll do you as much as he can;
> You bet he will collar,
> Your very last dollar,
> In the Valley of the Saskatchewan.

Lloyd's version of the indignation meeting was written in 1940, and it agrees with the other accounts until the point at which the letter was passed to Lloyd for verification of Barr's signature. Lloyd said that Barr shouted over the catcalls and heckling that the man who had produced the letter could not come to the colony, and then Barr left the tent. Lloyd said that he then climbed on the box in response to the demands of the crowd and urged them to get on the trail, presumably without waiting for their luggage.

Both Lloyd and Speers presented themselves as being the voices of reason, the quiet conciliators. Speers had a week to think about the indignation meeting before he reported at length to his superiors. He said that after Barr spoke, the confusion was so great that Speers took over the meeting and asked people to reconvene the next day.

Barr had all but admitted that he had asked for commissions from the various merchants he dealt with in the West. But he blustered and denied what he had done, rather than explaining that he had borrowed a great deal of money to purchase goods on the colonists' behalf and that, in the absence of government bonuses he still hoped to receive, he had been forced to look for other ways to raise money in order to pay the interest charges on his loans. It is ironic that the *Saskatchewan Herald* in Battleford, understaffed and underfinanced as it was, had deduced what Barr was doing almost two weeks before and had reported it in the following way.

> Mr. Barr and his managers are surprised at the business ethics of the West. They are quite willing that an extra percentage should be placed on the goods supplied to their friends provided it was returned in the shape of a rake-off to the promoters.

"Mr. Barr and his managers" were themselves running several businesses inside the camp. In response to an early report that Saskatoon restaurants were charging one dollar each for meals, Barr had arranged for the dining tent to supply the same for twenty-five cents. He also arranged for shaves and haircuts at prices lower than those offered in town. In close proximity to the dining and barber tents in the south end of camp was the Saskatchewan Valley Emporium, the biggest of all the colony's business ventures.

The store opened in a large marquee tent a few days after the colonists' arrival. Organized by the stores syndicate, unbowed after the resignation of two of its directors in Winnipeg, the emporium stocked everything that the colonists would need at reasonable prices. The *Free Press* described the tent so well that William Hutchinson copied their report almost verbatim for his articles in the *Weekly Telegraph*, and Lloyd paid the paper a similar compliment when he wrote his memoirs.

To paraphrase the admirable description, the store contained everything necessary to start work on a farm—rows of shovels and stable forks leaned against the wall; crates that had been roughly ripped open exposed their contents to view; stacks of brooms filled one corner; camp stoves were piled outside. There were barrels of coal oil and piles of bread and a wide selection of tinned goods. So brisk was the trade and so time-consuming the conversion of Canadian prices into British that the staff of six had little time for pleasantries. The majority of the customers had no idea what they would need and consequently bought everything they could afford and then some.

Ivan Crossley had eighteen pounds in his pocket when he arrived in Saskatoon. That was all he had left in the world. He and his three partners had decided to heed Barr's shipboard advice and pool their resources. They were able to buy a team of horses, harness, a wagon, a small camp stove, cooking utensils, flour, a large side of salt pork or sowbelly and several sacks of oats. But Ivan's share of expenses left him with very little money.

Some people discovered that they could save by shopping out of town. William Hutchinson and his brother Ted bought a team of oxen and a wagon from a Ukrainian farmer who threw in a lot of advice at no extra charge. At Rosthern they bought a pail each of peach jam, strawberry jam and treacle, as well as a twenty-five-pound box each of dried apricots and prunes. Stanley Rackham and Bernard Smith walked to the homestead of a former North Dakotan, where they were fed supper and given a place to sleep on the kitchen floor. The next morning they bought ponies and three oxen at prices much lower than those in Saskatoon.

Before leaving Britain, Barr had advised the people travelling ahead on the *Megantic* to be careful investing money in Saskatoon before he got there. "There will be unscrupulous men offering cattle and horses for sale not worth the money asked," he warned. Barr was in a position to know. His brother, Jack, was at that very time making arrangements for hundreds of horses to be brought to Saskatoon, and not all of them were worth the price he planned to charge.

The *Free Press* reporter had seen some of the horses arrive and he had been fooled. He called them "very fine." He also mentioned that an entire carload of Jack's horses had smothered to death in a boxcar on their way from Calgary, which should have warned him that Jack Barr's concerns did not rest entirely with the proper care of this fine horseflesh.

Ivan Crossley called Jack Barr "the biggest old renegade I ever met—a real crook, a horse dealer." Ivan was at the corral one day when a colonist who claimed to know a good horse when he saw one matched wits with Jack Barr. The man wanted a good team of work-horses and Jack said he had just the ones for him—black mares, well matched, guaranteed good workers and quiet. Jack warned him, though, that they still had their winter coats and did not look very good. The colonist felt their legs and hocks, pounded their ribs and gave them a good looking over. Jack hitched them to a wagon and drove the settler around for half an hour. The team handled well. The settler paid in gold sovereigns for the team, the harness and the wagon and left well pleased.

Later, while taking the team down to the river to drink, the new owner noticed that they did not step clear of the tent guy ropes and wagon poles that lay like an obstacle course throughout the camp. One of the mares stepped on his foot and nearly knocked him down. He showed the team to a friend who sold horses in the Old Country and was told that both the horses were blind.

Next morning, the colonist was waiting at Jack Barr's corral when the dealer arrived for the day's business. In a north of England dialect further obscured by profanity, the frustrated man vented his spleen. "You sold me a pair of blind horses," he spluttered, "and you'll have to return my money or I'll have you arrested." Jack replied, "You told me you knew a good horse and nobody could fool you on a deal. I was honest with you when we made the bargain. I told you these horses did not look very good."

Some of the animals sold to the colonists were very old and some far too young. Some of the horses were half-wild range cayuses that refused to work with other horses as a team. Some of the oxen were nothing but big steers that had roamed the range wild for years.

The NWMP had assigned Inspector William Parker to safeguard the interests of the Barr colonists. The thirty-year veteran had just re-turned from service with Lord Strathcona's Horse in the Boer War, where he had earned the nickname "Old Hardface." In the understated terminology of a well-trained policeman, Old Hardface "interviewed the vendors" of some of the more outrageous livestock transactions, who then saw the error of their ways and provided their customers with better animals or a refund.

Barr had insisted that horses were the best animals for his colonists to buy, but old prairie hands knew that inexperienced people were better off with the slow but steady oxen. Horses required stabling in the cold weather and not everyone would get a stable built before winter. Horses had to be fed oats and hay, which would be in short supply in the colony until the first crops were harvested. But despite the department's frequent warnings, many people bought horses. It suited their image of themselves as gentleman farmers. No self-respecting gentleman could see himself behind a pair of plodding oxen.

According to one of his daughters, Robert Holtby was a good judge of horses and purchased a beautiful team. His son, Bob, agreed at the time. Although not perfectly matched, the two chestnuts were the best of the bunch, and Holtby paid Jack Barr $375 for them. So sure was Robert that others would covet his horses that he ordered Bob to get up during the night to make sure they were safe. He bought specially made harness. When the horses were hitched to the new wagon with its four hoops and canvas cover, the outfit looked very grand. The Holtbys were going to travel first class.

Lloyd went them one better. He bought one of the best teams in camp from Jack for $500—$200 cash plus an I.O.U. for $300. Jack was to give the I.O.U. to his brother, Isaac, who had been keeping Lloyd's $300 for him—the $300 Lloyd had been given by the colonists on board ship.

Livestock prices moderated somewhat when local farmers offered some competition. In addition, the government offered teams at no profit for $250 to $300, and the CPR sold livestock for cost plus freight.

While some colonists prepared for the trek, others were distracted by the power struggle being played out between Barr and Speers, with Lloyd hovering close at hand. The meeting arranged by Speers to deal with the problem of insolvent colonists had been called for the afternoon of April 23, but early that day a new player had entered the field. James Clinkskill was a Member of the Legislative Assembly of the Northwest Territories. In response to a petition bearing 140 signatures, he had called a meeting for that morning.

As a sizeable crowd of people gathered outside the dining tent, Barr walked among them, warning that the meeting had been called by Ca-

nadian political factions set on creating dissension. The tent filled with
people nonetheless. When Clinkskill rose to address the crowd, Barr
jumped up and, calling the MLA an infamous scoundrel, shook his fist in
his face. Barr said that if Clinkskill did not leave his tent he would put
him out by force.

When Clinkskill replied that the tent was not pitched on private
ground, Lloyd entered the fray on Barr's side, telling Clinkskill that if
the meeting was for

> stones, stumps and grass, well and good, but the people are
> our people, not [yours]—we have our difficulties—but if
> dirty linen has to be washed we do it ourselves. We will not
> have outside interference.

Lloyd threatened to frog march Clinkskill and his delegation out of
the tent with the help of twenty or thirty men.

Clinkskill, to his credit, remained polite. When none of the 140 pe-
titioners interceded on his behalf, he and his delegation withdrew quietly. Obviously, an insufficient number of these new immigrants
acknowledged the authority of the government of the Territories, although they were very glad to attend the afternoon meeting at which
the government of the country, in consultation with the management
of the colony, promised relief for those in need.

Barr did not attend the meeting, and although Lloyd was there,
Speers was clearly in control. He explained the futility of going on to
the colony in hopes of finding a job. When he asked for a show of
hands from those who had less than ten pounds, two hundred hands
went up, some of them belonging to men with families. He announced
that each would be interviewed and given a job. In the end, 40 men
were sent to Prince Albert and 110 to Moose Jaw for railway work,
and a few found jobs in Saskatoon with surveying parties.

When William Hutchinson wrote his next article home to an audience full of people interested in emigrating, he commented benignly,

> The Dominion Government keeps a fatherly eye on those
> who go to make a home within its borders, and seems to
> have a happy knack of doing the right thing at the right
> time.

Clifford Sifton, the minister in charge of immigration, had made it plain years before that he was opposed to giving immigrants financial help of any kind. It was his opinion that

> Once a man is taken hold of by the Government and treated as a ward, he seems to acquire the sentiments of a pauper, and forever after will not stand on his own feet or try to help himself.

Obviously the department had softened this policy temporarily.

Before Speers adjourned the meeting that Thursday afternoon, he also announced that the entire route between Saskatoon and the colony would be patrolled by competent teamsters equipped for emergencies. Lloyd, apparently untroubled by this particular kind of government interference, announced that he would ask Barr to go to the colony at once. At the colonists' request, Lloyd would stay in Saskatoon until everyone had left.

A large number of colonists seemed reluctant to leave the relative comfort of the camp at Saskatoon. In the south end in particular, where the wealthier people camped in the vicinity of Barr's tent, things had settled into a routine. It was there that the ladies put on afternoon dress and paid calls, and the men affected sporty garb and strolled around with their dogs at heel.

But the fine ladies had to return to their tents after making their calls and cook their suppers bent over tiny tin camp stoves just like their sisters in the north end of the camp. And north end or south, many of the women had never learned how to cook, domestic help being available for such low wages in Britain.

The smart people learned some of the basics for survival before they left camp. They clustered around the farming instructors, cheering enthusiastically at almost everything they heard. New owners of horseflesh practised harnessing and driving; new owners of shovels dug holes through the prairie wool—a thick mat of roots and dead grass—to look learnedly at the soil beneath, and new owners of stoves discovered the most effective methods for lighting fires.

Ex-soldiers were pleased to show anyone who cared to watch the techniques for survival they had learned on the South African veldt. The presence of these veterans accentuated the military atmosphere in the camp. Reveille was sounded every morning at 5:30, an army tradition that may not have been appreciated by all of the camp's occupants.

But no one seemed to mind the presence of the many guns in camp. The *Free Press* wondered facetiously if the colonists had come armed to protect themselves from Indians or perhaps to hunt a little buffalo. But people were excited about the possibility of shooting game, and many carried a gun just in case a rabbit came into sight. Random shots were heard day and night. One colonist came out of his tent and fired both barrels of a 12 bore shotgun into the air. When the NWMP came looking for him, he hid in his tent.

Life in the camp had a dark side. Some of the men spent their evenings in the saloons and woke the camp with their drunken attempts to find their way home in the darkness. In her book *Gully Farm*, Mary Hiemstra describes how a man's repeated drunkenness led to his wife's suicide. Two other colonists died when they contracted scarlet fever while they were confined to the hospital tent with pneumonia. Doctors Amos and Keating had arrived in camp to be put to work immediately in the hospital marquee near the river. Soon there were several other cases of scarlet fever. Proper quarantine was established, the blankets and pillows of the two dead men were burned, and the families of the sick resigned themselves to staying in Saskatoon a little longer.

The general hygiene of the camp was satisfactory. The river water was a "nice coffee colour," but everyone knew it had to be boiled. Toilets were newly dug holes in the ground surrounded by canvas for privacy. Most people took it in stride.

But there were a few for whom it had all become too much. On April 22, the *Free Press* noted that two or three families had bought tickets to return to England. The word trickled out. Bernard Boden noted in it in a letter to his fiancée. William Hutchinson had no patience with the people who quit.

> What are wanted here are men, real men, who are prepared to rough it. . . . I have seen enough of people who have come out here who have managed the journey by boat and train very well; that was an easy and enjoyable time, but when the dream passed away, and they were faced with stern realities, such as a 200 mile trek up country . . . they have turned tail and fled back home to give Canada a doubtful reputation in the eyes of the Mother Country.

Mr. Speers knew that many of the men he had placed in jobs in the area would be subject to pressure from the local people to stay rather than continue on to the colony. He took heart in the knowledge that, having already given Barr their homestead fees, they would resist these blandishments.

And there were people who should have reconsidered, people whose future in Canada looked shaky indeed. They were people with insufficient money, widows with too many children, husbands with reluctant wives, wives with husbands unequal to the task at hand, pregnant women and sick men, women and children.

But as the wagons were loaded up and the teams harnessed, most of the settlers were able and optimistic. Few realized yet how little they knew, and even fewer would have welcomed any outside advice. As Speers noted, "The English like to use their own judgment in many of these matters."

William Holtby drew $600 from the bank, leaving a balance of $366. He loaded farm equipment, tents, bedding, clothing, dishes, cooking utensils and nonperishable food supplies into the wagon, being careful to avoid jostling Agnes's tin trunk with its precious cargo of breakable treasures wrapped in cloth. There being room left in the wagon for only one passenger, his two older boys, William and Stanley, were required to walk. Agnes slung her one-year-old son Redvers, the apple of her eye, onto her hip and announced that she would walk as well. Her sister-in-law, Kate, was walking, too. Kate's daughters, Bessie and Dorothy, took turns riding beside their father, Robert, until they could endure the lurching and swaying of the wagon no longer.

The huge loads on the wagons could not be blamed entirely on the colonists. Most of them had brought an abundance of belongings, it is true, but they had been promised transport for their excess baggage, and that had failed to materialize. The last-minute arrangements by Speers with the Metis freighters did not begin to fill the need, as the majority of those wagons were used by people who could not afford to buy a wagon for themselves.

Twenty-five people had left on April 21. On April 24 the general exodus began. The Holtbys left on April 28, the two families having joined up with a Mr. Crawford to ensure that there would always be two wagons to pull the third wagon out of a mud hole.

The plan had been for the colonists to travel in groups of twenty or more accompanied by experienced Northwesters who would give directions and advice. But by now the authorities had learned how hard it was to tell an Englishman what to do. Despite all advice of the government and the local inhabitants, the colonists had chosen to listen to Barr, the leader many of them no longer trusted, who wanted them on the land to claim it as quickly as possible. No matter that the night temperatures were still well below zero. No matter that the frost was beginning to come out of the ground during the day, softening the trails and leaving water standing in huge sloughs. No matter that their baggage had not arrived. No matter that many of them had not mastered the harnessing and driving of a team. No matter that just one month before, they had been city dwellers used to travelling on trains and buses and buying their food from the corner grocery. No matter that their wagons were overloaded and top-heavy, that their destination was far beyond the edge of settlement and out of reach of the good advice of seasoned farmers. The members of the All-British Colony would go, they would go now, and since no one seemed to be organizing any larger groups, they would go by themselves or with one or two other wagons.

Isaac Barr dressed for the occasion in a high-crowned fedora with a white scarf tied cowboy-fashion around his neck. With Dr. Amos beside him in his heavily laden democrat, he led a cavalcade of several wagons that carried, in addition to marquees and hospital, library and store supplies, his fiancée Christina Helberg and his secretary George Flamanck.

The trail to Battleford ran through the middle of the camp. Over the course of several days, it carried a varied and colourful parade. Jaunty buggies bore young men done up like gentlemen in flared riding breeches, knee-high leather boots and tweed jackets. Other men, having abandoned their jackets in the heat of the day, wore their sleeves rolled up ready for the business at hand. Many still wore ties, as if the narrow adornment gave them some slight connection to a world they understood but had left behind. Many of the men had learned why westerners wore wide-brimmed hats in the hot noon sun, but few had realized the impracticality of the thin English boots they stubbornly persisted in wearing.

The occasional woman had chosen comfort and common sense over convention by wearing a wrapper, whose loose fit gave her more freedom of movement, and a man's wide-brimmed hat. But the majority of the women wore crisp white shirtwaists, the necks high, the sleeves long and the fronts ruffled and decorated to cover, modestly, bosums thrust stylishly forward by whalebone corsets. They wore

dark-coloured serge skirts with extra fullness in the back to accommodate a small bustle and a petticoat or two to add volume and rustle as
they swept the ground. High-laced boots with little heels crunched on
the prairie wool. Only the hairdos had adapted to present conditions,
the wind having won the battle over fashionable rolls and pompa-
dours.

The prairie stretched away to the northwest, bare and gently rolling. An April wind caught the leafless branches of the gnarled poplar
trees huddled in clumps here and there across the landscape. On the
south slopes of the small hills, the sun had flushed out a hint of green
in the straw-coloured prairie wool.

In knots of two and three, the wagons set out. Here a well-matched
team surged ahead, glad to be free of the camp and as eager as the
driver to be on their way. There a balky nag struggled in its harness
and fought against its partner and its driver. Ox teams covered the
ground with maddening slowness. Sprightly buggies took advantage of
the openness of the plains to dance between the prairie schooners,
whose white canvas covers hid heavy loads of furniture, farm implements and trunks. Tethered to some of the swaying wagons were
milk cows, and riding on top of some of the loads were crates of domestic fowl, cackling and crowing in distress. Women and children
followed behind some of the wagons, the women striding out in determined fashion, the children darting here and there playfully. In the
buoyant mood created by the prospect of adventure, one driver was
heard to call out, "Westward the star of Empire wends its way."

A sombre 1894 portrait of the Holtby family seems to presage later problems. Kate, pregnant with Dodie, stands beside Kitty; Bessie sits on Robert's lap; Oliver *(left)* and Bob are in front. *Author's Collection*

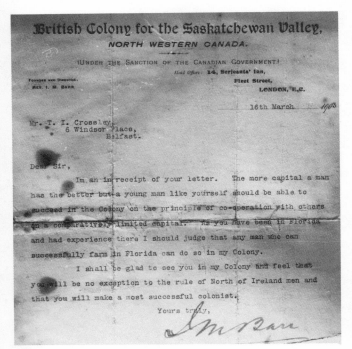

British Colony for the Saskatchewan Valley,
NORTH WESTERN CANADA.

(UNDER THE SANCTION OF THE CANADIAN GOVERNMENT)

Head Office: 14, Serjeants' Inn,
Fleet Street,
LONDON, E.C.

FOUNDER AND DIRECTOR:
REV. I. M. BARR.

16th March 1903

Mr. T. I. Crossley,
6 Windsor Place,
Belfast.

Dear Sir,

Im an in receipt of your letter. The more capital a man has the better but a young man like yourself should be able to succeed in the Colony on the principle of co-operation with others on a comparatively limited capital. As you have been in Florida and had experience there I should judge that any man who can successfully farm in Florida can do so in my Colony.

I shall be glad to see you in my Colony and feel that you will be no exception to the rule of North of Ireland men and that you will make a most successful colonist.

Yours truly,

I M Barr

Just two weeks before nineteen-year-old Ivan Crossley sailed for Canada, he received this letter from Isaac Barr. *Author's Collection*

The captain of the *Lake Manitoba*, the Reverend George Lloyd, two colonists and George Flamanck, secretary and future controversial postmaster, stand behind Isaac Barr, who still wears his clerical collar. *Saskatchewan Archives Board, Saskatoon/A2521*

A boxing match relieves the monotony for some of the 1960 passengers crammed onto the *Lake Manitoba*, a ship built to carry 700. *Saskatchewan Archives Board, Saskatoon/B174*

Men's top boots and fur coats and women's large hats and city clothes are in evidence as passengers from the Immigrant Special Train disembark at the Saskatoon station.
Saskatchewan Archives Board, Regina/A4586

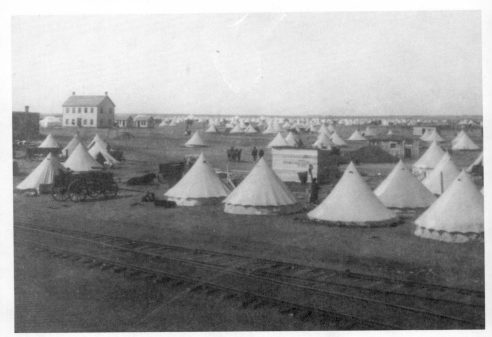

Secondhand bell tents, veterans of the Boer War, provide "head-lowering, back-bending" accommodation for the settlers at the colony camp near the immigration hall at Saskatoon.
E. Brown Collection, Provincial Archives of Alberta/B-2360

Green-boxed, red-wheeled Bain wagons are viewed by eager purchasers. Spring-mounted seats, bought separately, were essential; the hoops and canvas covers were luxuries. *Saskatchewan Archives Board, Regina/A2310*

Halfway between Saskatoon and the colony, settlers stop on the trail near Battleford. Only some of them wear clothing that is practical for life on the prairies. *Saskatchewan Archives Board, Saskatoon/B4*

A sod house was a practical choice for settlers short on cash. Collecting buffalo bones to sell to fertilizer companies helped add a few dollars to empty pockets. *E. Brown Collection, Provincial Archives of Alberta/B-2348*

With no land broken, only the rudimentary log fence, the livestock and the single haystack mark this homestead, alone on the vast prairie, as an agricultural enterprise. *E. Brown Collection, Provincial Archives of Alberta/B661*

Hands clenched and face set, a woman stands beside her husband by the door of their log house with its sod roof and store-bought windows. *E. Brown Collection, Provincial Archives of Alberta/A-1247*

Irregular poplar logs fashion a house and a stable. Firewood stacked "teepee" style awaits the winter, when there will be ample time to bucksaw it for the ravenous stove. *Provincial Archives of Alberta/A-4920*

Boxing Day celebrants pose in front of the unfinished Hall and Scott's store after the Village Well Diggers beat the Telegraph Gang Bull Frogs at football. *Provincial Archives of Alberta/A-4929*

In his Norfolk jacket, wing collar and tie, sometime storekeeper and committee member Nathaniel Jones strikes a wintery pose before "the soddery," his house in town. *Dorothy Reinhardt Collection*

Before deep snow and frigid temperatures allowed only the properly clad to go outside, a family prepares for an outing. Most of the colony's horses did not survive the winter. *Provincial Archives of Alberta/A-9387*

Bell tents and a covered wagon flank the new immigration hall in the spring of 1904 as mounted police, settlers and a visiting cowboy gather around the last patch of snow. *Provincial Archives of Alberta/P444*

The temporary premises of the Lloydminster Hair Dressing, Shaving and Bath House were built from twisted poplar logs like the ones that lie in the foreground.
E. Brown Collection, Provincial Archives of Alberta/B-2345

The business section of Lloydminster, August 1904, shows some signs of permanence as firewood is stockpiled and the Minster Restaurant announces its continued presence.
E. Brown Collection, Provincial Archives of Alberta/B2344

Articulate, methodical Stanley Rackham strikes a serious pose, as befits a successful farmer. He was one of the few colonists trained in agriculture before he emigrated. *Lloydminster Exhibition Association*

Prosperous citizens of a new town in a new province, Ivan and Bessie Crossley pose with their children, Muriel and Desmond, just before World War One. *Muriel Bick Collection*

CHAPTER
VII

Raw Englishmen
Loose on the Plains

AS DAWN BROKE ON THE MORNING OF APRIL 29, A THIN BLANKET OF SNOW LAY bleak and cold on the first government camp ten miles west of Saskatoon. A scattering of shabby tents surrounded the bright new government marquee, which had filled quickly the previous evening with travellers exhausted from the first day on the trail.

Drivers had climbed down wearily from their wagons; women and children had straggled in behind. There were some who had travelled with little incident, following one of the sets of parallel tracks that led across the wide prairie, encountering no troublesome hills or sloughs. There were others whose choice of track led them to swampy ground where they had been stuck once, twice, even three times.

The plan for the trek, as explained by Barr on board the *Manitoba*, had sounded sensible. Moving in organized groups of twenty or thirty, the colonists were to proceed in an orderly fashion from government marquee to government marquee. They would be preceded by an advance party, who would have freshly baked bread and freshly slaughtered beef waiting at every stop. Doctors and trained nurses with a mobile hospital would keep pace. A special sanitary staff would be in attendance, although the details were left unspecified in the interest of delicacy.

Reality bore little resemblance to Barr's plans. Instead of travelling in organized groups, wagons stretched out along the trail in one continuous, if somewhat irregular, string. The colonists arrived at the first camp to find no one in charge and none of the promised food in evidence. Although there was an excellent stove in the marquee, there was a line-up of people waiting to use it. Those who were impatient resorted to eating, unwarmed, something from a tin can, while the more adventurous shot prairie chickens, ducks and rabbits and experimented with ways of cooking them over a campfire or on a portable tin stove. With the promise that there would be bread available the next day, everyone retired early, bundled up against the rapidly dropping temperatures.

The day had been bitterly cold, too. Many of the colonists were inadequately clothed. Shivering children cried. Bernard Boden and Bob Holtby had walked the whole way and still were not warm. Jim Ashton and his companions went against all good advice by setting up their camp stove inside their tent and passing the chimney through an opening in one of the seams. With no asbestos or tin to protect the canvas from the hot chimney, they risked burning the tent down but judged that the alternative was freezing to death in their sleep.

The tethering of livestock was a problem for many. One man who had tied his horse to a small tree woke during the night to see the animal disappear at a gallop into the distance, dragging the uprooted tree behind him. Hobbles were the restraint of choice on the prairies, but the stiff-legged rocking-horse hop of an animal with its front legs manacled looked dangerous to many greenhorns, who feared that they would be trodden on in their sleep. The Holtby boys jumped out of bed several times to scare hobbled horses away with a whip. One of their Uncle Willie's horses broke loose and, while cantering wildly through the camp, caught its shoe in the ropes of a tent. The tent was torn past mending.

Since they were not able to sleep anyway, the Holtbys decided to get an early start. Wishing to avoid disturbing their neighbours, they applied oil to their wagon wheels, hoping to still the piercing squeal that could wake the dead. Soon they discovered why wagon wheels should be left to squeal—dirt clinging to the oil caused them to bind. The wheels had to be removed and the oil wiped away.

The sound of reveille caught very few people asleep. The snow, the cold and the prospect of a new day on the trail were as good a deterrent to sleep as many had ever experienced. There was much to be done before camp could be broken—breakfast to prepare, tents to fold, wagons to load, teams to fasten into a complicated harness—and it was twenty miles to the second marquee, twice as far as they had travelled the first day.

Water lay everywhere. The warm days of the previous week had turned every crevice into a stream and every depression into a shallow slough that often covered the trail and stretched as far as the eye could

see. Fearful of losing their way, the inexperienced drivers stuck tena-
ciously to the trail, urging their teams into the water and praying that
they would make it through.

Even if a driver, schooled by bitter experience, wished to avoid
driving through a slough, his team usually made up their own minds
about where to go. Oxen seemed to be especially determined to walk
deliberately into sloughs. Fresh water lured team after team, and the
animals refused to obey commands. There were colonists who explained this by pointing out that some of the teams had been bought
from "Red Indians" or Doukhobors. They reasoned that oxen coming
from such owners would not understand English commands. But even
an English ox would have been baffled at the barrage of conflicting or-
ders that emanated from the driver's seat of a wagon firmly bogged
down in a prairie slough. And no amount of profanity would dislodge
the imprisoned vehicle.

The Barr colonists would become experts at getting wagons out of
sloughs, their expertise honed by repeated practice. It seemed impossible to avoid getting stuck. It even happened occasionally to the experienced freighters.

The first step in getting out of a slough was to avoid tipping the
wagon. This was not always possible to do, given the combination of
nervous horses and inept drivers. Many a precious load—crates of fine
china, carpets, pianos and baggage—tipped slowly over into water
made muddy by the efforts to free the wheels. Even if tipping could be
avoided, it was still necessary to unload the wagon. Box by box, crate
by crate, the men carried the large loads to shore through knee-deep
water, the soft bottom of the slough tugging all the while at their feet.
Once empty, the wagon could sometimes be pulled free, but if the
mud was particularly tenacious or the animals too young to pull with
enough strength, a second team had to be harnessed in to help.

It was all very time-consuming. Once the wagon was freed, luggage
had to be reloaded, mud scraped off, clothes dried, empty stomachs
filled and aching muscles rested. If it was late in the day, the tent
would be pitched right there and a campfire lit to dry wet boots.

Sloughs were difficult to avoid, but at least they were easy to see.
Alkali flats were not. Reedy grass camouflaged them until it was too
late. One day, an alkali flat imprisoned eight wagons at the same time.
Harry Pick likened it to being stuck in a mixture of wet concrete and
quicksand. Bob Holtby was sure alkali flats had no bottom; the soft,
slushy muck seemed to go down forever. William Hutchinson's wagon

was stuck up to the axles in the grey ooze for four hours until he and his partners hitched a second team to the wagon and placed a man behind each wheel. When the wagon was free of the alkali, the men were caked in mud to the knees and splashed with dirty water to the tops of their heads.

That evening someone vented his frustration on the pristine canvas sides of the second government marquee. Written with a stick blackened in a campfire were the words "The land flowing with milk and honey" and "Barr's lambs" and, lest anyone think their author a quitter, "On to the promised land."

In the days ahead the government camps would become better equipped and staffed, but increasingly the colonists camped wherever they found themselves at the end of the day. They learned to pick a spot that was sheltered from wind and weather, with water and firewood in close proximity.

There was little firewood available near the trail, the poplar bluffs having been decimated over the years by other travellers and by frequent prairie fires. It was necessary to pick up firewood from the marquees, where it was supplied free, although at considerable expense to the government. Drinking water was abundant and was available in two forms. Dark brown slough water was easy to obtain, but it contained various species of minute aquatic organisms that made straining advisable, and it caused swamp fever, a disease fatal to horses. Much better for horses and much more appetizing in colour was the pale amber water from a seepage well. But since someone had to dig a pit to make such a well, most people on the trek got used to drinking water from the sloughs.

Bernard Boden found he had no trouble at all drinking the water. He announced rather proudly to his fiancée that he was not as particular as he used to be. As she read his letters, Madeleine must have wondered what change had come over her beloved Bernard. If she could have seen him, she would have been truly alarmed.

When Bernard looked in a mirror, he saw a young man with very brown skin and very long hair who was badly in need of a shave. And he liked what he saw. There was not a trace of the office clerk he had been two months before. He was amazed to find that the rough life he was leading suited him. He was impatient to get settled on his homestead so he could take some photographs of himself and his brother to send to their fiancées.

The transformation of clerks into trekkers was hastened by the urgent need to acquire new skills. Barr had promised that bread would be available on the journey. When it became apparent that this was not true, some people returned to Saskatoon to be instructed in the fine art of making trail bread or bannock, but others learned by trial and error. Bannock was a mixture of flour, baking powder and water that could be baked in a cooling oven or fried in bacon grease on a griddle. Few of the bachelors perfected the art but the products of their labours—burned on the outside, raw in the middle—were wolfed down eagerly all the same.

Bernard Boden was proud of his bannock. Baked in an iron jack pot over the campfire, it was edible, and he actually sold some of it to an Indian freighter for fifteen cents a loaf. William Hutchinson was equally proud of his bannock or damper, as he called it. Although it was made with slough water that contained "enough living insects to stock an aquarium" and the resulting bread was "somewhat sad and heavy," it was always eaten quickly and with gusto. He had to insist that his companions leave some for later in the day.

Prairie chickens made fine eating too. "Any man with a prairie chicken and a loaf of damper need not starve," Hutchinson declared. Ducks were also good to eat and plentiful, but they were not as sought after since they tended to be near sloughs and thus fell into the water when shot, making it necessary for the hunter to wade in after them. It was so much easier to catch a prairie chicken. Being naturally curious, the birds allowed the hunter to get close enough to break their necks with a stick. That being accomplished, it took no time to remove the breasts, fry them in bacon grease and gobble them down.

Hutchinson and his partners were astounded at how much they could eat. It seemed as though their appetites were out of control. They tried to cut down on their bread intake by filling up with rolled oats. They tried to cut down on their food intake by adopting the Canadian system of three meals a day instead of four. But they counted the hours until their next meal.

Kate Holtby, despite her unhappiness, rose to the challenge of camp cooking. She plied her family with rousing breakfasts of porridge, bacon, bread and coffee and, for the other meals, the staples of tea and porridge rounded out with wild game birds cooked to a turn. Although she found Canadian yeast a mystery, her bannock was superb.

Her son Bob could not get over how hungry he was all the time.

This Canadian air does give you an appetite. I can eat any-
time in the day or night. I am pleased to say I never had a
cough or cold since I left England despite being wet
through four or five times and many a time walking all day
without bothering to take my boots off and let them dry.

Most of the young single men on the trek wrote in their diaries
with wonder and delight at the effects of the open air on their health
and appearance. Nothing marred their optimistic view. Brown drinking water full of insects and muddy battles with stubborn oxen were
tossed off as amusing incidents. Hair grew long, skin peeled and then
turned brown, beards replaced clean-shaven cheeks and soap became
an unnecessary commodity.

Neither is the use of soap in much demand. We lay down at
night just as we have been dressed all day, but use our
great-coats and blankets for warmth, so that in the morning
to get up and just shake ourselves like dogs isn't much trouble and it is wonderful how fit and fresh we feel.

But young wives and mothers and older women did not greet the
harsh conditions with nearly as much gusto. A pail swinging from
under a wagon box said that there were women and children in the
party; the pail contained soiled diapers and, if anyone had been im-
modest enough to admit it, bloody squares of winceyette as well. For
nature did not stop her natural processes just because a young woman
was tramping across the prairies following her husband while he
chased a dream.

Martha Topott was determined to keep up with her husband, nine
months pregnant though she was. They had left Saskatoon with two
other couples, one with a child, all crammed into one wagon. On their
first night out, they were forced to pitch their tent on soggy ground
beside a slough because their wagon was firmly stuck. The temperature was dropping, and Martha had a chill. When two men came by in
a buggy and offered to take the women to the government marquee,
they accepted eagerly. The caretaker at the marquee sent word back to
Dr. Keating in Saskatoon, who drove out to bring Martha Topott
back to the immigration hall. A hammock was fixed for her on the second floor.

It was after the hammock collapsed that she discovered Betsy Lee was in the immigration hall too. The new mother took Martha down-stairs and fixed a place for her to sleep on the floor. A young man gave her some money, which she used to buy oranges, buns and cookies. One week later, she drove to Battleford with Dr. Keating, his wife and two nurses. In the fast-moving democrat, the ninety-mile journey took only two days.

It took most of the settlers two days just to go the first thirty miles. The trail had become a quagmire, and there were rumours of flooded streams ahead. There were other rumours about a strange group of Russian peasants who lived in a village farther along the trail.

The colonists had heard of the Doukhobors—how they had been persecuted in Russia for their pacifism, and how certain Quaker groups and the novelist Leo Tolstoy had helped thousands of them to emigrate to Canada. Just the year before, some of them had sold all their belongings and begun a pilgrimage. The rumours spoke of herds of cattle being abandoned and nudity being practised.

But in Saskatoon some of the colonists had encountered Doukhobors selling fine-looking yokes of oxen for a decent price. Despite their limited knowledge of English, the Russian settlers did not seem to be very threatening. After he left Saskatoon, Jim Ashton had seen some sturdy-looking Doukhobor women pulling a plough. They did not look very threatening either.

The trail led across a plain and over the brow of a hill. Suddenly, in a valley below, the travellers saw the Doukhobor communal village. Whitewashed log and clay-plastered houses, their ridged roofs shaggy with thatched grass, squatted along one side of the trail. Sparkling windows trimmed in pale green and blue peeked out from beneath sheltering verandahs.

Everywhere was evidence of the Doukhobors' prosperity. Their machinery was up-to-date; their pastures and corrals were full of cattle; their bountiful stores of butter, eggs, potatoes, oats and poul-try were for sale. Ivan Crossley bought a huge cheese. The Holtbys bought fresh bread and, impressed by the friendliness of the Rus-sian peasants, camped nearby for the night. As Bob watched the sun set behind the village, he thought he understood what the Doukhobors meant when they said they had found the Garden of Eden.

Next morning, a solitary figure walked away from the Holtby camp, her feet crunching on the prairie wool, her head lowered, her eyes on the winter-dead grass as it moved nervously in little gusts of wind that never quite stopped. Tiny spears of new green pushed up through dry brown, where clumps of crocuses, soft and subtle, hid shyly. The young woman raised her head slightly. Tiny wild rosebushes, twigs bare except for the odd shrivelled red hip, thrust up through a tangle of brown grass. Here and there low shrubs held onto a few dead leaves.

Bessie Holtby thought of English primroses growing wild in the hedgerows, of dainty English robins and English church bells calling Sunday worshippers. She remembered how intricately English larks sang. Then the raucous cries of thick-billed black magpies brought her back to the Canadian prairie, and the fainter calls of even larger birds made her lift her head to search the sky.

Large dark hawks, ten, maybe twelve of them, wheeled and drifted in the sky to the northwest, then banked to the south and turned white in the sun. The land below them looked rough and disturbed, as though an ancient earthquake had opened a jagged slash in the rolling prairie. Bessie saw wagons approaching from the south, stopping in the village and moving on towards the rough terrain. She hurried back to camp.

The colonists had been warned about Eagle Creek. It was one of several big streams they had to cross before they reached Battleford. The farm instructors and Metis freighters had tried to prepare them for the difficult task of getting their wagons across streams swollen with run-off from the melting snow, but the advance instructions served only to fill everyone with dread.

The trail down the bank of the creek was the steepest Bob Holtby had ever seen. A man was stationed at the top to make sure the wagons were properly braked so that they would not gather too much speed on the way down. Drivers were advised to pass a strong pole or a logging chain through the back wheels to stop them from turning. But there were drivers who refused to follow the advice, drivers who were sure that their wagon's dragshoe would be all the brake they needed.

One after another the wagons inched their way down the bank, their uphill side slightly raised on the uneven track, their heavy loads tipping towards the gully and the stream running swiftly below. Wagons without effective brakes overtook their teams, their drivers jumping as the entire outfit crashed out of control down the bank. Drivers who reached the bottom safely removed their braking pole or chain and prepared to ford the creek.

It was important to stay on the tracks while going through the water, but the stream bed became boggier as each set of wheels cut through it. Anyone planning to avoid the mud by crossing above or below the trail invariably dumped his load when his wheels hit the large boulders that lay on the bottom of the creek.

The ascent of the other side presented new problems, for now speed and power were of the essence. Properly prepared drivers instructed their helpers to have stones ready to lay behind the wheels should the teams lose momentum. Harnessing a second team to their wagon, Bernard and Percy Boden began the slow climb behind another wagon whose driver allowed his team to veer slightly to the downhill side of the track. As the wheels on that side sank into the soft ground at the edge of the trail, the wagon slowly overturned, dumping the load, injuring the animals and stopping everyone behind them.

Most people made it through without incident, glad to have had good advice and already composing their version of the crossing to tell at the campfire that night. But even the successful had to deal with the sight that met their eyes as they struggled over the top of the embankment. A horse lay dead, its last breath expended getting a wagon to the top. It had been there for several days. The settlers passed with eyes averted, hoping to forget the lolling tongue and the evidence that the hawks already had been feasting.

That night, at the third government marquee, talk turned to other distressing news. More settlers were deserting. Everyone knew that two or three families had returned home from Saskatoon. Bernard Boden had heard the news from his fiancée in England, which meant that the British newspapers were still talking about the colony. Boden had warned Madeleine that, in his opinion, half of what the British papers wrote was exaggerated or untrue. The *Free Press* reporter travelling with the colonists delivered a similar warning.

> The unusual interest taken in the Barr Colony shows no signs of subsiding. The people composing it have been criticized and held up for inspection so often that everyone spoken to about them has an opinion of his own and a great many of these opinions are exaggerations of the most sensational character.

Some of the sensational stories had to do with how green the colonists were, but most centred around the numbers who were deserting.

Downstream from where the colonists crossed, Eagle Creek flowed into the North Saskatchewan River. Just upstream from there, a small ferry took passengers across the river to the fledgling communities growing up on the other side near the proposed route of the Canadian Northern Railway. Maymont, Ruddell, Denholm and Brada welcomed Barr colonists who could not afford to go any farther or who were discouraged by the difficulties experienced so far. Some colonists learned that by taking this detour it was possible to find a homestead without trekking off to the outer reaches of the country.

Between Eagle Creek and Battleford lay the Eagle Hills. They reminded Stanley Rackham of the treeless English moors. Former soldier Jim McCormick thought of the South African kopjes. For William Hutchinson, the rugged hills and peaks stretched across the horizon like "a barrier across the trail."

The Eagle Hills had seen bloody confrontations between the Native people and the fur traders of the Northwest Company. But the hills owed their name to a time before the white men came, when the sparsely treed slopes provided the perfect setting for the pursuit of precious eagle feathers.

On the west side of the hills were several conical knolls, at the tops of which Native men dug shallow pits where they covered themselves with willows and grass, hoping to induce eagles to dive for the large piece of fresh meat lying on their chests. As a giant bird descended, talons first, the man kept very still. He had one chance to grab the feet, bash the bird on the head to kill it and win the eagle feathers— proof that he had passed the rigorous test.

British settlers raised on tales of the bloodcurdling deeds of "Red Indians" were not reassured by such stories. It was only six years before that Almighty Voice, a Cree outlaw, had held off a force of one hundred Northwest Mounted Police and civilian volunteers for two days, killing several of his would-be captors before he himself was dispatched by the bombardment of a nine-pounder gun. One of the constables involved had retired to a ranch near Baljennie in the midst of the Eagle Hills, and he was pleased to tell the story to the parade of Barr colonists who stopped to buy bread from his wife.

Inspector William Parker, "Old Hardface," had been on the Almighty Voice campaign too. Now he was shepherding the Barr colonists. Although Parker had respect for the group, whom he referred to in his memoirs as "a refined class of settlers," he would remember for the rest of his life the many examples of their inexperience as they fought their way through the Eagle Hills.

The trail had been established by the Metis, who had become freighters to support themselves after the great buffalo herds were exterminated. Driving wagons loaded with goods, they had searched for the best route, threading their way through ravines, around rocks, down hills and over streams. Each year in the spring they repaired the rough log bridges and laid new corduroy where the muskeg encroached upon the trail. Now, as they stood beside their worn and dingy wagons, they eyed the brand-new gear of the colonists, bright wagon paint still showing through the mud, the schooner tops of the more affluent still mostly white. The Metis men scoffed at the canvas tops. Waste of money, they thought. Blocked the view to the rear and made the wagon harder to unload. Sure sign of a green-horn.

Even with the advice of the freighters, the Eagle Hills presented a huge challenge to the novice drivers. They were either whipping their overburdened teams up a steep hill or trying to hold them back as they plunged pell-mell down the other side. The animals reacted to the lack of assurance in their drivers' commands by galloping out of control along creek beds, missing bridges and frequently overturning loads. One man was rumoured to have hobbled his oxen to keep them from running down yet another hill; unable to move their feet, the animals were pushed over a steep embankment by the weight of the wagon behind them. Men's legs were fractured. Horses were left broken-winded. Some people, tired of constantly unloading and reloading their wagons, left possessions by the side of the road, not really believing their own vows to return later for their belongings. Others, more energetic, unloaded their wagons before they crossed each stream in order to avoid a spill in the middle.

Robert Holtby was in a hurry to get to Battleford. He had been urging the horses on ever since they left Saskatoon, whipping them up to a trot whenever possible, driving like a man possessed, forcing Kate and the children to trot as well. Bob had argued with his father, questioning the need for such haste, but that did not stop the older man. Now, as the Holtby party limped into the fourth government camp in the early evening under a drenching rain, one of their horses was obviously ailing.

The government marquee was full of wet, tired people trying to dry their sodden clothing around the large stove. Someone joked about the rain, saying it was a nice change from the snow that had fallen several times since they left Saskatoon. Four veterans of the Boer War put everything into perspective by telling stories about South Africa that made this trek seem like child's play.

Most people slept soundly that night, undisturbed even by the fussing of fretful children that had kept them awake on previous nights. The morning was time enough to worry about a lame horse, a shortage of rolled oats or whether there would be any land left worth farming by the time they got to the colony site.

In the outside world the Wright brothers were trying to develop an engine light enough to power their glider, and Britain had just established a twenty-mile-per-hour speed limit for motor cars. In the southwestern corner of neighbouring Alberta, seventy people lay buried beneath millions of tons of rock that had slid off Turtle Mountain the week before and covered the town of Frank. But deep in the Eagle Hills, cut off from the world, the colonists slept in ignorance and woke early to begin the final drive towards Battleford.

A nearby farmer agreed to nurse the Holtbys' sick mare back to health. In just two days, they were on the road again too, their spirits revived, their horse apparently rehabilitated with a mash of barley, oats and linseed, and their bellies full of porridge served for once with milk. The farmer's wife had given Bob a special roast beef dinner—a "first class feed worthy of an English table."

Perhaps it was the roast beef that did it, but as he walked along through an expanding landscape that stretched to an impossibly distant horizon where it met the immense dome of the prairie sky, all Bob could think of was the cricket fields back home "and the happy time some people would be having." His homesick reverie ended abruptly when, without warning, the Holtby party found themselves in the midst of a sea of green and yellow striped snakes. The snakes were not very big around, but some of them were as long as a walking stick. The ground seethed with thousands of them, and the trail was greasy with their bodies where wagon wheels had crushed them. The men found them annoying and aggressive as they slid up pant legs and slithered down collars. The women and children were horrified and climbed onto the wagons, clinging there all day and refusing to stop for lunch.

By nightfall the snakes were gone. The Holtbys pitched their tents with trepidation but passed the night unmolested. It had been their misfortune to be in the way as the snakes proceeded from their breeding den to their favorite slough. Settlers travelling a day later saw only the carcasses.

For the last twenty-five miles before Battleford the trail ran through thick stands of poplar and spruce along a height of land above the ice-choked North Saskatchewan River. Though the trail was graded, the colonists needed logging chains to brake their wagons as they descended to the river valley. Every so often they could glimpse Battleford through the trees, but the town never seemed to get any nearer. Then the Battle River deflected their path away from the North Saskatchewan, the trees thinned out and an open plain revealed itself before them.

Telegraph Flat, so named when the Dominion Telegraph Company built its western terminus, was renamed Battleford when it became the first capital of the Northwest Territories. It was here that Patrick Laurie had founded the *Saskatchewan Herald*, the territories' first newspaper. When the Crees and the Assiniboines, in support of their Metis allies, laid seige to Battleford during the 1885 Northwest Rebellion, the white inhabitants fled to the safety of the NWMP barracks across the Battle River. In the eighteen years since then, the town had moved permanently across the river, closer to the protection of the mounted police.

It was to this new town, on the site of an old Hudson's Bay Company fur-trading fort between the Battle and North Saskatchewan rivers, that the colonists drove their wagons, crossing the Battle River on a proper bridge of iron and wood. William Hutchinson thought Battleford was much prettier than Saskatoon, but that was not saying much. It was certainly more orderly, its houses and buildings—post office, telegraph office, Dominion government land titles office, two churches and two hotels—laid out in military fashion.

The people were friendly, their good humour enhanced no doubt by the trade that hundreds of Barr colonists were bringing to this outpost of civilization. Harry Pick opened an account at the new branch of the Bank of British North America. Jim Ashton bought his supplies in Clinkskill's general store and was charmed by the optimism he sensed all around him. Jim McCormick wished he had enough money to play billiards at the Queen's Hotel. The citizens of Battleford were so friendly and helpful it made some of the colonists think the town would be a good place to settle.

But the prices were high. Goods had to be brought by barge down the North Saskatchewan River from Edmonton in the summer and by freight wagon from Saskatoon in the winter. The only vegetables available were onions, and bread was very expensive.

The government camp lay on the open prairie some distance from town. Set up on the banks of the river, the marquee tent, with a stove, hot water and a good supply of wood and hay, was surrounded by a community of bell tents. Next door to the marquee was the immigration hall, a rough agricultural building converted to quarters for married people. The citizens of Battleford had raised a special subscription to finance it. The newly boarded walls, the tables, shelves and curtained partitions all seemed very luxurious to people who had been living in tents for several weeks, and the hall was soon filled to overflowing.

Bob Holtby liked Battleford. He went into town to buy oats for the horses and discovered a race course where he could exercise them. The locals entertained him with stories of the rebellion. They told him that while the farmers had taken refuge in the NWMP barracks, their cattle had been stolen, their crops destroyed and many of their buildings burned by the rebels. The experience was still so fresh in their minds that it was hard for Bob to be convinced by assurances that all the Indians were living quietly now on their reserves and the Metis went about their own business quite peaceably.

The Holtbys had arrived in Battleford two days after Isaac Barr, just in time for Barr's confrontation with the Dominion land agent. Mr. Chisholm was still smarting from his battle with Mr. Bromhead, Barr's advance man, over Bromhead's insistence that Barr had exclusive right to assign all the homesteads. Since then, Chisholm had been accosted repeatedly by colonists who demanded first choice of land because they had been among the first to join the movement. Having received Chisholm's support, a group of them had left for the West, anxious to be among the first to arrive at the colony.

When Barr heard what had been happening, he was furious. He accused Chisholm of advising people to defy his authority and challenged the agent's jurisdiction, refusing to believe that his colonists might want to choose their own land. If they did not abide by his choice, Barr said, they could settle elsewhere. Chisholm's reply was stinging: "Your people utterly distrust you." "They are liars and troublemakers," the angry Barr retorted, threatening to withdraw. But the land agent called his bluff. Barr backed down and apologized, then stormed off to cable the department with his version of events. He fumed about articles published in the *Herald* describing the meeting Clinkskill had tried to organize in Saskatoon.

The *Herald* was facing a crisis of its own. Mr. Laurie's opposition to large reservations of land had found a focus in Barr's scheme, but just when the perpetrator was within his reach, Mr. Laurie fell seriously ill. The journalistic battle was about to begin, and he was too sick to join the fray.

Laurie succumbed to his illness, but his helpers fought mightily to persuade Barr's people to stay in Battleford. Contrary to what the settlers had been promised, the paper warned, there would be little work available in the colony. Most people could not afford to pay wages and there were no established farmers in the area looking for hired help. The newspaper warned them not to count on the promised railroad for construction jobs.

Among the colonists reading the paper were some, described by Chisholm as the most inflamed members, who took this advice to heart. Colonization agent Speers decided to stay in Battleford until he could see them settled. A delegation of twelve colonists inspected the country just north of Battleford near Jackfish Lake, reported back favourably and took the disenchanted group to the area to choose homesteads the next morning. They found Canadian and American settlers ready to help them in every way possible.

Although many struggled with the decision, the majority of the colonists decided to stay with the original plan. The Holtbys talked about settling near Battleford, but they decided that all the good land had been taken up. A lot of people found themselves in Jim McCormick's position. McCormick could not afford to keep going, but he could not afford to quit, either. He was glad he did not have a family. He had been out of money for some time and was able to continue the trek only by selling the pipes he whittled in his spare time. Chisholm found temporary jobs for about twenty of the colonists in Battleford, cutting firewood at the convent, herding cattle and digging gardens.

Everyone had heard the rumour that a large number of their group had returned to England. In the years since, no one has been able to put an accurate figure on how many did go back in the first year, but the number is smaller than most people believed that spring. Most of those who did not reach the colony stayed in Canada and settled somewhere else on the prairies. But the press harped on the subject, no doubt spurred on by British and European editors demanding evidence that the rumours of mass defection were true.

A year later, the *Herald* quoted a letter that Lloyd had written to a church newspaper in England commenting on the persistent rumour. England was producing two distinct classes of men, Lloyd said. The first were "those who, like their forefathers, can build up nations, men of grit, tone, force, and bull-dog stick-at-it-ness, and unfortunately, the second are the toast-and-butter, warm-slipper, return-to-Liverpool-with-a-weary-smile men." William Hutchinson would write later that fall that "every year thousands of people emigrate to Canada, and scores of them return home at once—plucked." It was not hard to tell what the colonists who persevered thought of those who went home.

Ivan Crossley and his partners decided that, since they had come this far, they might as well see the colony for themselves. Since they missed having milk to pour on their porridge, they agreed to buy a cow from a local rancher for $35. Accompanying the cow was a wild-looking calf, whose constant bawling unnerved the men and upset the mother. She planted her feet firmly, refusing to lead even when tied to the wagon axle. Out of a conference of the new owners came the brilliant idea to capture the calf, tie its legs together and hoist it on top of the load. This accomplished, the sweating men, breathless from the chase, attempted to untie the mother, reasoning that she would follow her offspring.

The mother had fire in her eyes and a set of impressive horns. No one could get near enough to her to loosen the rope. When one of the men crawled under the wagon and cut the lead with an axe, she chased her new owners around the wagon until they scrambled onto the load. The driver called to the team, and wagon, luggage, partners and calf lurched down the trail pursued by an angry, bawling cow.

After ten miles common decency required that they halt the wagon to let the calf feed. Untying its legs, they let it down still holding onto the rope while it nursed. But when they tried to climb down from the wagon to push the calf up again, the cow attacked them. The partners began to argue. They were wasting time. If they let the calf go they would be wasting money. Time won. They let the calf loose and mother, child, and $35 trotted off home together.

The country west of Battleford looked very promising. Even a city man could see that this was good farmland. The vanguard of settlers anxious to reach the colony travelled along the Old Fort Pitt Trail, over ruts cut deep by Red River carts, and were reminded again of the 1885 rebellion. The campsite on the first night out lay near Poundmaker's reserve, scene of the Battle of Cut Knife Hill. In that very week, eighteen years before, the Cree war chief Fine Day had used the wooded ravines south and west of their camp to great advantage in his battle with Lieutenant-Colonel William Otter. Their own

Mr. Lloyd had been wounded and left for dead during that battle.

That night Stanley Rackham, who had set out with the advance party, avoided the government marquee and camped instead near Bresaylor, a prosperous farming community named for three Metis families, the Bremners, the Sayers and the Taylors, who had come west from Manitoba and settled the rich plain in 1882. Rackham felt as though the worst was over. The road was dry and well maintained, the residents were prosperous, the land was rich. This was what he had come to Canada to find.

On the night of May 6, Barr camped near Bresaylor too. More anxious than ever to reach the colony, he had left his entourage and the main body of settlers in Battleford. His confrontation with Chisholm had made him more angry and fearful than he had been in Saskatoon. Things seemed to be slipping out of his control.

Travelling light to save time, he arrived at the headquarters camp of the colony, deep inside the land reserve, late on the evening of May 9. He had hired a man in Saskatoon and sent him ahead to locate the site and put up the store tent, but no provisions had arrived. Barr was greeted by enraged colonists who had pressed ahead, many of them with no money or supplies. He attempted to placate them with promises. He tried giving advice. He was sure he could satisfy everyone if they would only give him the chance.

Very early the next morning, Barr crept out of his tent and hoisted a large Red Ensign. This was the culmination of his dream. He had organized the largest number of British colonists ever to come in one group to the Canadian prairies. He looked out over the flat, empty land and imagined an all-British town surrounded by prosperous farms as far as the eye could see.

He knew that the dream had become tattered. There were so many problems. He had discovered the night before that there was only one surveyor in the camp, and he knew that it would take one man far too long to replace all the survey pegs that had disappeared. He knew that the land guides were having trouble finding people's homesteads for them. He knew that some colonists had dropped out along the way to settle nearer civilization. Since leaving Bresaylor, he had passed hundreds of wagons full of travel-worn and mud-spattered colonists. The women had shaken their fists at him as he rode past.

But Barr did not blame himself. Instead, he formulated a plan. He would return to Battleford as soon as possible and telegraph the deputy minister. He would demand that Smart supply more surveyors and that incompetent land guides be replaced. He would urge the railway to begin construction through the settlement at once. He would save the day.

That afternoon in the headquarters camp, a spark fell from a stove onto the dry grass. The grass ignited, and the fire spread rapidly. Stanley Rackham and a few others were the only men around, since most of the others were out looking for their homesteads. They tried beating the fire with shovels. They harnessed teams of horses to ploughs and struggled to carve fireguards around the camp, but their efforts were hampered by their inexperience. By the time the fire burned itself out, two or three outfits were completely destroyed, and the ground for miles around was left blackened and desolate.

An irregular line of wagons stretched back along the trail as colonists continued to straggle in from Battleford. Some distance back, an ex-soldier sat slumped over the reins as his team plodded along. Hearing the sound of galloping horses, he looked up and felt a thrill of recognition. A three-man detachment of the NWMP, under the command of Inspector Thomas McGinnis, rode quickly by on their way to the new colony. The scarlet tunics and dark blue riding breeches of the policemen were the same as those worn by the British army. The ex-soldier had worn a khaki version of the uniform during the fight with the Boers. The Stetson hats were a Canadian touch, to be sure. He had seen them worn by the Canadian regiment Lord Strathcona's Horse in South Africa, and many people wore them in the Northwest Territories, too. But the familiar uniform reassured him. The uniform that had become the most Canadian of symbols told him that British order and civilization were within reach even this far from home.

CHAPTER
VIII

Starvation Camp

A YOUNG MAN WHISTLED AS HE WALKED. WHAT MATTER THAT HIS HAIR WAS shaggy, his shirt dirty, his trousers torn and his army puttees hanging in ribbons around his ankles? It was mid-May, the sun was shining for a change, the road was firm and sandy, the land looked as if it would grow something and all was well with the world.

The young man had just left Battleford on his way to the Promised Land. There were many more like him—people still on the trail—and there were more back in Battleford. None of them knew that the worst of the journey was yet to come, and they were only vaguely aware that the leadership of the colony was in doubt.

Many Barr colonists had lost faith in Barr, and most of those who still believed in him did not know where he was. An increasing number of people wanted Lloyd to take over. Each time Barr had faltered, Lloyd had been there to pick up the pieces. But Lloyd had stayed behind in Saskatoon until all the scarlet fever patients were well enough to travel.

As each group of settlers left the government camp in Battleford, they found the first miles of the trail wonderfully invigorating. They strode along undisturbed by the flagging footsteps of their livestock, the tattered appearance of their wagons and the loud squealing of the wagon wheels. Behind the wagons, the women herded their children over the flat plain, the breeze carrying snatches of familiar nursery songs whose rhythms set the children's feet to marching.

But just when the New World dream seemed possible again, it all went wrong. The fertile plain gave way to rough bush and the firm, sandy trail to huge sloughs. Bob Holtby thought they had learned everything there was to know about driving horses and staying out of sloughs, but he was wrong. His uncle Willie's wagon got stuck in mud up to the axles almost as soon as they started one morning. In the afternoon, one of the horses refused to go any farther. Various members of the Holtby party took their turns at whipping the poor animal until some Canadians who were passing by told them it was obvious the horse was tired and that she would have to be rested and fed as much as she could eat. A farmer stabled the mare and gave them oats for the other horses and milk for themselves. While the men pitched the tents nearby, the farmer's wife allowed Kate to bake some bread in her oven. Agnes and the children rested in the warmth of the large kitchen.

Two days later the Holtbys resumed their journey. Before very long, they came upon another giant slough. Having wasted an hour trying unsuccessfully to find a way around it, they finally plunged in, one wagon at a time. Their travelling companion, Mr. Crawford, led the way. When he got stuck, they pulled him out. Willie Holtby was next, and though it was a struggle, he managed to get through. Then it was Robert's turn. Following what he was sure was a better route, he drove straight into a quagmire that grabbed the team and wagon in a firm and mucky grip. Willie's team was hooked on in front of Robert's to no avail. The horses, trapped to their knees in mud, started to plunge and splash, pulling Bob, who was trying to lead one of them, off his feet and submerging him completely.

The only solution was to unload the wagon. As the men ferried the boxes and trunks through the waist-deep water, Bob, wet from head to toe already, stepped into a hole. As he dropped, he managed to keep his feet under him and hold the precious bag of flour he was carrying above his head. Once the unloading was complete, they dug the wheels out, freed the wagon, reloaded, had dinner, resumed their journey and came to another slough.

So difficult was the terrain between the first two government camps after Battleford that when the colonists came upon the Paynter farm it seemed too good to be true. Peter Paynter had come west from Toronto to join the mounted police in time to serve during the 1885 rebellion. Since his retirement to an isolated farm, he had prospered. Barr had visited him the previous autumn and seen fine herds of cattle, thousands of bushels of oats and other grains, and farm machinery of the very latest kind.

Rumour had it that during that visit the year before, Barr had struck a deal with Paynter regarding oats to be sold to the colonists.

Barr had bought the oats at twenty-five cents a bushel, then asked Paynter to charge the colonists fifty cents a bushel, thus giving Barr a twenty-five cent per bushel profit. But the rumour also said that Paynter would tell the colonists Barr's price and then offer his own oats at twenty-five cents a bushel, thus saving the colonists twenty-five cents per bushel and allowing Paynter to make a profit. Paynter was a generous man. Everyone who passed through his yard received something—good advice, a drink of milk, the opportunity to buy bacon, eggs or a few hens. The rumour about the oats, whether true or not, also gave the colonists additional reason to distrust their leader.

By this time, almost everyone was prepared to believe anything bad that was said about Barr. Stories travelled back and forth along the trail. There had been no food at headquarters. Now there was food, but the prices were exorbitant. Barr had no authority to sell CPR land. There had been fires at headquarters and, even more ominous, there had been fires en route to the colony.

The colonists on the trail had seen smoke on the horizon for several days. Sometimes it blocked the sun. A hot, drying wind blew from the southwest. As they walked over the prairie wool, the dry crunch, crunch under their feet sounded like a warning. The matted mass of dead grass lay in wait for a carelessly thrown match or an badly tended campfire.

Fires had swept over the prairies for longer than humans could remember. Every spring and fall, hundreds of fires burned over thousands of acres of dry grass land, blackening everything in their path, a disaster for any person or animal caught in the way but necessary to the process of rejuvenation, as the dead grass was burned to make way for the green shoots of the new.

Sometimes the fires were set deliberately. Since the end of the buffalo, the Metis had set fire to the grass to reveal thousands of skulls and bones that could be sold to fertilizer manufacturers. But now, as more and more white settlers arrived on the prairies, most grass fires began unintentionally.

William Hutchinson and his partners were not particularly concerned by the warnings they had received about fires in the West, even though they had seen several on the horizon. The fires were especially visible at night and made an awesome show, but none had ever threatened the party. Even when their steady westward path took them through a recently burned area, the ground still hot and smelling strongly of soot, tree stumps charred and ground blackened as far as the eye could see, they were not unduly alarmed, nor did they alter their direction.

Having passed through the burned area, they found an inviting clump of trees near a slough just in time for their noon meal. After dinner, everyone stretched out for a nap except Hutchinson, it being his turn to make bannock. Suddenly he became aware of a loud crackling sound close by. He ran to investigate and was met by blinding smoke and overwhelming heat. He woke his friends, who scattered to find an escape route but encountered fire wherever they ran. The changing direction of the wind had created a circle of flames. Their only hope now was to light another fire to burn back to the one that threatened them on all sides.

Several of the party struck matches. Instantly the backfire became a thing beyond their control, roaring through the grass and trees but clearing a patch of safety in the midst of the inferno. As they drove their teams and wagons into a clearing, they heard shouts. A wagon and team appeared through the dense smoke, the driver desperately trying to control his animals. Hutchinson and his partners scrambled across the two-hundred-yard-wide strip of burning ground that separated them, grabbed the oxen by the harness and charged back through the fire to the relative safety of the clearing.

Now it was smoke that threatened to overwhelm them. For two hours they stood in the shelter of the wagons, faces grimy, bodies sweating, eyes stinging and half blind, throats burning. When the smoke finally cleared a little they moved out into "a wilderness of ruin." As darkness fell, they advanced slowly through the monotony of a prairie devoid of life. Finally, they found a small patch of unburned ground in the lee of a slough. They camped there for the night, surrounded on all sides by the blackened prairie and a dull red glowing sky.

Almost the entire triangle of land enclosed between the Battle and North Saskatchewan rivers from Battleford west along the trail to the colony reserve, and through it to the headquarters camp, had been blackened by the huge fire. There were small green patches only where sloughs had diverted the blaze. The next morning Hutchinson's party passed several badly scorched wagons heading east, each one carrying settlers with horrifying tales of hairbreadth escapes, of belongings consumed in the fire, of choking smoke, of pell-mell charges as they drove their wagons into sloughs and jumped into the water, submerging themselves to the neck.

Hutchinson heard the rumours that the fire had been started by a careless settler. He fumed over the inability of some of their number to appreciate the consequences of such lack of caution.

> It has seemed impossible to awaken these men from the Old World to a sense of the dangers attending carelessness in small matters. . . . It is no uncommon thing to come across patches of blackened ground strewn with half-burnt wearing apparel, boot tops, portions of boxes and remnants of a tent. . . . So general have the fires been that not 1/20 part of the prairies in the whole reservation, to say nothing of the scores of miles down the trail . . . have been left unburnt.

None of the colonists were killed in the fires that spring, but many lost their belongings. They had to return to Battleford for more supplies and then join the rest of the group still pressing on towards the colony, each person looking for someone to blame.

Agnes Holtby knew who to blame. Her husband, Willie, was responsible for this. Because of him she was here, thousands of miles from England, walking towards God-knew-what over a landscape destroyed by fire. A black powdery dust covered the ground; the wagons raised clouds of it, covering everything and everyone in sight. She strode along behind Willie's wagon, her year-old son cradled in a sling around her neck, her shoulders thrown defiantly back. The smell of soot permeated the air. Her hands and face were smudged, her clothing filthy. Her darling Redver's little face was splotchy with dust. Her two older sons followed behind, ignored by their diminutive mother, their adolescent legs barely a match for her determined stride. Agnes was angry at Kate, too. Her sister-in-law should have put her foot down and refused to come. That would have nipped this silly business in the bud. But no, Kate had gone along. She had not looked happy about it, but then Kate never looked very happy about anything.

Agnes Holtby set high standards for herself. She made it a rule always to wear at least one heavy petticoat, even on the hottest days. As she strode indignantly over the blackened prairie, her boot heels kicked up the flounces of her skirt, showing flashes of a once-white petticoat and sending little puffs of soot out behind.

Kate ignored Agnes. She had something much more important to worry about. Her fifteen-year-old daughter Bessie was not well. By the time they reached the last government tent, it was clear that Bessie had scarlet fever. The disease was nothing to trifle with, and the girl must rest. She would have to be kept in quarantine, anyway. The family decided that the men would continue on to find the land and the women would stay in their own tents near the last government marquee.

The last government camp was just inside the boundary of Barr's reservation and thirty miles from the colony headquarters. "Starvation Camp" was a dismal place with a dismal slough nearby that someone had named "Duck Lake" in honour of the disappearance of that very bird. All the creatures at Starvation Camp, human and animal alike, were hungry. The settlers were running out of food. The oxen's forage had been destroyed by fire. The horses, already suffering from a shortage of oats, were now beginning to sicken from drinking slough water.

Throughout the trek, heavy snow had alternated with equally heavy rain. When the snow melted it seemed as if the whole area was underwater. People kept track of the height of the water by watching how far up the sides of Noah's Ark the water had risen. Thomas Edwards's bizarre wagon with its heavy wooden peaked roof stood stranded in the middle of the slough, a symbol of the frustration and futility that they all felt.

But among the people at Starvation Camp was a fair sprinkling of the sort who thrive on difficult situations, who are determined to be as cheerful as possible no matter how hopeless things are. The Hills were people like that. They shared their small amount of flour with others who had run out of food. They lured people to the campfire in the evening with the sound of singing, their voices blending in four-part harmony, familiar melodies lifting spirits and driving away present woes for a time.

A few managed to keep their sense of humour. William Hutchinson's pancake recipe was a good example. He and his partners had arrived in Starvation Camp soaking wet and with little food. They rationed themselves by allowing each man a little rice and one pancake per meal.

> The pancakes were made of flour and water, mixed with snow to make them light—our calculation on this occasion being, one handful of snow equals one egg.

Despite the bad conditions, it was necessary for some people to stay at Starvation Camp for an extended period. Scarlet fever and now dysentery delayed several families. While wives and children waited, some men went ahead to scout out the land. With the prairie black for miles around and rumours of a shortage of supplies and inflated prices at the headquarters camp, many opted to stay where they were. At the very least, it meant that they did not have to fight their way through any more sloughs. The last one before Starvation Camp had trapped almost everyone.

On May 15, the Holtby men left their wives and young children in camp and set out to find their homesteads. Later that afternoon, Kate and several other women assisted Martha Topott as she gave birth to her son, lying on several blankets thrown on the frozen ground in a borrowed tent.

Several days before, Martha had arrived in Battleford with Dr. Keating to find her husband waiting for her in the government camp. The other men in their party, their wagon and most of their possessions had gone on ahead. Anxious to get to the colony as quickly as possible, William bought a horse, borrowed a buckboard and loaded Martha onto the seat in front. Accompanied by their friend Alice Hall, who perched in the back of the buckboard on top of a small tin trunk that contained baby clothes, they set out, their only supplies a borrowed tent, some blankets, some bread and a five-pound tin of Upton's jam.

They sped over level plain, then through rough scrub, unimpeded by an excess of baggage. By the time they reached Paynter's farm, however, the collar pad on the harness was badly worn. William sent his young wife to buy a new one from the veteran farmer, thinking that she would appeal to Paynter's sympathy. Martha was prepared to be rebuffed. She told him that if he could not spare a pad she would get one at the next place. Her heart sank when Paynter replied kindly, "You won't see another place." But luckily he did have one to spare.

Driven forward by a sense that time was running out, they pressed on after dark over land still smoldering from the recent fire. Alone on the dark prairie with just her husband and her friend, the young woman from a settled English town mistook glowing embers for house lights and the darker shadows for wolves.

It was late afternoon of the next day when they saw the white tents of Starvation Camp stark against the fire-blackened ground. Several women greeted them with disbelief. For days everyone had been speculating on Martha's whereabouts, and now here she was, still pregnant and still on her way to the colony. But no one knew the whereabouts of the Topotts' travelling companions or their wagon. It was the need to wait for their friends and the presence of a seepage well that persuaded them to stay in camp. The desire for good water without "wigglers" in it had filled Martha's thoughts for days. They pitched their tent and arranged their blankets. The next day, Martha's labour pains began.

Middle-class women raised in the late Victorian era went to their first confinement ignorant of what to expect, it being generally held among proper English mothers that a knowledge of physiological facts destroyed the air of innocence so desirable in a young woman. The completion of a young woman's education therefore came only with the birth of her first baby.

With no medical aid or equipment, the birth of Martha's first baby was very difficult. But women who may well have shrunk from preparing their own daughters for such an ordeal were there to help her. Having given birth themselves, they were able now to perform in deed what they would have found difficult to explain in words. Centuries of experience passed down from one generation to the next guided their hands. The baby was wrapped and laid in his mother's arms. All seemed well, but within a few days Martha developed a heavy cold that settled in her chest. As her condition worsened, the temperature outside dropped and it began to snow again.

Aided by the other members of the Topott party, who had arrived in camp with the wagon, the women attending Martha used ingenuity and common sense to save her. Reasoning that a smaller space would be easier to keep warm, they built a cosy enclosure over the new mother by using two hoops taken from the wagon and set into the ground at her head and feet. A tent was then draped over the hoops. Kate emptied the prairie grass from her own tick into Martha's empty one to provide a settler's version of a quilt. Inside her little tent within a tent, Martha fought off the infection.

On the day that Dickie Topott was born, Isaac Barr was travelling as fast as his horses could pull his light wagon in the direction of Battleford. He had left the headquarters camp at daybreak the day before. By the next day, he was in Battleford.

Barr was an embattled man. He had experienced the animosity of the colonists ever since they had blamed him for the overcrowded conditions on the *Manitoba*. They blamed him for the failure of his transportation company, too. He had been criticized and taken to task. People complained when he did not deliver on his promise of fresh bread and meat on the trek. There was even one outrageous rumour that the tents and blankets he had sold to the colonists had been infected with disease. Now people had started to talk about all the money he had collected for absentee homesteaders, or for CPR land, or for shares in the hospital or the stores syndicate.

In the weeks since he had left Saskatoon, he also had been threatened on several occasions. He had given his travelling companion, Dr. Amos, a revolver and asked him to act as a bodyguard. He told Amos it was to protect the large amount of money he carried with him and stored under his mattress each night, and that was partly true, but he had also begun to fear for his own safety.

In later years, everyone had a story about seeing Barr on the trail between the colony and Battleford in those middle days of May. Usually the stories involved midnight rides and hurtling horses. Often there was a posse in pursuit. The stories are very hard to confirm and harder still to fit into the sequence of events. Bessie Holtby, sick with scarlet fever in Starvation Camp, thought she heard Barr go by one night. When her mother looked out to see what was happening, a wagon full of men with guns pulled up. They asked if anyone had seen Barr go by and said they were going to kill him if they caught up with him.

Not everyone blamed Barr for everything. Some would admit that the problems on the ship and the missing baggage were beyond Barr's control. They saw that he had tried his best to satisfy everyone when he arrived at the headquarters camp. When people complained about the lack of fresh meat, Ivan Crossley said that Barr took an axe and knocked down one of his own oxen, crying, "There's fresh meat for you all now, help yourselves." Ivan said Barr was "worried to death." Harry Pick said that Barr was drinking. And Harry Pick said that one night Barr just disappeared.

Barr had come back to Battleford on May 16 to inform the Dominion government by wire of the situation from his perspective and to demand some action. As he vented his frustration at the telegraph office, Land Agent Chisholm anxiously watched a crisis in the making. He reported to the deputy minister that "the mere mention of Barr's name inflamed [the people]." Settlers were returning to Battleford from the colony headquarters full of indignation at the conditions they had found there, and most said it was the fault of Isaac Barr.

Chisholm could sense the desperation in Battleford. The child of a colonist had died that morning of scarlet fever and the mother, crazy with grief, had thrown herself into the river. The Anglican minister, Mr. Parker, had followed the poor woman and was able to rescue her from drowning, although she fought him fiercely. The NWMP had been required to deal with a man who had consumed too much bad whiskey. Everything seemed to be getting out of hand.

As if in answer to a prayer, George Lloyd arrived in Battleford from Saskatoon late that evening. He and his family reached the government camp in the middle of a snowstorm. As they pulled up outside the roughly built temporary immigration hall, people swarmed out. "Everybody had a different tale to tell," he would report. Some of them had not even been to the colony, so horrendous was the news from farther west. Pleading extreme fatigue, Lloyd promised he would call a meeting in the morning. He and his family spread blankets to cover the large cracks in the floor and settled down to sleep in the small space that had been cleared for them in the corner of the hall.

Early the next morning a deputation asked Lloyd to be their leader, and although he could not have been surprised at the request, Lloyd avoided giving them an immediate answer. He said he would need the permission of his employer, the Colonial and Continental Church Society, before taking on additional responsibilities and suggested they all attend the meeting he had called for the afternoon.

Included in the deputation that visited Lloyd that morning were Robert Neale Blackburn, an engineer, Arthur Still, a farmer of some means, and Nathaniel Jones, former manager of a Manchester safe company. All three men were at or near middle age, all had travelled cabin class on the *Manitoba* and all were determined to be rid of Isaac Barr.

Nathaniel Jones was full of ideas about how the whole venture should have been organized. Having left his wife, Elizabeth, and one son temporarily behind in England and having sent his other three sons to Prince Albert to find work for the summer, he was free to devote himself full-time to putting things in order.

When George Lloyd looked back on that day, he was sure that the majority of the colonists were in Battleford at the time. He was mistaken. Many of the settlers had reached the colony headquarters already, and many more were on the road between Battleford and the colony, including a large number at Starvation Camp. Although some people had returned to Battleford, few of the people whose diaries and letters have survived were in Battleford on that day. The actual number attending the meeting was quite small. Barr's biographer, using Lloyd's figures, wrote that there were 140 people at the meeting, approximately 7 per cent of the original group.

And they were a particularly disgruntled lot. They were the people who had stayed behind, or who were thinking of taking up land outside the colony, or who had been burned out by the fires. Nathaniel Jones rose to make a motion that they no longer look to I. M. Barr as their leader and that the name "Barr" no longer be applied to the British colony. The crowd offered Lloyd the leadership, and though he declined at first, they urged him to reconsider. Lloyd promised that if he could send his employer "the unanimous resolution of that mass meeting" and if a committee of twelve men was elected to share the duties, he would consent to assume the leadership.

Jones, Blackburn and Still were elected to the committee on the spot, and it was agreed that the rest would be voted on later. Word came that Barr was in town staying at the Queen's Hotel. The time was ripe for a showdown. The people were instructed to congregate again that evening.

In preparation for their confrontation with Barr, Lloyd and his committee met with Inspector Griesbach of the NWMP, who had been watching the situation closely and told them that no laws had been broken. If any legal action was taken against Barr, it would have to be in a civil suit. The Dominion government also had been watching with great concern. Having assumed control of the colony in all but name, the Department of Immigration was careful to have nothing to do with the overthrow of Barr or the selection of Lloyd. Mr. Speers, however, was instructed to "take such steps as he deems wise regarding oversight to ensure success of the colony irrespective of Barr or any other person."

Although Speers was present, it is Lloyd's account of what happened at the Queen's Hotel that survives—one man's version of an event where emotions ran very high. Barr was afraid for his life. He said that the colonists "were a rough lot . . . a crowd of ruffians" and that they had threatened his life with a revolver. Considering the frustration of the colonists and the large number of firearms in their possession, this is not an impossibility.

In the crowded hotel room, Nathaniel Jones read the resolution of the mass meeting. Adamant that he would never return to the colony,

Barr agreed to bow to the will of the group. Then, with Speers taking an active part, the discussion turned to the details of transfer of medical supplies, syndicate shares and inventory, and contracts for absentee homesteaders. Speers "seemed to be more anxious to let I. M. Barr out than to help the committee carry on," Lloyd reported peevishly.

Then the issue of potatoes had to be addressed. On Barr's instructions from the previous fall, a merchant named Secord had floated a scow loaded with $2000 worth of potatoes from Edmonton down the North Saskatchewan River. The plan had been for him to meet Barr with the scow north of the colony headquarters, at the point where the river crossed the Fourth Meridian. But when Secord arrived, he discovered that Barr had just left to return to Battleford. Unable to float the scow back to Edmonton against the current and not wishing to be left with such an abundance of potatoes, he took his cargo farther downstream to Battleford.

Secord was in the hotel room when the committee arrived for their meeting with Barr. He watched as Barr agreed to step down, then demanded payment for his potatoes. In the first flush of victory, the committee foolishly agreed to take responsibility. Some potatoes were taken by settlers, and the rest of "the murphies" were to be transported by freight wagons paid for by the new administration. The committee had been in control for a matter of minutes and had already agreed to spend a large sum of money.

Not surprisingly, the next step for the committee was to secure operating funds. The manager of the only bank in Battleford asked them what they could offer in security for a loan of $3000. Lloyd replied that all he had was his good name and his boots. He warned the manager that if the colony broke up it would set immigration back ten years. When that failed to impress the banker, Lloyd agreed to give the bank the right to garnishee his cccs wages if necessary.

The new leader of the British colony sent a telegram to Obed Smith, commissioner of immigration for the prairies.

> By unanimous resolution British colonists Battleford Lloyd and committee replace Barr. Leave for front at once. Have asked Minister for Special Commissioner.

In his use of military terminology, Lloyd may have inadvertently revealed his state of mind. A reporter for the *Saskatchewan Herald* was on hand that evening as Lloyd presided over a second meeting with the colonists. It was time to "take the bull by the horns," the new leader cried. He "rehashed" all the grievances and reported on his meeting with Barr. Nathaniel Jones read the resolution proposing that the appointed committee remain in charge until a proper form of government could be elected. The resolution was passed unanimously and signed by all present. Three cheers were offered for Lloyd and one for his wife. Having instructed the assembled people to proceed to the colony as fast as possible and to tell everyone they saw on the trail of the change in leadership, Lloyd adjourned the meeting.

It was important not to delay. The next morning, Lloyd, Still and Jones departed for "the front." They hoped to prevent any further desertions, and they were anxious to check on the supplies in the colony before returning to Battleford to settle matters finally with Barr. Because Lloyd wished to travel quickly, he left his wife and children in Battleford, promising that he would be back soon to collect them and their belongings. Mrs. Lloyd was to handle the colony mail while she waited.

Back at the headquarters camp, the weather had been terrible. A cold north wind blew fitfully across the flat prairie, carrying snow and rain with it and making life in the tents a misery. The land guides refused to go out in such bad weather. No one was in command. It seemed as if the colony were about to collapse.

Then, on May 20, a democrat pulled by two Indian ponies arrived in camp, carrying Lloyd and his committee. Word spread quickly. People gathered around the wagon cheering and shouting questions. The committee instituted a system of rationing to control the distribution of the last of the rolled oats and flour. There were no eggs, cheese, butter or sugar, but a bakery started by three or four men was an instant success. The colonists were notified that the government was sending three surveyors. The very presence of the new leader served to stop the people who had been leaving. Settlers who had camped along the trail waiting to see what would develop now started to arrive at headquarters.

Barr spent the next two weeks roaming the country between Battleford and the colony. Although he had officially relinquished leadership, he seemed unable to walk away from the idea that had dominated his life for the past year. So much had happened since his first contact with Canadian immigration officials in February of 1902. The plan had grown from an idea in his head to the emigration of over two thousand people. Now he wandered from camp to camp talking to the colonists, abused and threatened by many but sympathetically received by some.

He visited the Topott homestead not long after William had brought Martha and Dickie, by then ten days old, to their new home, a tent in the middle of the prairie. The controversy over Barr's leadership had gone almost unnoticed by the Topotts, so preoccupied were they with their own problems, but the couple had heard the gossip. They knew that Barr had been deposed. He asked them if they could spare a change of horses. William made him a cup of tea. When Barr left, he handed the new father fifty cents for his little son. As Martha said years later, "In those days fifty cents was quite a bit of money." Then the deposed leader headed east yet again, back to Battleford for a second meeting with Lloyd and the committee, who were also driving east with fire in their eyes.

They had seen the conditions in the colony and on the trail. They had listened to the tired, the sick, the penniless and the just plain angry. They were even more furious with Barr and determined to see justice done. But their anger had limited their efficiency. Speers characterized the activity of the committee in the days after Barr stepped down in the following way:

> The absence of all business methods was conspicuous among the leaders. This may be due to contention and quarrelling and a good deal of running about, as the Committee had secured control of Mr. Barr's books, and they were both determined to go to court, and a very acute stage had been reached when I convened Messrs Barr, Lloyd and the Committee in my room in Battleford.

Speers was being somewhat unfair to Lloyd. By his presence in the colony alone, the new leader had reassured the colonists and achieved some measure of order. But it took a determined Speers to cajole Barr and Lloyd into an amicable settlement and, although both agreed to withdraw their lawsuits, Lloyd would not allow Barr access to Barr's own accounting books. Because of this, Barr was able to say that he had done the best he could in returning people's money but that he could not be blamed for any oversights because he could not refer to his figures.

In his memoirs, Lloyd did not remember the settlement as amicable. He was particularly obsessed with the contents of a crate marked with a red cross, which he said was supposed to have contained all the surgical instruments. When the committee opened the case in the presence of Doctors Amos and Keating, they found a six-foot iron cot with one leg broken, a mattress and a pillow. Lloyd would have posterity believe that Barr had tried deliberately to cheat the colonists of medical equipment. But the new leader had forgotten about all the equipment the doctors had been using to treat scarlet fever in Saskatoon. That equipment was now in the colony.

When Lloyd left the Queen's Hotel after the meeting with Barr, he went in search of his family. Anyone used to seeing the tall, elegant curate in his customary clerical garb would not have recognized the apparition that strode through the government camp. A mosquito net covered his hat and head; a large dirty cloth concealed the boils that infected his neck; his clothes were dirty; he was obviously unwell, and he could not find his wife and five children.

Someone told him to look for them at the NWMP police barracks. He found Marion standing in the doorway of an old shack near the stockade, under a sign that said "Scarlet Fever." One of his daughters had contracted the disease and she and her mother were in quarantine for several weeks. The rest of the children were with a nurse from the colony.

The roof of the shack leaked, and there was a space around the floor where gophers ran in and out. Lloyd's daughter slept on a canvas stretcher, her mother on a steamer trunk. Mr. Parker, the local Anglican minister, brought them drinking water every day, but Marion herself carried water for washing up the long hill from the river.

Lloyd pitched a small tent in the vicinity of the shack, and Marion prepared him a disinfectant bath, some poultices and some food. Having washed and eaten, he felt more normal. He could spend only a day with his wife and daughter, however, visiting at a distance, before he had to return to the colony.

Barr seemed reluctant to leave the territories. He was seen at various locations between Battleford and the colony during the month of June and into July. There were the final documents to sign, and he said he wished to make himself available to anyone to whom he owed money. And he did not seem to have lost his enthusiasm for colonization schemes, telling some people that he was returning to England to bring out a group to the Vermillion River.

When he finally left to travel to Ontario, where his fiancée had gone to wait for him, he was reported to have been pelted with rotten eggs as he waited to change trains in Regina. Two days later, on July 10, he was in Winnipeg when the House of Commons in Ottawa debated the Barr Colony situation. A member of the Opposition commented on an interview with Commissioner Preston published in London in late May in which the department official had said,

> In regard to Mr. Barr, I have only to say . . . that the department has welcomed his intervention, and are perfectly satisfied of his honourable conduct in the whole matter.

The newshounds were not taken in by the smooth talk of department officials. On May 19, 1903, the *Globe* of Toronto had run the headline "Mr. Barr deposed." The *Toronto News* crowed, "All-British Colony Comes to Ignominious End. Promoter has returned cash and settlers are scattered." The Reuters dispatch to London reported that hundreds of settlers had arrived in Saskatoon on their way back to England. In London, Commissioner Preston was not content with the department's denial of this dispatch and demanded further proof. The department responded,

> Premier Haultain, Hon. Bulyea, B. Prince Legislative Member for Battleford and Saskatoon agents join with me stating without reservation absolutely no truth in statement that Barr colonists returning to England in large numbers. You can assure public ninety-nine percent are remaining and settling.

Sensational headlines and the premier's denials meant very little to the people at the headquarters of the colony. They were much more concerned with the latest tribulation to be visited on them—mosquitoes. The warmth of the spring sun, making a belated return appearance, hatched millions of the tiny pests from the sloughs. Few of the colonists except the ex-soldiers had ever seen a mosquito before, and now the insects swarmed all over them. They breathed them in, they ate them, and their horses and oxen were covered with blankets of them.

Mosquitoes tormented Jim McCormick as he sat in the buggy behind his ailing horse Belle, going so slowly he could write legibly in his diary. It was very hot. He had spent more than two weeks searching for several missing horses, retracing his steps as far back as the

Eagle Hills and returning now to the colony, his mission a failure. As he neared the last government camp it had taken him one and a half hours to go five miles. Finally he could stand it no longer. He un-harnessed Belle, tied her on behind and pulled the buggy half a mile into camp himself. "It was," he said, "a laughable farce."

That night he washed the buggy, gave Belle a rubdown and slept soundly. In the morning he walked the mare to the homestead where his partners had been camped for the past two weeks. As he ap-proached the tents, pitched on the open prairie, he was greeted with the news that the horses had been found several days before.

CHAPTER
IX

Being Green Altogether

ALICE AND WILLIE RENDELL WERE THE SORT OF PEOPLE THE CANADIAN GOVERN-ment would have called ideal immigrants. They were British, they were experienced farm managers, they had some capital, and they were young and strong. Now that Isaac Barr was no longer the leader of the colony, now that Lloyd and the committee had taken over and were attempting to bring order to the headquarters camp, it was people like the Rendells who would provide an example of how things should be done.

The Rendells had left England after the other colonists, arriving in Saint John on the S.S. *Lake Simcoe* just in time for the fire at the train station. Their journey to Saskatoon was miserable, a situation which the Rendells, as Canadian Pacific Railway shareholders, found reprehensible in the extreme. But through it all Alice had kept her sense of humour in the lively letters she wrote to their friends back in England.

Nothing stood in the way of her letters—not her two small children, not her pregnancy, by then entering the seventh month, not the many times the family "felt faint and famished from hunger," and not even the painful abscess on her face. So faithful a correspondent was she that she had every right to expect there would be letters waiting for her when she and her family reached Battleford. But the postmaster refused to give out any Barr Colony mail because he was not being paid to do so. Alice, undeterred, took time to write another letter, ending it with the words,

> Our thoughts are constantly wandering to our dear old
> friends and the dear old country, but although we have

passed through so much already our courage is still undaunted. Dear friends, don't forget our address is P.O.
Battleford, N.W.T., Canada.

Then she and her family made the final push towards the Promised
Land, arriving there well ahead of the main party.

The Rendells reached the colony during the brief period when Barr
was at headquarters camp before he was deposed as leader. When
Willie decided that the homestead allotted to him before he left England simply would not do, he went directly to Barr, who helped him
find another piece of land. And what a piece of land they found. The
soil was fertile. There was plenty of wood and water. It was close to
where Barr said the railway station would go, a few minutes from the
land set aside for a school and only a half-hour buggy ride back to
headquarters. There was an adjacent quarter section available for their
hired man.

A day later, the prairie fire that swept through the colony left their
homestead blackened and bleak. Back at headquarters, the Rendell's
daughter Doris had a high fever, their hired man was fighting off
pneumonia and Alice had collapsed with a bad chill, bronchitis and a
recurrence of her abscess.

But nothing daunted the Rendells. Within two weeks, they had
moved to their "estate," named Doris Court in honour of their daughter, and Willie had started to plough. "It is a glorious feeling," Alice
wrote, "to be able to look around on our own property and feel that
each day's work is for future benefit, no landlord and no rent to pay
nor taxes!"

A few miles to the east on the Holtby homestead, eight-year-old
Dodie was trying to come to terms with her new home. There was
nothing there—"no house, no garden, no fence—nothing!" Was this
how she was to be rewarded for being such a good girl on the trip? On
the *Manitoba* she had been the only Holtby who was not seasick. She
had looked after herself, wandering all over the ship watching the sail-
ors at work, only disturbing her parents to tell them how a "nice gentleman" had taken her to his cabin and given her an orange.

The camp at Saskatoon had been just as much fun. She occupied
herself all day exploring and had to ask for help only when she could
not find her way back home for supper because all the tents looked
alike. As for the trek, she knew she would remember the steep hills,
the wagons overturning, the garter snakes, the snow, the heat and the

smell of burned grass all her life. Dodie had come to think of life on the wagons as normal, but she looked forward to seeing her new home. When they got there, however, she was horrified. There was nothing but another campsite sitting alone on an empty stretch of prairie.

Her father, her uncle and her two brothers had gone ahead to lay claim to the land, arriving at dusk in a driving rainstorm. They had pitched a tent in the shelter of a bluff of poplars and gone through the familiar ritual of lighting a fire in the stove, draping their clothes around it to dry.

Because each of the four men was eligible for a homestead, the family could claim an entire section, but it was important that they be sure they were in the right place before they registered. When they checked their location, they realized they were too far south, but when they moved, they came too far north. Finally, with the help of guides, they found their land. Some of the corner posts were missing, but they were "almost reasonably sure" they were in the right place, and that made them surer than most people were.

The settlers who *were* sure were not necessarily pleased with what they found. Barr had said that all the land was good, but much of it west of the Fourth Meridian and north of Big Gully Creek was rough and swampy. Someone estimated that half the land in the entire reserve was unsuitable for farming. There were unrealistic expectations among the settlers, too. Some of them had imagined nothing less than a piece of English park land with "grassy, gently rolling slopes interspersed with clumps of trees, a sparkling stream and possibly a silvery lake thrown in." Others were more realistic but had genuine grounds for complaint. One man pointed out that his land was full of stones, and since he was not a lime-burner, it would not be any use to him. Another man needed a canoe to reach his land. A third man had no land at all, his entire quarter section being taken up by a slough.

Early every morning, George Langley, the sub–land agent, would emerge from the land titles office tent to post a list of vacant homesteads. Then he would go back to his office to deal with the people who were unhappy with the land Barr had assigned to them. Their indignation turned to panic when they heard that there was not enough good land inside the reserve to provide for everyone.

Most people needed a guide in order to find their land; the lack of markers rendered them helpless to an "inconceivable degree," according to Langley. The pressing need for land guides gave birth to a new set of rumours. The land guides were not competent; the land guides were competent but they had no compasses; the sub-agent was indiscreet and was giving out confidential information. Whether the rumours were true or not, the waiting list for the land guides was long. Once the services of one had been procured and the homestead had been viewed and deemed suitable, a quick return to camp was necessary in order to register the claim before someone else did.

William Hutchinson and his brother, Ted, joined a group of eighteen men who had agreed to share the services of one guide. A convoy of wagons set out, heading east along the main trail. Several men, including the Hutchinsons, followed on foot, carrying blankets and food for three days. Soon the convoy left the trail and struck out across the prairie, maintaining the compass bearing in a straight line no matter what—over hills, down ravines and through waist-deep sloughs. When it became dark, they made camp and slept fitfully on the hard ground under the stars. They woke with the first glimmers of light to fill their pockets with food and set off behind the guide in his light rig, leaving their blankets in camp.

As each homestead was located, the claimant doubled back in a race to headquarters to register, but the afternoon shadows were long by the time the Hutchinsons saw their land. They set off on foot for headquarters, trying to keep the compass bearing and trying to ignore the clouds that were rushing in to block the sun. A drenching rainstorm did not slow them down, nor did they stop when it became dark. They pressed on, taking turns leading, stopping to read the compass by the light of a match when the clouds made celestial navigation impossible. So dark was the night that when they hit the main trail at one o'clock in the morning, they had to feel with their feet to stay on the path.

They reached headquarters at 3:00 A.M., just as dawn was breaking. Since the land titles tent was not open for business until seven, they had plenty of time to change their wet clothes, eat some breakfast and be waiting at the tent when Langley arrived for the day. Sixteen of the men in their group had been able to register their homesteads, but the land claimed by the Hutchinson brothers had been taken by somebody else.

The next day William went out alone, leaving Ted to tend their livestock. This time, he was searching for two homesteads that Langley assured him were empty. He was able to find them himself, and having determined the boundaries and sampled the water from a stream that ran through the property, he prepared a camp in a poplar bluff and lay down to sleep on his own land.

Back in camp, a story was making the rounds about a man who had been checking over a piece of land when he heard noises behind a clump of poplar trees. Walking quietly to investigate, he had come upon two big men so intent on fighting over who would claim the same quarter section that they failed to notice his presence. The observer, knowing himself to be no match in brawn, slipped quietly away, returned to camp and registered the land for himself.

For those colonists determined to find their land without the help of a guide, the obstacles were daunting. Only the township markers, iron rods one inch thick and two feet high, remained from the survey done twenty years before. The section and quarter section markers had virtually disappeared. In response to Barr's demands that they be replaced, the department had sent three men who simply checked the township stakes and told people to work out the sections and quarter sections for themselves.

The amateur surveyors encountered many problems. Those with compasses forgot that their instruments had been calibrated in Britain, where the deviation for magnetic north was over thirty degrees different from the deviation at the Fourth Meridian. Thus many calculations were inaccurate, and many settlers wandered about unable to find the township lines.

Once the township line had been determined, the individual township markers had to be paced out at six-mile intervals. To do this, one man drove a wagon while a second man rode behind him holding a compass to keep him precisely on a straight line. Before the men set out, they had measured the circumference of the right back wheel and tied a red cloth to it. A third man walked behind the wagon, counting the wheel's revolutions. At the six-mile point the horse was unhitched so that the wagon would stay exactly in place. Then everyone fanned out, looking for the four holes that were dug at the diagonal corners of the compass around each of the iron township markers. This exercise was made more difficult by the plenitude of badger holes, which looked just like the surveyors' diggings.

When the township boundaries had been established, the sections could be paced off and then the quarter sections. Like most of the colonists, Ivan Crossley had absolutely no idea what one hundred and sixty acres looked like. He thought that all farms were just nice little places laid out with a road past them. . . . This was nothing but a howling wilderness with no semblance of roads or anything else.

Some people, like the Holtbys and the Hutchinsons, were fortunate to find their land with only a minimum of false starts. Others, like the Joseph Hills, built a house and did a great deal of ploughing before they discovered they were on land that belonged to someone else.

The good land on the reserve filled up quickly, leaving many people to look for suitable quarter sections south of the colony boundary. But the quality of the soil was everything Barr had promised it would be. The rich black loam made the ordeal worth it, although William Hutchinson noted wryly that the views of some of the men on the quality of the soil should be taken with caution, since they had "never even dug a back garden before."

The land was beautiful as spring gradually gave way to summer. The blackened landscape had turned green again with surprising quickness, little shoots of new growth appearing through the charred grass in three or four days. The wildflowers were showing, and the perfume of willow and wild thyme floated on the breeze.

Most of the land was flat as a table, but on the edge of the reserve were hills with clumps of poplar trees growing so thickly that it was impossible to walk between them. In the small spaces between the trees, raspberry cane and berry bushes sought the shade. Northeast of headquarters, Big Gully Creek ran through a steep-sided valley, the thick spruce and poplar on its north-facing slope interspersed with patches of rich hay land.

Not far to the south of Big Gully Creek, Bob and Oliver Holtby were heeding the advice of the farm instructors who were urging people to start ploughing immediately. There were only a limited number of weeks when the land could be broken; after that it would dry out and become too hard. The first time either of the Holtbys had touched a plough was when they loaded their new Massey-Harris combination into the wagon at Saskatoon, but now they managed to put the handles on, fix the eveners on the front and hitch up the horses without too much trouble.

Oliver drove as Bob held the plough. They discovered how to make adjustments until they liked the looks of the furrow. Then Bob took the reins, knotted them together and hung them over his shoulder, leaving him free to grip the handles. As the team went along the furrow steadily and easily, Bob felt a thrill at seeing "the beautiful black wave" of overturned soil.

Things did not go nearly as well for Bernard and Percy Boden. Their first problem was making the whiffletree wide enough for three oxen. Because they had positioned the holes for the harness incorrectly, the pivoted crossbar broke when they tried to plough. And the animals would not pull evenly. Someone pointed out that it was obvious the oxen had never been broken to a plough. Bernard pretended not to care, saying, "[They] are quiet, willing enough, and I do not repent buying them."

Again and again the Bodens tried to drive their oxen in a straight line. Again and again they were unsuccessful. Boden confessed that he often lost his temper. The oxen caused them other problems, too. The beasts had taken to walking all over the seeded garden. Then they started to wander away. The brothers scoured the countryside, scanning the prairie for the wayward animals, their opera glasses a poor substitute for binoculars. Sometimes the Bodens' animals travelled six miles before they were found.

Everyone who came by Bernard and Percy's place gave advice about ploughing, much of it contradictory. Someone said they should trade for older oxen, but someone else said young oxen were too valuable to trade. The farm instructor's assurances that the animals would plough next year were little consolation. They needed to plough this year, if only to build a sod roof for their house, so they persisted until the ground was too hard and they had to wait for a softening rain.

The Boden oxen continued to wander away. The brothers tried staking them to the ground. The bullocks either broke their ropes or pulled up their stakes. By now the animals could lift the bars off the log fence the men had built around the garden and were eating the new plants as they sprouted.

The decision was made to exchange one ox for a milk cow, but ploughing was no easier with the two remaining oxen. The brutes were unevenly matched in strength, and the stronger was also the more willing. Bernard confessed to his fiancée that he had lapsed into a bad old habit of "having too free a tongue." Something was always breaking or going wrong. "It is enough to vex a saint," he wrote. It was not until November that the Bodens discovered most of their problems had been caused because their plough was too heavy for their team.

Long before November, Bernard Boden had begun to pin his hopes on "next year." His letters home reflected his philosophical attitude.

> We do not seem to have much to show for our time here, and I suppose it is on account of our not knowing how to go about things . . . next year things will come much easier when we get the knack of doing the work.

Bob Holtby was philosophical too.

> We could have done a lot better the first summer if we had not been so green and being green altogether without anyone in the community who was really well acquainted with prairie conditions, we had to find out how to do things the hard way.

As the hot sun of summer made a welcome appearance, it was easier for the colonists to enjoy the good weather than to worry about all the things they did not know how to do. Langley reported that "a number of them seem unable to free themselves from the idea that the whole thing was not a sort of picnic." Bernard Boden, observing that he often slept late, said, "I have grown more fond of my bed since I came out here than ever before." But on July 1, Bernard was up early and rummaging through his portmanteau for his dressy clothes. It was Dominion Day, an unfamiliar Canadian holiday but a good excuse for a celebration.

A special event required special dress, not the underwear and overalls that Jim Ashton had been wearing; not the dark shirts that hid the dirt or the slouch hats that were crammed into breeches pockets when their owners came inside; not the top boots that had become scuffed and worn or the collarless shirts that made so much sense to a man doing manual labour. For Dominion Day, proper hats, shirts, collars and ties were required. Stanley Rackham unpacked his flannels, and Jim McCormick found his regimentals. Women got out their summer dresses and extra petticoats from the bottoms of trunks. From squashed boxes under a pile in the back of the tent they took their summer hats, which they decorated with the wildflowers that now covered the prairie.

July 1 was a beautiful day. The headquarters camp was decorated with flags and flowers. A few of the celebrants adorned themselves with orange and green in premature recognition of the Battle of the Boyne, the tiger lilies of the prairies an inadvertent confirmation that William of Orange was remembered by Protestants in the territories too.

At the pony and horse-and-wagon races in the afternoon, three mounted policemen maintained the boundaries of the course

> in a very businesslike manner hustling the crowd about with their horses as if we were tight packed in the Strand instead of a handful of people in the middle of thousands of acres of almost uninhabited land.

Metis cowboys with long matted hair brought wild ponies to test the mettle of the men. None of the colonists managed to stay on board the bucking broncos, but the crowd cheered when a dark-skinned, range-hardened cowboy rode one successfully.

With group photographs to be taken, tea and dinner to be eaten, and a football match to be played, it was a wonder that anyone was on time for the big event of the day—the Patriotic Concert. The crowd, which included French settlers from nearby homesteads and local Metis, Cree and Blackfoot people, was seated on upturned wagon boxes. Before the musical program began, it was necessary to endure a few speeches. Then came the banjo and mandolin solos and singers in various combinations. When the evening ended at 10:30 with the singing of "God Save the King," there were some of His Majesty's subjects who were not ready to go home. Jim McCormick and several other young men stayed behind and danced outside the marquee until four in the morning. Jim had never seen anything like it before, especially with a teetotal crowd.

And the colony was teetotal in the early summer of 1903. Barr had made mention of temperance in his pamphlets, but as he himself indulged in alcohol, it must have been more for the stirring sound of the words than from any conviction. There were the usual number of people among the colonists who considered moderate consumption of alcohol acceptable, but the chaplain did not. Lloyd wanted the colony to be absolutely dry. His resolve was further strengthened by incidents of drunkenness as the summer progressed. Jim McCormick made reference in his diary to these activities with the cryptic remark "scandal rife in camp and women and whiskeys." By winter, Lloyd's battle with the "liquorites," as he called them, would be joined.

As the summer wore on, even the consumption of water would become problematic. Barr had called the reserve "the best watered part of the North-West," but soon it would be obvious that Barr had been wrong again. The land began to dry out, the dust turning people "as black as colliers." The farm instructors and department officials knew that soon the streams and sloughs would disappear, but the colonists were not worried. There was still enough water in the sloughs for the stock. People dug little seepage wells that provided most of them with enough water to drink, and since the majority of the colonists were bachelors, there was little interest in doing laundry. Besides, after the hot weather in June and early July, it began to rain, copiously. It was hard to get concerned about a lack of water when the wind drove the rain through the tent door, or when a puddle collected on the side of the tent where the bed happened to be, or when everything inside the tent was soaked, including the glue on the envelopes.

Water, or the lack of it, did not concern Lloyd and the committee either. At the headquarters of the Promised Land, on Section Eleven, Township Fifty, Range Twenty-eight, West of the Third Meridian, they had other priorities, inappropriate ones according to Colonization Agent Speers. "They seem to be more concerned about townsites and other matters that would bring them profit than they are about the people," Speers reported to his superior.

The permanent town site would be situated one mile south of headquarters camp, close to the school land and near the point where the proposed railroad would cross the Fourth Meridian. Barr and three of his close associates had chosen the section immediately south of the school land for their homesteads. When Lloyd pointed out to Langley, the sub–land agent, that Barr would have no further use for the land and suggested that Barr's name and those of his friends be replaced with Lloyd's and three others, Langley agreed.

Having dealt with Barr's homestead claim, Lloyd and the committee now attempted to expunge Barr's name from any association with the colony. From now on, the twenty townships near headquarters were to be called "the Britannia Colony." The original plan had been to call the town itself Barrview, but now a new name had to be found.

It was all very democratic. George Flamanck, Barr's former secretary and now the postmaster, had instructions from the Dominion post office to name the town. At a series of meetings held throughout the colony, he proposed "Lloydminster," which blended the name of the new leader with the old English term for a church of considerable size or importance. The choice was a popular one and passed easily.

As it turned out, the only good thing about the new town site was that it was on the proposed railway line. It was the worst possible location for water, laying equidistant from two major rivers and near to neither. There was even less water available there than on the homesteads, and what there was had a high iron content, which left pails coated with rust. But the railway was too important to ignore and so Lloydminster was established. A few settlers who were reluctant or unable to become farmers, or who had no money, became the first residents of the village.

Gradually the centre of activity in the colony moved from the headquarters camp to Lloydminster, but the stores tent tarried in its old location until midsummer. At a meeting in late May of all the shareholders, the stores syndicate had been reincarnated as a co-operative, a concept familiar to the British working class. Anyone with enough money could purchase shares and receive a portion of whatever syndicate goods were left—a pathetic collection of pitchforks, axle grease, knapsacks and very little else. Nathaniel Jones was elected unanimously by the committee to be the storekeeper.

Jim McCormick doubted that Jones was ever meant to be a storekeeper, but he conceded that the man's dignified bearing and his advanced age were probably advantageous. Lloyd thought Jones's even temper and honesty were to be admired, but whether he was the man to make some sense of the mess that had been Barr's stores syndicate was debatable.

Supplies for the store came by barge from Edmonton or by freight wagon from Battleford. The barges got through only when there was enough water in the North Saskatchewan River to clear the sandbars. The freight wagons got through without fail but were driven by a stubborn breed of men used to thinking for themselves. The shortage of coal oil was a case in point. Although the colony needed this commodity badly, the freighters always found some excuse not to bring it, complaining that coal oil always slopped on the other goods in the wagons.

Storekeeper Jones seemed unable to obtain the food supplies he wanted. At the beginning of July, the entire food stock of the store consisted of flour, bacon and a large number of Mr. Secord's potatoes. There was seldom any butter or syrup available, treacle and lard were so scarce they were regarded as luxuries, and the butcher who was supposed to slaughter fresh beef every Friday rarely appeared. Moving the stores tent from headquarters to the new town site did not improve Jones's ability to provide supplies nor quiet the continual protests from the colonists. When three brothers from Edmonton named Miller opened a rival store in August, they promised good management and cheaper prices. It was the beginning of the end for the store tent.

The disbanding of the stores co-operative in September was mourned by no one. Members were to receive one dollar and forty-two and a half cents for every one pound share held. Stanley Rackham's share was seventy-eight dollars and thirty-seven cents worth of small hardware, axle grease, string, soap, linseed, corn flour, some "not very palatable bacon," six sacks of flour and thirty-three army knapsacks.

It was fortunate that good food could be had at Jane Posthuma's restaurant tent. A big woman with tendrils of red hair hanging over a large pair of gold-rimmed glasses, Miss Posthuma had emigrated as the major-domo for Barr's entourage and was now in need of a means of supporting herself. The Minster Restaurant was an immediate success.

On Sundays, the young men hung around town after church waiting for dinner to be ready at the Minster. One day the conversation turned to the corral full of wild steers and broncos brought into town by local ranchers to sell to the colonists. The young men boasted that they could probably tame them. Since the owners had no objection, lots were drawn to see who would ride.

The wild steer contest became a weekly event, with a small monetary prize for the winner collected from the crowd that always gathered to watch. One Sunday morning Ivan Crossley drew the long straw. He watched in some trepidation as a cowboy led the steer towards him up a narrow alleyway between two rows of tents. His feeling of dread increased as the animal fought to resist the blindfold, the stock saddle and the crupper.

As the enraged steer kicked and danced around, the former peach plantation worker eyed his adversary, then climbed aboard and held onto the saddle horn with all his strength. The steer was turned loose to a yell of "Ride 'em, cowboy." With no other thought in his mind than to hold on as hard as he could, Ivan was not aware that the steer was heading for the open door at the back of the Minster Restaurant until he and his mount began knocking down chairs and tables. The sound of breaking crockery could be heard above the screams of Miss

Posthuma, who ran out the other end of the tent pursued by the bucking steer.

Ivan let go of the saddle horn. The steer pitched forward, catching the tent with his horns as he bucked and careened down the alleyway, dragging large pieces of canvas with him. In the aftermath, a collection was taken up to compensate Miss Posthuma for the damage, and the committee put a stop to the bucking steer contest.

This may have been the committee's finest hour. Their other activities caused controversy at every turn. They clashed with the government whenever the officials gave advice. They were especially outraged by the department's efforts to encourage those who could not support themselves to look for work elsewhere. In the opinion of the committee, the government was doing this to break up the colony.

In order to avoid the loss of any more colonists, the committee realized it must provide work at home and accordingly initiated a project that paid colonists to plant potatoes. The plan was successful, but only insofar as a great many potatoes were planted. The workers had to fight for weeks to receive their wages.

Then committee member Arthur Still, a man of some means, agreed to take on the railway grading contract. The Canadian Northern Railway, under pressure from the Dominion government, had agreed to the clearing of one hundred miles of right-of-way at a site two hundred miles ahead of their present location, in order to provide jobs for Barr colonists. Only men with teams could apply. Work was to begin in July.

Week followed week. The promise of railway jobs kept men at home who would otherwise have looked for employment elsewhere. When several disillusioned settlers finally did leave to find other work, Still made a long speech accusing the government and the town of Battleford of deliberately drawing the colonists away. The waiting continued. It was not until the third week in August, with the summer weather soon to end, that work on the railway grade began.

Critics had found fault with the committee from the day it was formed, but the longer it was in control, the worse the criticism became. George Langley called it "one of the most incapable bodies of men ever got together." The way it had run the stores was "one succession of blunders," reported the sub–land agent. The farming instructors agreed, and Charles Marlow, a colonist with experience in municipal government, wrote to a friend in Britain describing the committee as "a clique of faddists who are not at all competent" and blaming them for the sorry state of the post office.

The mail distribution system was still haphazard at best. When the postmaster in Battleford refused to handle Barr Colony mail during the trek, some of the colonists who were expecting cheques manoeuvred him out of the post office door while others searched for and found several bags of mail. Lloyd arranged to have the bags sent to the Battleford immigration hall, where Mrs. Lloyd agreed to sort and distribute the mail while she waited for her husband to return from the colony.

When Mrs. Lloyd and her daughter were quarantined for scarlet fever, the mail had to be fumigated before it could be sent on. Once in the colony, the bags of letters, parcels and newspapers were dumped inside a vacant tent to be trampled on by people trying to find mail for themselves.

Moving the mail to the store tent made postal activities only marginally less chaotic. Mail arrived when someone happened to be coming from Battleford, there being no person officially designated to bring it. Often there was a gap of two weeks between mails. Finally, in mid-July, the postal authorities approved the name Lloydminster and a post office tent was established in the new town site with George Flamanck as postmaster.

Postal service did not improve. Charles Marlow described the situation to his friend in England.

> I am sorry to say the present postmaster, although one of our colonists, does not take any trouble whatever to distribute the mail regularly. It is now no uncommon thing to have a letter lie in the post office a week after being received although asked for.

The mail was supposed to arrive every Friday afternoon and go out every Saturday morning. Demonstrating a great deal of faith, Bernard Boden went to town every Friday to check for a letter from his fiancée. Sometimes he came away empty-handed, but just as often he would receive several letters at once, some of them having taken only three weeks to get from England. How welcome they were. He urged his fiancée to make her letters as long as possible and told her how he carried them with him, reading them over and over until they became quite dilapidated.

Stanley Rackham had left no woman behind to send him letters and fill his thoughts, but his family were generous with news from home, of trips planned to Paris and Switzerland and of impending weddings. When conditions in his new home became too much to bear, the self-sufficient Rackham was just like everyone else. He thought fondly of the green countryside and cosy settled communities of his beloved homeland, which unfortunately had not been able to offer him very much of a future.

Mosquitoes added to the misery of homesickness. They came in clouds and were especially bad just before it rained. Their animal victims huddled stoically against the onslaught, and the humans on which the insects feasted were a mass of itching, pea-sized lumps.

Men could gain a certain amount of protection by smoking a pipe, but this was not an option open to the women. Some of them made net bags on drawstrings that fitted over hat and head. The trick was to make sure no skin was exposed by wearing long sleeves and high collars, torture on a hot day.

The best remedy for mosquitoes was the smudge, a fire designed to produce as much smoke as possible. A good stick fire with turf on top gave off a dense smoke that lasted all night. Green grass smoldering in a jam pail would protect the interior of a tent. Opinion varied on the best way to build the large smudges required to protect the animals. Ivan Crossley liked dry branches mixed with sod and horse manure. Jim Ashton favoured pure manure. Others thought manure and straw was the best combination. Everyone and everything smelled of smoke.

Oxen seemed to adapt to mosquitoes very well. They headed for the nearest slough, submerging themselves in cool water. Unfortunately, they often were hitched to a wagon or plough at the time.

Understanding and tolerating the oxen seemed to be the key to mastering the art of ploughing, and the few who did were progressing well with breaking their land. Twenty colonists, having no ploughs, tried to break their land with shovels. After the ribbons of sod had been turned, they were allowed, ideally, to lie and rot, but since time was of the essence, some of the colonists took a short cut by working the sod into smaller pieces with a harrow. Seeds were broadcast by hand early in the morning before the wind got up and then harrowed into the ground.

The majority of colonists did not come anywhere near harvesting a crop. The seed oats bought from Peter Paynter at a bargain price had been heavily frosted and as such had little chance of germinating. But the most common reason for having no crop was that so little plough-ing had been done. Langley reported at the end of July that 70 per cent of the colonists would not have crops in 1904, let alone 1903.

Most of the colonists concentrated their efforts on digging vegeta-ble gardens. Bernard and Percy Boden planted a variety of seeds, which came up fast in the splendid soil. A visiting woman said that their plot looked like "a real English bit of garden." The Holtbys were discouraged by the toughness of the sod, so they removed it and planted in the subsoil. The few plants that actually came up were spin-dly and soon died. That happened to Ivan Crossley too, among others, and resulted in the loss of all the seeds he had brought from home.

Many mistakes could have been avoided if the colonists had listened to advice, but nothing had changed since Mr. Speers had observed in Saskatoon, "There is something in the English character that leads me to believe they would like to use their own judgement in many of these matters." And Lloyd was more determined even than his prede-cessor to exclude non-English settlers, the very people who could have shown the newcomers how to farm and survive.

The colonists were prepared to listen to the farming instructors, having been assured that they were of British descent. As they made the rounds of the homesteads, the instructors worried about the late-ness of the season, the expensiveness of the seed and the poor condi-tion of the livestock. The most pressing need now was for people to build a house for winter, get in a good supply of fuel to last through the cold weather, build stables for the livestock, earn extra money and acquire supplies. A tall order.

Since it was there for the taking, the easiest job was to harvest the hay. Following the demise of the great buffalo herds, the prairie grass had grown tall and luxuriant. It was especially rich in the dried-up sloughs, where it was sometimes as high as a man's head. When it was cut it was so thick it stayed standing. Here was a crop that everyone could harvest.

William and Ted Hutchinson bought a mowing machine and cut hay near the sloughs. They cut ten tons of green grass in a day and a half and left it lying on the ground to cure. Two days later, when the sun had turned it golden, they loaded it onto a square rack they had made of poplar poles and willow branches to fit on top of their wagon box and "got the hay home" in a week.

Bernard and Percy Boden were not so fortunate. Without the funds to buy a mower, they attempted to cut the hay with a scythe. Hampered by not having "the knack" and by a dull blade, their progress was very slow. Once they had the hay cut, it began to rain. The hay lying on the ground had to be forked over several times to dry before it could be stacked. Since dry days alternated with wet ones in early August, the Bodens had to repeat the process several times.

Just when they despaired of making any progress, they received a visit from their neighbour, Stanley Rackham, who offered them the use of his mower in return for their help in getting his hay home. Now they progressed rapidly and were stopped only when the wind blew too strongly. Their haystack joined the others that dotted the countryside. Each one was a slightly different shape and some were decidedly irregular, but they made the homesteads look more like farms and filled the rookie farmers with a strong sense of satisfaction.

Willie Holtby did not wait around for the satisfactions of haying. The sight of his wife fussing unhappily over their youngest child had soured the whole project for him. Willie had been carrying a small brown diary in his pocket, which he seldom remembered to write in, but on July 6 he had been moved to record two words—"very downhearted." On July 7 he had written, "made up my mind to go back." On July 16, Willie and Agnes and their three boys were headed back up the trail to Battleford and on to Saskatoon. The official reason given for their leaving was that the climate was too severe for a small child, but Willie had hedged his bets. By the time they sailed from Montreal on August 12, Willie had taken steps to ensure that they would return, severe climate or not. Just six days before, he had filed for his homestead.

Lloyd had an eye to the future as well. He had been receiving letters from people in Britain who had delayed their departure to wait for the second wave of colonists that Barr had planned. They had heard the rumours of the colony's failure and were anxious to know what was happening, so Lloyd prepared another circular letter to answer their concerns.

Six hundred homesteads had been taken up, he reported, and additional applications were being received, but there was still room for more in the Britannia Colony. He advised newcomers to wait for spring and to come via the railroad to Edmonton and then down the river on barges. Those determined to come at once should send their homestead receipt and their land would be held, but anyone wanting a refund would have to deal with the government. They were warned to expect no refunds for any of the money they had paid to Barr.

Because the letter was to be circulated as well to colonists already in Canada, both in the colony and elsewhere, Lloyd reported that luggage was still scattered at various points. The only advice he could offer in that regard was to "keep writing until you get it." Later that summer Lloyd discovered that much of the luggage was in a large corrugated iron building in Regina, having been impounded by customs officials after being mistakenly routed through Boston. According to customs, it could be released only when the individual owners had filled out three copies of an affidavit at a cost of one dollar for each piece of luggage. After several long telegraphs charged to the immigration department, Mr. Lloyd received permission to make one declaration for all the luggage.

While Lloyd and the committee were looking to the future, Barr was in Ottawa still struggling with the past. The department wanted money for hiring the transport teams in Saskatoon and to reimburse people who had left the colony. Barr in turn wanted money from the department. In a press interview he said that the only money he had received for his troubles was the commission on the steamship tickets, all of which had been spent on projects related to the colony. "I was not in this work out of a feeling of pure philanthropy," the former leader told the paper, "and would think it would only be fair that I have my services appreciated."

In London, Commissioner of Immigration W. T. R. Preston had told a magazine interviewer two months before that Barr would probably receive a commission from the Canadian government of approximately three thousand pounds, the amount that would have been paid to any agent for the same class of emigrants. The minister, Clifford Sifton, told Parliament that Preston was incorrect. He said the department had no agreement with Barr to pay him anything. But later that summer Deputy Minister Smart gave the impression that had Barr's colonists not cost the government so much money, the department would have given him the bonus usually paid to agents.

Far away from Barr and the bureaucrats, on a homestead in the Britannia Colony, one of those colonists sat down in front of an upturned jam pail and with a blunt-stub of pencil began to write home. Bernard Boden was tired, dirty, unshaven and unshorn, and very content.

Here a person is without restraint and can do just as they like so long as it is within reason, this coupled with the outdoor life which gives one an unfailing good appetite enables one to enjoy a sense of freedom quite unknown in the old country.

The rain fell and the sun shone, the flowers bloomed and the hay ripened, the streams dried up and the days grew noticeably shorter, and one day in early September, Bernard looked up to see geese flying south.

CHAPTER
X

Their Curious Dauntless Demeanour

BUYING PLYMOUTH ROCK HENS IN ONION LAKE, FORTY MILES TO THE NORTH OF colony headquarters, made Bernard and Percy Boden feel like real agriculturalists. So they took it in stride when, during their return trip to Lloydminster, they had to chase a runaway hen through a slough. And three weeks later, when one of the hens got into their tent while they were outside kicking a football around, and that hen ate a recently baked cake of which Bernard was inordinately proud, the two men accepted the event as retribution for playing ball on Sunday.

It was good to have fresh eggs to eat, and soon the brothers had enough to sell. It was for the chickens that the first building on the homestead was constructed—a house made of woven willow branches plastered with mud—but the ungrateful birds continued their depredations. They ate nine of Bernard's freshly baked spice and raisin buns and only a few days later ate a whole loaf of bread, which was inside the tent and covered to avoid detection.

It was clear that the tent had to be made chickenproof, and accordingly, the brothers tied the door shut and anchored the bottom with a log. Undeterred, the hens gained entry and created havoc by breaking open a bag of oats and spilling a bucket of milk. By late August the chickens had discovered the garden, dug up the turnips and eaten the peas and broad beans. Bernard felt like shooting his feathered tormentors. There were times when he thought that the hawks hovering over the homestead could have them.

Bernard blamed it on the hawks when the hens stopped laying eggs until six chicks hatched from eggs that he had set. This redeemed the hens until November, when they ate all the putty out of the window frames in the new cabin. By then three of the chicks and some of the hens had died of the cold or been trodden on by the oxen, making the decision to retire from the poultry business an easy one.

When all was said and done, it was the chickens' foraging in the garden that had most hurt the Boden brothers. Until that time, the garden had been healthy and productive. It had survived the oxen's attack and had received no damage from the gophers ravaging many other vegetable patches. No matter what else had gone wrong, the garden had continued to flourish. It gave the brothers a feeling of accomplishment. But then the chickens got into the garden, followed by the cow, and on September 3, Percy and Bernard woke to find that a killing frost had destroyed every remaining plant.

Many other colonists also lost the vegetable crop they had planned to make central to their winter food supply. Before the frost, the new peas and tiny potatoes, picked fresh, had provided a welcome break from the monotony of a frontier diet. A lack of ice had limited the meat most people ate to sowbelly, and only those with deep wells could keep butter. Bernard Boden had counted it a red-letter day when he found a salted, six-pound ox tongue for sale in town. Since the price of seventy-five cents included the enamel bowl the meat came in, it was hard to imagine a better bargain.

The routine acts of cooking and eating were fraught with difficulty for the settlers. Even experienced bread makers had to learn how to use the hard Canadian yeast cakes. Since most of the stoves were outside the tents, no cooking could be done on rainy days. On breezy days, aluminum plates and cups were easily tipped, and on windy days soup blew off the spoon.

By midsummer, some bachelors had become expert cooks and some women had become wizards with a camp stove. The countryside provided a welcome change in diet as, one after another, raspberries, gooseberries and chokecherries ripened and offered themselves for the picking. Everyone had an appetite, one that increased as the reality of the coming winter finally spurred people into feverish activity.

The signs that winter was on the way were subtle at first—a gradual shortening of the day, a light brownish tinge to the unploughed prairie. The northern lights on clear August nights seemed, in their icy midnight display, to warn of things cold and dark, but the killing frost of September 3 took the colonists by surprise.

The Department of Immigration and the Northwest Mounted Police knew what a prairie winter would be like, and they knew how ill-prepared the colonists were. Mr. Speers had seen how poorly the houses were built and how unaware the people were of what they faced: "They seem contented; perfectly composed; but they lack the individual application that they should possess." He judged inevitable the notion that at least a few of the families would have to be looked after if they were to survive "the rigours of our winter."

Inspector Thomas McGinnis of the Lloydminster NWMP detachment also reported the lack of preparation for winter. His letter set in motion a co-operative effort between the police and the department to stockpile basic food supplies and convert a ramshackle police barracks in Battleford into emergency accommodation. But Mr. Lloyd and those closest to him were not concerned about the coming winter. Lloyd said that everything was under control in that regard. Rather than tending their own homesteads, the committee and its followers concentrated on establishing a proper town.

Lloyd had learned from the Canadian Northern Railway agent that an English syndicate had purchased the railway land to the west of the town site. The railroad was to be built through the middle of the syndicate's section, with the station in the centre. Lloyd made a counterproposal. He offered the railway agent every second lot in the town site if he would locate the station on the Lloydminster boundary line.

Soon after, Lloyd made the arduous journey to Ottawa. He did not intend to discuss the welfare of the colonists, as the department might have expected, for he was determined that the Britannia Colony could manage on its own. But he wanted to make sure his plans for the town site were properly explained and approved. He proposed that the section be surveyed and divided into town-sized lots, and that alternate lots be given to the CNR. The remaining lots would be offered free to any member of the colony who wanted to build a house in town, thus ensuring that a good portion of Lloydminster would be populated by colony members. The deputy minister agreed to everything except the railway provision. Only in Lloyd's own quarter section would the alternate lots be made available to the railroad. Lloyd would retain one lot for his own home.

Reporters in Ottawa, alerted to Lloyd's presence there, were much more interested in the stories about how green the colonists were. Lloyd admitted that some of the stories were more or less true—one man had indeed driven for ten days without removing the harness from his team because he was afraid he would not be able to put it on again. True too was the story about the man who tied strings around the legs of his chickens. The man showed good sense, in Lloyd's opinion, because when the chickens were released from their small travelling cases to exercise and feed, the strings made them easier to catch.

But the story about the man who bought oxen instead of horses because he could milk the oxen was a story told about almost every greenhorn who ever ventured onto the prairies. And the one about the man who bought split peas thinking he could plant them was probably not true either. However, the *Saskatchewan Herald* stood by the story reported in its pages about a Barr colonist who commented that he often saw sticky flypaper advertised but could not think what use it would be, as he had never seen any "sticky flies."

If the reporters who had travelled with the Barr colonists on the trek had stayed in Lloydminster for the summer, they would have had stories aplenty about how green the colony's inhabitants were and how unprepared for winter. Many had not broken any land, and many more were still living in tents. But when Lloyd came back from Ottawa with news that free town lots were available to anyone who built a house on one, the colonists gave him their full attention.

Stanley Rackham was one of the many people who gathered to hear from Lloyd at a September mass meeting. The leader of the colony spoke for two and a quarter hours about the plans he had for Lloydminster. Much of what he said was based more on wishful thinking than on any concrete proposals from the department, but when Rackham left the meeting, he noted that Lloydminster had been promised a police barracks and a telegraph office. Two weeks later, when surveyors arrived to begin the town-site survey and lay out the main street, it seemed as though it would all come true.

Bernard Boden left the meeting with a sense of time running out. Since the early frost had ushered in what the locals called "squaw winter," he had become aware of how little he and his brother had done. Now this news of the town lots gave him something else to worry about. A man would be a fool not to avail himself of free land, but the necessity of building a house in town added one more thing to the long list of jobs that had to be done, the most important of which was building a house and stable on the homestead.

In his first pamphlet, Barr had advised that "the first thing to do is not build a house." Instead, he told the colonists to plough a few acres and plant them at once with potatoes and vegetables. This was good advice, but Barr betrayed his inexperience with his next sentence. "When this is done, which might occupy ten days, or perhaps two weeks, the settler should proceed to erect himself a house."

Having failed to anticipate the settlers' ineptitude and lack of motivation, Barr went on to miscalculate the availability of building materials and the amount of money necessary to procure them: he strongly advised building the first house of logs and cheap sawn lumber with boards and shingles for roofing.

> Much of the work . . . can be done by any handy man with a little instruction from a practical carpenter. . . . Ready made factory doors and window sashes, with glass already inserted can be purchased at very low prices.

It may have been that the prospect of building a house was so daunting that many postponed it, hoping for some sort of miracle to occur. Or it may have been that they believed those among them who said that the reports of severe winters were grossly exaggerated. Whatever the reason, house construction did not begin for many until well into the summer, and when it did, only the wealthy could afford to buy enough lumber for a frame house. Everyone else had to settle for what Speers called "available material."

Available material in the Britannia Colony consisted of poplar logs, the gnarled and twisted victims of prairie fires, which stood and lay in the bluffs all around; sod, which was there for the taking; mud, which increased in quantity as the sod was stripped off the home sites; long grass, which grew on dried-up sloughs, and cow dung, of which there was no shortage.

The farm instructors, already diverted from their original purpose to serve as land guides, were ordered now to devote themselves full-time to advising on house construction. But with many more houses to be built than farming instructors to give advice, the final products varied greatly in method of construction and in appearance and durability.

Alice and Willie Rendell were among the few who could afford to build a frame house. Doris Court was a bungalow thirty feet square with a large attic and two large cellars for winter food storage. It was "quite the best house in the colony," and it was located close to town. Because there were so many people without homes and the men of the NWMP detachment also needed a place to live, Doris Court became a boardinghouse where Alice Rendell housed and fed fifteen people.

The materials for Doris Court had not been easy to find, there being very little lumber in the colony. The Rendells' hired man had

had to drive twenty-five miles to a point on the North Saskatchewan River near the ruins of the Fort Pitt post office. There, flat-bottomed barges from Edmonton were unloaded of their cargoes of lumber, groceries and machinery, and then broken up into lumber to be sold at a good profit.

The Indian reserve at Onion Lake produced lumber for sale at a government-controlled sawmill. The rough, unplaned boards were sold for cash, a sign over the door of a log shanty summarizing the policy of the proprietors regarding credit. There, below a drawing of a dead dog, were the words, "Poor trust is dead, Bad pay killed him, Not ask for Trust."

The majority of colonists looked to what was available on their own land for house building. Fire-killed logs were plentiful, well-seasoned and already bark-free, but there were very few straight ones. And cutting them down was a problem. The bluffs were so densely treed that when the first logs were cut, they became wedged into trees still standing. Removing enough logs to make a trip worthwhile and loading them onto the wagon frame was an exhausting process that had to be repeated many times.

On the advice of the instructors, the Boden brothers dug into the side of a small hill to prepare a protected site for their log home. Then they built a framework by sinking one end of each of nine supporting logs three feet into the ground, a task whose difficulty was soon surpassed by having to cut the six-inch-thick logs to size with a bucksaw. "It does not half make the hands and arms ache," Bernard told his fiancée.

Unlike most of the other log homes, the Bodens' was built entirely of upright logs, but they followed the general pattern when they built their roof using a frame of logs covered with sod. The framework was almost complete when they were advised that their supporting logs were not strong enough and would require a new ridgepole to strengthen them. Two weeks later one of the instructors came by and told them their house was too large, and as such would be difficult to heat. He advised starting again and reducing the size by half. It being too late to do so, they decided to ignore him.

With their ploughing problems as yet unsolved, obtaining sod for the roof and cutting it into straight blocks took much longer than it should have. Then they had to lift the heavy sod bricks to the roof and lay them on the log frame with six inches of hay in between. The cracks were filled with clay. Then the cracks in the walls were filled with a mixture of mud and grass on the inside and mud and cow dung on the outside.

The Bodens' lack of money was especially evident when it came to building the window and door frames. Being unable to afford lumber, they sawed logs into boards that they used for the frames. By joining several boards together they made a door. Their one extravagance was glass for the three windows.

There were log houses more grand. The Hutchinsons had a board floor. Stanley Rackham lined his house with shiplap. But Jim Ashton could afford only half a floor and had to leave bare earth on the other side. Packed dirt was the most usual floor in the colony, at least until there was more money to buy boards or more time to cut rounds of logs and lay them like paving bricks.

Sod houses evoked images of eastern European peasant hovels and as such were considered by some to be unsuitable homes for the English. But having been advised in Saskatoon that sod houses made the most economic sense, many Barr colonists chose to build them. Agent George Langley called it a "regrettable idea." The sod houses he saw in his travels around the colony were some of the poorest in the Northwest. One problem was the sod itself, which was more porous than the sod near Saskatoon, but the main problem was the skill of the builders.

The west wall of Thomas Edwards's sod house collapsed under the onslaught of a strong northwest wind accompanied by a three-day downpour. His wagon, the notorious Ark, was a veritable fortress by comparison. His replacement for the collapsed sod edifice was a board house so spare and lacking in comforts that his daughter described it as "a glorified granary."

The Holtbys chose sod too, because they knew nothing about building with logs. They were informed that they could choose between two building methods for the walls. The first required marking out a space on the ground the size of the desired house and then piling the four-inch-thick sods up, brick by brick, to the height needed. The Holtbys chose a second method that started with a framework of poles, one for each corner and one on either side of the door, and finished by filling the spaces between them with sod bricks.

It was when they chose the method for the roof that they made a serious mistake. Instead of resting the framework for the roof on the walls, they rested it on the corner posts. Had the roof sat directly on the walls, the house would have settled as a unit when the sods dried and shrank, as they inevitably did. As it was, the framework kept the roof in place, leaving a space at the top of the walls big enough to put a cat through.

Sod houses were dark and dirty. Some had no windows at all; others had only a bottle plastered into the thick wall or a tiny frame covered with glazed muslin. But they were easier to heat than log houses, and the holes that inevitably appeared in the walls could be mended by stuffing in more sod. Jim McCormick dressed his sod house up by plastering the front wall, smoothing the mud on with his bare hands after working it to the proper consistency with his bare feet. As far as he was concerned, it made the house look like a Swiss cottage. He further improved his home by papering the kitchen walls with newspapers and pictures from magazines, a decorating feature that relieved the darkness of the room but was marred somewhat when the weather turned cold and he and his partners had to stable their horses in the house while they finished building the stable.

Those who had enough money could hire Native workers to make a thatched roof, the type favoured by the department. The long slough grass could be plastered with a good layer of mud to make it less flammable. But sod roofs were the most common because they were the cheapest. When the heavy rains came, they were also the wettest and the dirtiest.

The sod could absorb a certain amount of moisture, but when it became saturated, after three or four days, the ceiling started to drip. Soon the dripping became so widespread that there was scarcely a dry place in the whole house. Bernard Boden likened it to having a shower with one's clothes on. Alice Edwards considered herself fortunate that she had more than one umbrella and that she was not superstitious about opening them inside. Ivan Crossley's clean white dress shirt, which he had worn especially in honour of a visit to a neighbour's shack, was splashed with dirt when a chunk of wet sod dropped from the ceiling into his tea.

It was a funny thing about those sod houses. In later years, on a prominent wall in many proper frame houses, a picture of the family's sod house would be proudly displayed. But there are people today, latecomers to the colony, who argue that no one lived in a sod house. They ignore the pictorial evidence and dismiss the idea as preposterous.

In 1903, in the Britannia Colony, just to have a house was a relief. Months of living in the crowded, back-breaking tents had been difficult—the mosquitoes hard to control and privacy impossible. With a house to live in, trunks could be unpacked and dishes placed upon rough plank shelves. And though the new beds were often made of poplar poles or unplaned lumber, it was such a relief to be sleeping up off the ground that few complained. For the men, the act of building a house, any kind of house, gave a sense of accomplishment that was a reward all by itself.

In the third week of September, one foot of snow fell, but the days were warm and the snow melted. Though the pale yellow leaves dropped from the poplar trees and the patches of scrub turned crimson, it was sometimes possible, just for a moment, to imagine that summer had not gone. Then the stillness of autumn wrapped the prairies in silence again. There were no bird sounds, and even the northern lights had stopped their ching, ching. And though it was warm enough some evenings to sit outside, in the morning there was frost on the blanket and ice on the water bucket.

Indian summer was upon them. There were no mosquitoes. The sky was clear blue, the air dry and exhilarating. It was so warm during the day that people could lie on the grass and bask in the sun, whose rays turned everything the colour of hay and whose angle, just past its fall equinox, gave a golden quality to the light.

But the golden tint of Indian summer had a sinister side, for it meant that the grass was dry, and dry grass burns easily. From their experiences on the trek, the colonists knew what prairie fires were like, and they had prepared for them by ploughing fireguards around their farm buildings and assembling a collection of sacks to beat out the flames. But they knew that a big fire could jump even a river, and that being so, their fireguards seemed puny.

During the third week of October, seven large fires were reported to be advancing on the Lloydminster area from the west and the south, destroying grazing land, trapping unwary freighters in their wagons, and surrounding and burning homesteads. Stanley Rackham noticed a faint red glow in the west on Sunday evening. By noon the next day the air had become hazy and smoky, and the wind carried particles of burned grass. By Monday evening, the fire showed itself plainly—"a huge lurid cloud of smoke"—and though Rackham lay down on his bed, he kept his clothes on, and he did not sleep.

On Tuesday morning, Jim McCormick was mesmerized by the magnificence of the fire, which was advancing at a rate of about three to four miles an hour in a forty-mile-wide front towards his homestead. That night the Rendells could see fire all around them. It was driven by a tremendous wind that roared in unison with the fire and carried the smell and the stifling smoke.

Some people ploughed furrows in haste as the fire advanced, believing the advice that the best fireguard was a freshly made one. The smoke and ash made breathing difficult. Under such adverse conditions, the sod often did not roll over properly, making it necessary for someone to follow behind the plough turning the heavy ribbons by hand to expose their damp, black underbellies. One woman performed this heavy task in an advanced state of pregnancy, trying to keep up with her husband as he struggled with an unfamiliar plough and nervous horses.

William Hutchinson and his pregnant wife, who had arrived from England a short time before, had been watching the darkened horizon for a week. Each night they climbed a hill to look through field glasses at the leaping flames reflected in the sky. One night the light was so bright they could have seen to read. Lines of flame were creeping towards them from three directions.

The wind and flames were devastating allies. The wind fanned the flames and carried the heavy smoke in advance of the fire; the black and brown billows of rolling smoke filled the sky. The hot wind seared the lungs and sent burning ash flying and spears of flame darting across the grass. The flames swayed, reared back, darted ahead. They licked at the trees in the poplar bluffs, and the wind sent the burning branches flying.

The Hutchinsons' fireguard was two ploughed strips four furrows wide, separated by a fourteen-foot grassy space. With the flames creeping closer, William backfired the grass to deny the big fire any fuel should it jump the ploughed strip. As long as the wind direction stayed constant, the backfire would be easier to control, because it burned against the wind. Then he, his wife and his brother turned to face the flames coming from the south. In the heat and fury of the wind, they did not hear the thunder, see the lighting or notice the drops of water at first. Then, as they became aware of the cooling rain, they turned their faces upwards and let it wash over them. Soon it was coming down in torrents. Now the fickle wind changed sides and became an ally of the rain. It blew in gusts, sending water whipping across the blackened landscape and smothering the flames.

The people burned out during that week were forced to join the small but growing group of settlers who would need government assistance. It was hard to see how anything good could come out of the fire, but someone pointed out how neighbours had been brought together as they fought the flames side by side. It was not unusual, however, for a man to be away helping a neighbour when the fire struck his own place, leaving his wife and children to fight it alone.

Five months in the colony had changed most of the women from urban homemakers into seasoned settlers. The work they did was valued highly, especially by the men who did not have wives. Bernard Boden, in a misguided attempt to assure his fiancée yet again that he had made the right decision by emigrating and that she would love Canada when they could afford finally for her to join him, told her, "A wife is a great source of saving time and help to a new settler in this country and most people I have spoken to admit this fact."

And well they should have. The men accompanied by women were relieved of all domestic duties. They concentrated on the farm work, work that the women often helped them to do in addition to their own tasks of cooking, cleaning, laundry and tending children. And both the men and the women set high standards for those domestic duties. William Hutchinson described the ideal wife as one who was

> a sensible woman who can adapt herself to circumstances, and who, with a few tin cans and a stove can bake and cook with results equal to those obtained with all conveniences. This is a large demand but it can be done.

Hutchinson went on to tell his readers in England, many of whom he hoped to lure to the prairies, that despite living in a house with a dirt floor, a house crammed with trunks and packing cases and furnished with rough plank furniture, the ideal woman made sure that "not a speck of dust was to be seen." Describing a sterling example, he wrote, "The stoves were a picture, and were evidently no strangers to black-lead brushes. The beds were spotless with white counterpanes." An admirable housewife in Hutchinson's estimation utilized the resources at hand. Vegetable "down" was used to stuff pillows, the lead covering from packets of tea was fashioned into picture frames, empty flour bags were transformed into hearth rugs and dark brown camp blankets into children's coats. Mrs. Hutchinson's opinion was not recorded.

Such perfection required hours of labour, which began with sawing, splitting and carrying firewood to feed the stove, followed by a trip to the slough through a swarm of mosquitoes to fetch water. The house scoured, it was then time to scrub the clothes over a washboard with strong soap, the men's clothing stiff with dirt from long days behind a plough and the children's caked with black from the earth floor.

Of necessity, every job had a makeshift quality. Freshly washed clothes came out brown from the slough water. They were dried by draping them over bushes or laying them on the grass. Diapers were bleached by the sun, butter was churned in a tin can, children were bathed in pails, meals were prepared in the cramped corner of a tent or shack.

These hard-working women were portrayed as being cheerful and compliant. It was a picture painted by men and reinforced by the reluctance of most women to disagree even in their diaries, which make curiously flat reading. There is a lack of emotion demonstrated, and the cheery acceptance of their lot does not ring true. It was as if they could not admit, even to a diary, how difficult their lives were. The letters written by Alice Rendell, a truly remarkable woman whose talents and fortitude were a genuine inspiration to many, sound like the perky Christmas letters of the modern age that reveal little of the difficult side of life.

In the fall of 1903, as winter approached, there was no use a woman complaining. She swallowed her anger and got on with the business of survival. For many of the women in the Barr Colony that fall, "getting on with business" meant doing it alone, because any man who could find work was away earning as much money as he could to buy supplies for winter.

More than thirty married men were out of money when they arrived in the colony. Since then several single colonists had been able to find work outside, the men with survey parties and the women in domestic service, but employment within the colony was really a case of "taking in each other's washing." As one of the farming instructors described it, "Half the colony is dependent on the other half for employment," and since the employers too were starting to run out of money, he predicted there would soon be cases of destitution. How widespread that would be was difficult to estimate, as he could get very few people to admit that they had any financial difficulties.

The news that the long-promised work would begin on the railway right-of-way at Blackfoot Coulee, southwest of Lloydminster, was greeted with great relief. Any man with a healthy team was eligible for a job. The work went very slowly, though, many of the men having failed as yet to master the finer points of driving their teams. But despite the frustration, the work had its compensations. The men were paid not by the amount accomplished but by the time worked, and the food and coffee were better than most of the bachelors could make at home.

But the daily wage and the cost of the good food finished the contractor. When Mr. Still's funds ran out, the grading camp was closed. By April of the next year he still owed $1200 in wages, plus other monies totalling $3100. Since the contract was only valued at $3000, Mr. Still had paid dearly for trying to provide work for needy colonists. The cost in horseflesh was high as well, with several more fatalities being added to the growing list of dead livestock.

It looked as if the men would have to go farther away to make money. Beginning in August and continuing into the fall, hundreds left for the farming country west of Winnipeg, where work could be had bringing in the harvest and building the new railroad. As winter approached, there were jobs available in Battleford and in the forest around Prince Albert. Bob Holtby heard about work in a lumber camp west of Edmonton and made plans to travel there with six other young men as soon as he had driven his father to Saskatoon.

His father, Robert, had decided that it was necessary for him to find an outside job too. Having come to the conclusion that he was not cut out to be a farmer and citing his weak chest as a reason why he could not work on the harvest or build the railroad, he opted to return to his former occupation as a travelling salesman. He lined up a job with a firm in Toronto associated with his old employer in Leeds.

No one knows for sure what his wife, Kate, thought of him going so far away from home. One of her granddaughters thinks she was relieved when he left. But with winter facing her, even an unpleasant husband was better than no husband at all. Agnes and Willie had returned already to England. Her son Bob was due to leave soon. She and her two daughters would be under the protection of her other son, Oliver, a dreamy fellow more suited to painting a picture than working the land.

But Robert's mind was made up, and he was anxious to be gone. He prepared the homestead for winter by banking the walls of the house with dirt and fetching a lot of poplar logs, which he stacked tepeestyle, according to the custom of the area, outside the door ready to be bucksawed into lengths for the stove. A supply of groceries having been procured, he climbed on board the wagon beside his son Bob, and, ramrod straight and immaculately dressed, the man who had insisted that the family emigrate left for Battleford, Saskatoon, and the warmth and comfort of Toronto.

The summer-dried trail to Battleford and Saskatoon was much easier and quicker to drive. Besides the occasional traveller and the regular stagecoach, Bob and Robert encountered Metis freighters bringing mail and supplies from the railhead. With the increased population west of Battleford, anyone with a wagon and a healthy team could get work as a freighter, an opportunity seized upon by a number of the Barr colonists.

Before winter came, the men transporting freight slept under their wagons and cooked over a campfire. As the weather grew worse, however, it was necessary to stay with people on their route. The custom of the time was for travellers to cook for themselves on their host's stove and then sleep on his floor. Sleeping inside the one-room shacks could present a problem if their host was married. The prospect of preserving his modesty while getting ready for bed in such a situation preoccupied young Ivan Crossley. He need not have been concerned. When it came time for the adults to retire, the woman simply extinguished the light, and the darkness gave everyone complete privacy.

At Lloyd's request, Ottawa provided another form of employment just when it was most needed. The Dominion Telegraph Line, which ran from Qu'Appelle to Edmonton, missed Lloydminster by twenty miles as it passed through Fort Pitt. Now a branch of the line would be built to connect Lloydminster to the outside world.

By the time work on the line commenced in late November, the ground was frozen to a depth of at least two feet. It was necessary to dig with crowbars, the removal of each fragment of dirt a minor victory. As each man took a turn chipping at the frozen ground, the others, clad in British footwear, ran backwards and forwards to keep their circulation going. All but four of the eighteen-man gang suffered from frostbite. But despite the adverse conditions, the crew enjoyed the work. The daily pay was $1.50 and all found, the muskrat hunting was productive and the camaraderie of the crew was inspiring. The work was done in a month, just in time for the crew to return home for Christmas with money in their pockets.

Alex Carlyle-Bell's financial problems were not as easily solved. Lack of money was not his problem, merely lack of access to it. His considerable fortune was tied up in investments in London.

Carlyle-Bell was thirty-four, recently married and totally unsuited for his new life. Having paid too high a price to Jack Barr for his team, he had to destroy one of the animals when it injured itself. He had withdrawn two hundred dollars from the bank in Battleford, placed it in his pocketbook and then lost the pocketbook. By the time it was found by a local Native person, given to a priest and then to a policeman, there was no money left inside.

When Carlyle-Bell arrived at his homestead, he endorsed a bank draft for one hundred pounds and handed the draft to a passing freighter who was never seen again. When his agent in London advised him that there was no more money available until some of his investments matured at the end of November, he threw himself on the mercy of the Department of Immigration.

Mr. Speers investigated in person and reported that Carlyle-Bell was "very harassed for want of sufficient funds due to heavy charges and misfortunes." Carlyle-Bell had more problems than just a lack of immediate cash. His wife had been thrown from the wagon during the trek, he had ploughed seven acres on the wrong quarter section and, although he had purchased some lumber, he had not been able to build a house.

Speers bought the lumber from the wretched man and, leaving him with instructions to pack up and follow, took Mrs. Carlyle-Bell to Battleford. There he introduced her to the NWMP inspector, who saw her ensconced in a cubicle of the police barracks then being prepared to receive destitute colonists. Obed Smith dryly observed about Carlyle-Bell that "unless a great change comes over this young man, and he makes a greater effort, the sooner he decides to get a remittance from home and return to Scotland the better."

Remittances from home were ensuring the continued survival of another young man who came from the same town in England as Bernard Boden. He was the subject of much discussion between Boden and his fiancée. Because Madeleine requested years later that discretion be used in the matter of this young man's name, he shall be called Mr. Black, and his companion shall be called Mr. Roberts.

Black and Roberts had been terrorizing their friends and neighbours since their arrival in the colony, bunking in with another family from home, overstaying their welcome, spending money foolishly and, as Bernard described it, "going the pace pretty strong." So obnoxious had they become, and so difficult to dislodge, that their unwilling hosts had moved their entire family back to Battleford. Soon afterward, Roberts realized the folly of his lifestyle and began to establish his own homestead, but Black kept up the pace.

Bernard labelled Black's style "doing the gentleman." Having rented his horses to a man who wanted to work on the railroad, Black cast about for someone to move his belongings to his land and decided on Bernard and Percy. The Bodens were very busy, using every available hour from sunrise to sunset preparing for the cold weather, but they felt they could not refuse a fellow townsman.

When Black asked the Bodens what they would charge, Bernard foolishly offered to do it for nothing. While Black lounged about, Bernard loaded the wagon. Once at the homestead, Black "pottered around" while the brothers pitched his tent for him, fetched wood and water, and lit a fire for some dinner. By then it was raining heavily. Mice had made a nest in his long neglected belongings, and accordingly the brothers butchered a few rodents on his behalf. Before they left, a load of logs arrived for which Black paid twenty-five dollars. The paid work of cutting them had not been offered to the Bodens.

By early October, Black and the Bodens were constantly in each others' company. Having mustered up the courage to request that they be paid for their labour, the Bodens agreed to help Black build his house, although they often found him asleep when they arrived for work in the morning. Black spent much of his time either sending home urgent requests for more money or spending the remittances as quickly as he could. On Sundays he disappeared into Lloydminster and bragged, when he returned, that he had a standing invitation to dine at the Lloyds'.

The Bodens continued to assist their difficult neighbour, spurred on by loyalty to someone from their hometown and by the hope that they would realize some desperately needed cash. When Black hired Stanley Rackham to get his hay in for him and Rackham's mower broke down, Bernard did the repair. When Black decided to sell the hay, Bernard hauled three or four loads for him, discovering later that Black had cut the hay on Boden's own land. And as the fine weather of Indian summer stretched on day after day, Boden struggled to finish Black's house while Black and a new comrade lay on the grass watching him work.

By early November Black still had not paid Bernard and Percy a cent. He had taken to avoiding them but, when confronted, paid them half and promised the remainder when his next cheque arrived from

England. Before that could happen, Black and his new companion had adjourned to Battleford where, it was reliably reported, they were spending money in a manner that was "the talk of the town." When last seen, Mr. Black was spending his time in Battleford drinking, sleeping and playing billiards in the Albion Hotel. His last communication with Bernard and Percy was a short letter saying he would not be able to pay them the balance of their wages.

As Indian summer held, the industry of the colonists proved that men like Black were not typical. The majority of colonists had set aside their relaxed summer ways and were making up for lost time. The feverish activity on the homesteads was mirrored in the determined efforts of Lloyd and the committee to establish a proper town.

There were two general stores by then, a "rain and wind-swept" post office, a butcher's shop and a blacksmith forge. By far the most notable building in town, however, was the vicarage. It was more than thirty feet square and two storeys high, the first built of logs salvaged from a building in Onion Lake and the second made of lumber.

Upstairs, the seven members of Lloyd's family slept amid supplies from the store tent. Downstairs was a reception room divided from the kitchen and family living space by a large marquee canvas. The reception room was used for every meeting held in the town, for choir practice, for work parties, as accommodation for men visiting from the homesteads and for church services. People sat on packing cases arranged on either side of an aisle, with more seating provided by boards set on empty tinned meat boxes lining the walls.

Since the only artifical light came from two small stable lanterns, Evening Prayer was a dimly lit affair, but since the few hymnbooks were tiny, khaki-covered Boer War veterans with very small type, it did not matter that no one could see. One hundred people would fill every nook and cranny of the room so tightly that it had been necessary to reduce from four to one the number of violins accompanying the small portable organ, there being insufficient room to draw the bows.

Whether as a church, vicarage or meeting hall, the Lloyds' house was open to everyone. But everyone did not necessarily choose to be there. The colony had divided into two factions—those in favour of Lloyd and the committee, and those against. Many of those against were too busy preparing for winter on their homesteads to take anything but a passing interest. Mr. Speers was sure they would develop into a "thrifty and progressive community." One of their own, Charles

Marlow, agreed and went further in a letter to a friend in England, saying, "We have a great future before us if only the government will ignore the cranks who have been endeavoring to mislead both the people and the government officials."

Those who supported Lloyd and his committee were more likely to live in the town site, having chosen not to file for a homestead or, for a variety of reasons, not to move out and begin farming. A visiting journalist would describe the latter group in the following manner:

> Apparently they have taken, rather by ignorance, negligence, and devil-may-careishness than by intention, every precaution to accumulate difficulties and dangers in which to be jolly.

He went on to say that there were also a dozen or so of the "no good kind" who sat all day before the stove in the government immigration tent, while the rest of the townsfolk went about "the business of trying to shelter themselves as if merely making believe exertion to be necessary."

The houses being constructed in town, which had fallen so short of impressing the visiting journalist, were not meant to be proper dwellings. They were being built merely to fulfill the letter of the agreement between Lloyd, the CNR and the Department of Immigration. In order to ensure possession of one of the lots, which had been apportioned by ballot, a man had to build a house on the site—or something that vaguely resembled a house. The only requirement was that the structure be at least four feet high. As a result many colonists, already harried by the approach of winter, hastily brought in a load of logs and built a four-sided crib or something that resembled a frame for drying clothes up to the required height, positioning the structure at the back of the lot to allow room for something better to be built later. When left untended the logs were often stolen, to appear later on someone else's lot or disappear into someone's stove.

Those who had not yet ventured out to their homesteads put up a more useable structure on their town lots. Such a structure was Nathaniel Jones's soddery. Like most sod houses, Jones's house sagged unevenly. It was covered with vines and weeds that had grown from the roots trapped in the sod. Some romantic soul said it looked like a conservatory.

Inside, its tiny muslin-glazed windows let in no light at all. Piles of empty boxes competed for room with rough furniture. Jones's bed was made from a large box, flanked closely by the woodpile so he could feed the stove without getting out of bed. With his wife and sons elsewhere and his mind solely taken up with affairs of the committee, the house was all that Jones needed.

Mr. Speers visited Lloydminster in October to assess the preparedness of the colony for winter. He informed the colonists that the building of an immigration hall would soon commence. He listened as the contentious factions aired their grievances, then urged them to put aside their preoccupation with town lots and prepare more diligently for winter, requesting that those who needed assistance make themselves known to him. Rations would be given to families in need, he said, but men without families would have to hustle for themselves.

In his report, Speers accounted for approximately 1600 colonists, although many of those were working elsewhere. To his surprise, he found the majority of buildings on the homesteads to be satisfactory, "twice as good as any I have seen made by new comers during their first few years." But some houses would not do. "[They] are not habitable, not properly sodded, roofs insufficiently supported." And much else was wrong. The amount of cultivation was very small—two to three acres on average—with many having only a kitchen garden and some not even that. The quantity of hay put up was inadequate, the recent prairie fires having reduced even the small amount taken in; many horses had died and more would. Speers ended his report by saying,

> I beg to say that these people require attention; the conditions are not alarming; and the expenditure in connection with their care should not be great. The majority have done creditable work, but not enough of it. A few are helpless [but most] are profiting by their experience. . . . I can classify them as an industrious community; the women are exhibiting wonderful courage.

The weather continued to hold. The skies were a clear blue. The air was dry. No one, not even the most homesick, missed the raw damp days of an English November. But it was getting colder. The stores carried woollen stockings and vests, fur coats and capes, snowshoes, woollen rugs and leather driving mittens lined with wool. Those who thought the cold of winter had been exaggerated found that their English coats would not keep out the wind, that mere gloves were useless and that feet would freeze in five minutes in thin English boots. They learned that two pairs of stockings and a pair of moose-skin moccasins, though thin as paper, would keep the feet warm and comfortable. An autumn mania for hunting muskrat turned into a sensible pursuit when it was found that the skins, turned fur side in, made warm ear flaps for a winter hat.

Bernard Boden arranged with a Metis man from Onion Lake to supply him with moccasins. He built a porch on the house and closed it in. He bought heavy socks and caps. He mended the roof where the daylight showed through the cracks between the frost-shrunken sods. He tried unsuccessfully to dig a well through the frozen ground with a pick and resigned himself to melting ice or snow for the entire winter. He asked a Native man to teach him how to trap. He mended the day coat he used to wear when bicycling in England.

The article in the *Boston Evening Transcript* on November 21, 1903, had contained its share of misinformation, but the writer had spent several days in the colony and had come away with some lasting impressions.

> Even now they don't believe what they are told about winter; they are thinking of something "a bit worse than an English winter" as they gaze at the clear sunny sky; It is impossible not to like their curious dauntless demeanor. Going among them, one is strongly affected by their spirit. He half believes all will come right in the end—that once again the English will 'muddle through'.

Muddling Through

STARK AGAINST THE GLARE OF WINTER SUN ON PRAIRIE SNOW, A YOUNG WOMAN stood shivering in the open doorway of her sod house. Her world was silent, and she was utterly alone. By lowering her gaze to the side, she could see the outline of the stable where, just minutes before, her husband and his brother had hitched the horses to the sleigh and left for town with a cheery wave and a promise to be home soon with mail and supplies.

She had wanted to go with them. She had wanted to bundle up in wool and fur and drive across the prairie towards town. It had been weeks since she had seen another woman. Just to indulge in a few minutes of light conversation with someone of her own sex was what she wanted. But with money so scarce, they could not afford to buy outdoor winter clothing for her. Maybe next year she would be able to go out in the winter. Or maybe next year she would be back in England where she belonged.

She laid a hand on her bulging abdomen. She had to admit that even with warm clothing, she would have felt uncomfortable being seen in public in her condition. She also knew that she had been standing too long in the doorway. The hard-won heat from the stove would be sucked outside into the white emptiness. She swung the crude door closed and pulled a blanket down to block the cold air that leaked in between the uneven planks. Now her world was reduced to a single room with one small window whose dainty muslin curtains showed brightly against the dark sod walls.

Her hand still resting on her unborn baby, she thought for the hundredth time of her mother and sisters at home. At home a woman could rely on other women to see her through her confinement. At home they would have gathered with her in the afternoons to sew the baby's layette, to share with each other stories of other confinements, to tell her by their laughter and their presence that when her time came, they would be there with her.

She gave a thought to who would be with her here. If the weather was good enough for Dr. Amos to come all the way to their homestead, then it would be he who would bring her child into the world. Otherwise it probably would be her husband. Neither she nor her husband knew anything about babies being born. She had heard rumours of complications, lacerations, hemorrhages and third-day fever, but she knew nothing of the details. A midwife would be the best person to attend her. Such a woman would know from experience what to do and would be able to help with the housework for a little while, but she did not know if there was such a person in the colony. She wondered if her husband would remember to ask in town.

She heaved another green log into the stove. The frost that had formed on the walls and ceiling overnight was starting to melt, and the water was dripping onto the dirt floor. Soon a black tarlike substance would begin to dribble from every joint in the stovepipe, which ran the length of the room. The tar came from the green poplar, the only wood they had to burn since they had used all the seasoned poplar to build the frame of the house and the fences.

The woman's new chair sat beside the stove. Her husband had made it for her out of poplar and willow, calling it "Canadian Chippendale." After months of sitting on the ground or perching on an upturned box, she regarded the chair as a great treasure. It was the nicest present he had ever given her. She was surprised sometimes at how grateful she had become for small comforts. A year ago she would have refused to sleep on a straw-filled mattress. Now she knew that, compared to sleeping on the ground, a straw-filled mattress on a poplar frame was surprisingly comfortable.

Sharing the cabin with her brother-in-law was a problem not so easily solved. She knew that his presence made things easier for her husband. Two sets of hands were better than one when it came to hauling firewood and looking after livestock. Each man could claim the house as part of the qualification to prove his homestead. But two hard-working men required a great deal of looking after, and her brother-in-law's presence made privacy a scarce commodity.

The lack of privacy had been very hard to accept, especially when the three of them were confined to the cabin during a storm. She found herself postponing using the chamber pot. She became accustomed to undressing in the dark and, in the light of morning, to dressing under the bedclothes. Heaven only knew what she would do after the baby was born and she began to menstruate again. Hanging her freshly laundered rags to dry where her brother-in-law could see them was unthinkable. Perhaps she should delay the return of her period by nursing the baby, not the current fashion to be sure, but sensible given the shortage of cow's milk in the colony. Considering the birth-control options available to a respectable woman, breast-feeding made more and more sense.

The young woman chided herself for sitting so long. The fire needed tending; snow must be melted to water the livestock; water must be heated for washing clothes and for cooking some of the potatoes that had frozen inside the house before the cellar had been dug for food storage. She had learned the lesson about frozen potatoes the hard way. Letting them thaw before cooking made them soft, dark and inedible. Plunging them frozen into boiling water was better—they had no taste but at least they could be eaten. Next year she would cook them first, then let them freeze. It was all a matter of learning the right way to do things.

Bread-making in cold weather required special techniques too. The small round cakes of Canadian yeast had to be laid to sponge with some flour overnight. The next day flour was added and then the loaves could be baked. If the flour, her hands or the room were too cold, the yeast would not work. Experience had taught her that she must warm the flour and the bowl beforehand and then keep the batter warm through the night by wrapping the bowl in blankets or an overcoat and placing it close to the stove. In the morning, when she unwrapped the bread bowl from its protective cocoon, a sour smell would tell her instantly that the dough had failed to rise. But it had to be baked anyway. Even if the dough had frozen, she would have baked it. They could not afford to waste the flour. The most frustrating eventuality was when the dough rose well but baked unevenly because of the erratic heat given off by a stove fueled with green logs.

The stove gobbled firewood. The men spent most of their time gathering more, going farther and farther away in search of wood, leaving early and returning late. What spurred the expeditions was the knowledge that wood must be stockpiled before the heavy snows came. The cold weather had arrived suddenly on the heels of a brutal freezing wind that swept away Indian summer in mid-November.

Only small amounts of snow had fallen, enough to colour the ground white but not to prevent people from moving easily about the country.

Despite the arrival of temperatures so low that English thermometers would not register, there was still much to do to prepare for winter. A warm stable was needed for the livestock, as well as three to four big loads of hay for each animal. Clothing and food had to be purchased, houses made weatherproof. The lower the temperature fell, the more the sod bricks shrank, allowing daylight to show through the cracks in the roofs. Icicles hung from the rafters; hair froze to the pillow. A man with a badly fitted door woke up to find snow on top of his bed. Even though William Hutchinson's window was only seven feet away from his stove, it was always covered thickly with frost. Jim Ashton knew an ex-soldier who kept a cookstove and a drum heater going all the time; even so, water froze in a bucket on the ground between the two stoves.

At the end of November there were people with unfinished houses. There were people still living in tents, some with no stoves. The people with houses and stoves had to get up regularly through the night to tend their fires. If a colonist who lived alone were to become too sick to get up, he would have no way of keeping himself warm. There was no hospital where such a person could be looked after. Some of the women living in tents were pregnant. A tent in winter was no place for a newborn baby. It was all very worrying to Dr. Amos.

Dr. Amos was the sole practitioner in the colony, Dr. Keating having left in September. Despite their agreement with Isaac Barr for a salary and expenses, and despite their having submitted bills to the committee for services rendered, neither of the doctors had been paid since their arrival in April. But Amos had chosen to stay, supporting himself on whatever fees people could afford to pay him and involving himself in the life of the colony. As the cold weather tightened its grip, Amos's top priority was to have a hospital, and by early December a tiny wooden shack that held two beds had been erected.

The department's top priority was the people still living in tents. Some of them had been burned out in the October fires, but most were people who had been unable to cope on their homesteads and had moved into the village, where they threatened to swamp its limited resources. What was needed was an immigration hall, but there was no more lumber available at Onion Lake, and a shipment from Edmonton was stranded on a sandbar in the river. Accordingly, Mr. Speers ordered two large wooden-floored tents to be set up with three stoves in each, two for heating and one for cooking. One tent accommodated men and provided a place for concerts and lectures. The other contained a store and living compartments for women and children.

When Mr. E. W. Thomson, editor of the *Globe*, visited Lloydminster in November, he was touched when the woman tending the store asked him if he would like to see the baby who had just been born. Behind a curtain, on a straw mattress laid on a drafty floor, lay a beautiful young woman, her skin still tanned from summer, with a tiny baby in her arms. Snow drifted in under the edge of the tent. The woman's husband had begged Marion Lloyd to deliver the baby in the doctor's absence. Later, in her memoirs, Mrs. Lloyd confessed that though she had never delivered a baby before, she carried on as though she knew what she was doing, boiling water, assembling scissors and string, banishing the father and his little boy to the men's tent and breathing a sigh of relief when Dr. Amos made a last-minute appearance.

Some of the doctor's patients were less fortunate. A twenty-two-year-old lithographer named Francis Hurt died in a tent on his homestead. The family was destitute but asked only for enough timber to build a coffin. In the same week in November, twenty-four-year-old Norman Taylor, a stamper by trade, went out to water his horse, a rather nervous beast that Taylor sought to control by tying the end of the halter shank around his wrist. The horse bolted, dragging Taylor seventy-five yards. He was not missed until the following morning, when his body was found frozen stiff, still tethered to the animal.

Each case was reported to the NWMP detachment, whose role in the village had little to do with crime and a great deal to do with human welfare. Indeed, the constables rode a regular circuit checking on each colonist, making notes in a book signed by the settlers, distributing food and bringing people in need of assistance to the government tents. Needy settlers closer to Battleford were taken to the renovated police barracks there.

A warning came out from the NWMP. Given the reduced number of daylight hours in December, no one must set out to walk to his homestead after noon. Accordingly, the telegraph line gang struck camp early on the morning of December 24 to be back in Lloydminster in plenty of time for Christmas. One of their number, a lad named Jerry, was anxious to get home, a further nineteen miles to the east, to be with Laura Sisley, the woman who had brought him and several other orphaned boys to the colony. Miss Sisley's small fortune had been spent getting her boys established, and Jerry was anxious to give his paycheque to her for Christmas. A blizzard blew up that evening while he was still on the trail. His body was not found until spring.

No one in the colony that Christmas Eve of 1903 knew that Jerry had not reached home. The holiday season was upon them. The rest of the telegraph gang, Jim McCormick included, spent the first hours back in Lloydminster in a successful hunt for some whiskey. The more sedate members of the community were engaged in last-minute efforts to turn an unfinished general store into a church in time for the evening carol service. An enthusiastic if unbalanced choir of six sopranos, twelve tenors and twenty basses thrilled the assembled congregation with the familiar songs of the season.

The year before, Stanley Rackham had celebrated Christmas by attending the carol service at Westminster Abbey. This year, having dined on roasted prairie chicken and a plum pudding sent from home, he engaged in "a thorough spruce up" and, dressed in "more or less civilized style," walked the short distance into town. Bernard and Percy Boden chose to dine at home on prairie chicken, boiled potatoes, bread sauce, stewed apricots and blancmange. The Hutchinson brothers spent Christmas with a Shropshire family. No mention was made of how Mrs. Hutchinson, four months pregnant and unable to go outside without warm outdoor clothing, spent the evening.

Two hundred colonists celebrated Christmas Day in town at an eleven o'clock church service. Then Hall and Scott's general store, its roof completed only the day before and its unfinished front wall covered with a large canvas, was converted from a church into a dining hall. Food that had been prepared the night before was served on trestle tables covered with bedsheets. Guests had been instructed to bring their own cups, plates and cutlery. The walls were hung with evergreen boughs, coloured paper, flags and bunting salvaged from people's trunks. Also displayed was Lloyd's collection of one hundred of Cassel's Nation's Best Pictures; many were missing their frames and many more their glass, but the quality of their images could not be denied.

A large tree hung with sweets and gifts, "of the useful rather than ornamental kind," provided the focal point for the evening's concert. Following a program of music, the NWMP, in procession, carried in a huge plum cake. Bringing up the rear was Santa Claus, dressed in a scarlet robe, flowing white beard and boots trimmed with rabbit fur. Some colonists noted that he bore an amazing resemblance to

Nathaniel Jones. Included in the gifts distributed that evening were a number for Dr. Amos, a rocking chair for each of the restaurant proprietors, who now numbered three, $48 for the hospital fund and $135 for Lloyd, the latter gift intended to reimburse him for some of his expenses.

It was a time for celebration. Men who had not worn a starched shirt or collar for months came carefully dressed in "English clothes." Women wore dresses that had been packed away since March and hats, "the pride of the gentler sex," which William Hutchinson described as looking "none the worse for a good holiday." Just before midnight, the song "Home, Sweet Home" was received in hushed silence, a silence soon broken by a stirring rendition of "God Save the King."

New Year's festivities ended the season in fine style. The proprietors of the new general store, Mr. Hall and Mr. Scott, had decorated the room and waxed the floor. A band, described somewhat dubiously as "efficient" and consisting of several violins, two cornets and one harmonium, played until 4:30 the next morning. And, as if unable to end the fun and face reality, a large number of people gathered the next evening for a concert that ended with the singing of "Ho! ro! my nut brown maiden," "Star's Trembling o'er Us" and "Such an Educated Girl." Then the hall was cleared for dancing on mocassined feet, with the horses blanketed outside in the shelter of the building and the children asleep in the cloakroom watched over by a policeman who, in the interest of speedy identification, had pinned a large piece of paper to each child bearing the family name.

People went home that night in bright moonlight. What snow there was was hard and crisp, and it hissed as the runners of the sleighs slid over it. Skimming over the snow in a winter wagon on runners, even the makeshift ones made of two-inch thick planks, was a great improvement over the lurching and bumping of a summer wagon on wheels.

Because the heavy snow held off for most of January, people could come into town for meetings of Lloyd's Literary and Musical Society. The musical part consisted of sacred and secular singing. The literary was mostly lectures, the most popular of which by far was Lloyd's lecture on the Saskatchewan Rebellion of 1885, in which he had played such a heroic part. Bernard Boden thought the entire three hours was thrilling. His and Percy's social life was limited by their reluctance to accept invitations that they could not afford to return. Most of their entertainment consisted of reading newspapers sent from home and books borrowed from Stanley Rackham.

William Hutchinson was saving his few books until he really needed them. Instead, he read newspapers slowly, word by word, spinning them out by reading even the ads. After supper, he and his wife and brother talked and, if they had coal oil for light, wrote letters. Bernard Boden, now with a table to write on instead of an upturned jam pail, was able to use ink instead of pencil. Accordingly, his letters became more legible and much longer.

When Bernard had kissed Madeleine good-bye in England, his plan was that she would join him in three years. But in his letters that January, he began to warn her that it might take longer. She in turn begged him to express love more openly when he wrote, but he could not.

> I am afraid [my letters] are not very loverlike but you see life is so practical out here and although I am constantly thinking of you and longing for your society, I can't put all my thoughts on paper, but you know how I feel I think and you would not like me to keep telling you what you already know.

Perhaps a young man in his early twenties could not be expected to understand that a young woman could never get her fill of words of love. However, when Percy's fiancée, Madge, wrote to tell him that she could not bear the thought of coming to Canada, Bernard was sure that Madeleine would change her mind too, or that her relatives would persuade her to stay home. Desperation unleashed his pen, and he was able to write of his love in more flowery phrases. Included in his letter was a picture of himself in his new image, dressed as a farmer, his face weathered and his beard newly trimmed into a pointed tuft on the lower lip and chin, in the fashion set years before by Napoleon III. Madeleine's reply included a report on the lack of enthusiasm Bernard's sister had shown for his "imperial." Bernard defended his new look by saying that it suited him and protected parts of his face from frostbite.

In the neverending pursuit of ways to stay warm, the tobacco users were among the most adaptable. Ivan Crossley had been serious about smoking since working in Florida, but his devotion to the noxious weed was sorely tried when he was on the trail during a cold snap.

Knowing it was dangerous to remove his gloves and being unable to handle a cigarette with gloved hands, he resorted to chewing tobacco. But tobacco, whether for smoking or chewing, was not easy to obtain, forcing dedicated smokers to use dried tea leaves as a poor substitute. Canadian tobacco, when it was available, came in large cakes that the colonists called "gravestones." Nine inches long, four inches wide and three-eighths of an inch thick, the cakes were so hard the tobacco had to be carved off.

> Sometimes it is so hard that I don't believe it would be damaged if put under a waggon-wheel, and it only requires a chisel and hammer and one might engrave an inscription on it.

English tobacco was the most frequently requested item from relatives at home. But the parcels containing the tobacco and whatever other luxuries were sent from the Old Country had to withstand a difficult journey. The postal service had not improved very much. The postmaster at Battleford was still difficult, refusing to deliver parcels that then languished in Battleford to be chewed on by mice. In the eyes of some, Lloydminster's postmaster George Flamanck was no better. A petition presented to the village council, which had replaced the committee but whose membership was virtually identical, demanded the removal of Flamanck from his post, accusing him of "acts of flagrant inefficiency, carelessness and discourtesy." His position was saved with a counterpetition containing a longer list of names.

The postmaster and the post office had become pawns in a battle between the two factions in Lloydminster. On the one side were Lloyd, storeowner Herbert Hall and the members of the village council, all of whom wanted the post office in or near Hall's store. The other side included the Miller brothers from Edmonton who ran a rival store and had bought a building on Main Street, which they were prepared to offer to the post office rent-free for one year. The *Saskatchewan Herald* regarded the entire postal controversy as a joke: "The inhabitants of Lloydminster are thinking of applying for a post office on wheels so that they can have it on one street one week and another the next."

The continuing battle between the two factions continued on several fronts. They quarrelled over the stores syndicate, the provision of jobs, the location of the post office, the eligibility of ratepayers to vote, the suitability of the incumbent notary public and the granting of liquor licences.

Although some liquor licences had been granted "to thoroughly respectable people" in January 1904, Lloyd continued steadfast in his opposition to them and to the "liquorites," his name for those who favoured public drinking establishments. Lloyd's tactics included holding straw votes after church services, informing Premier Haultain of rumours of secret petitions, and making special appearances before the liquor commission armed with an endorsement from "a large public meeting," which had been attended only by those who lived in town.

It was accusations of drunkenness that made the notary public, a Canadian named Robert Ramsbottom, a special target for Lloyd's wrath, but Ramsbottom stood accused of other crimes as well—"violating a social usage in relations between a married man and a single woman," "being a disturbing element in the community" and "misappropriation of lumber." That the Supreme Court later found him to be guilty only of a muddle in bookkeeping did not save him from becoming the subject of a ratepayers' meeting where, according to Village Secretary Nathaniel Jones, "his name as a mischief maker was greeted with three groans very heartily given." "There is some that stay around Lloydminster," wrote Peter Paynter to a commission investigating the colony in 1905, "that do nothing but call public meetings, but they are not working the colony."

The people who *were* working the colony were on their homesteads waiting for the full fury of winter to descend upon them. When it came, it came in blizzards every other week. The snow drifted and blew; so much fell that drivers had to walk ahead of their teams, breaking trails that filled in again almost instantly. In places dry snow formed a crust so hard that teams could walk on top without breaking through.

People straining their eyes for some sign of a trail on the snow-covered prairie ran a real risk of snow blindness. Bernard Smith was blinded on his way home from town. His partner, Stanley Rackham, found Bernard lost, unable to see and in great pain. It required several days in a darkened room before he could see again.

Snow blindness made the eyes feel as though they were full of hot sand. Some relief could be obtained from poultices of cold tea leaves, but the stinging pain kept sufferers awake at night. Snow blindness could be prevented by wearing deep blue goggles, but the few pairs available in town were quickly sold, leaving people to make do with makeshift eye covers of green mosquito netting.

The prairie winter could rob a man of sight in other ways. While out in his sleigh, William Hutchinson was accosted by a howling wind that drove snow into his face, preventing him from looking ahead. With each step, the oxen kicked up another blinding gust of fine cold powder. After two hours of struggling, he decided to walk, jumping off the sleigh into waist-deep drifts, and plodded along for four more hours until suddenly he came upon Lloydminster, a strange, silent, deserted place whose buildings hid beneath huge drifts. Then the silence was broken by the jingle of sleigh bells. Out of the blowing snow burst the mail sleigh, pulled by four good horses kicking up clouds of snow that almost obscured their driver as he hunched down among the bags, wrapped in furs and rugs. The beauty was lost on Hutchinson.

> Snow, snow, everlasting snow. A moderate thickness of snow is all very well . . . but when we stand out on the lonely prairie . . . up to our waists in snow and ice as far as the eye can reach, and two or three thousand miles beyond that, you can well imagine that this wintery mantle receives anything but admiration.

William Laurence was a tall, strong ex-soldier who had a homestead forty miles west of Lloydminster. In the hope of receiving letters from his fiancée, it was his custom to walk the distance to town on a regular basis. One day he became lost in a blizzard. Realizing the danger, he dug himself into the snow and tried unsuccessfully to start a fire. It was only his fur coat that kept him alive until the storm abated two nights later.

By then, Laurence's feet and hands were frozen, forcing him to crawl. It was in this condition that a farmer saw him, a fur-clad being on all fours. Thinking Laurence was a bear, the farmer took aim with his gun, stopping only when the "bear" shouted, "Don't shoot." By the time Dr. Amos examined Laurence in the little hospital, his hands and feet were useless, but his head was clear. When his mail was brought to him, he refused to allow anyone to open it, and it lay on his chest unread as he passed into unconsciousness and died.

Kate Holtby wondered if she too would die before spring. She had been determined to survive the winter, but since the onset of the heavy snow, life was getting more and more difficult. Of the four Holtby adults who had come to the colony, she was the only one still

here. Her husband, Robert, had left her in the sod house months before, and now, as she faced the brunt of the winter, her children were
her only resource. They were also her main concern. Bob would be
fine. Strong, resourceful, optimistic, he would be bringing money
home in the spring from his logging job. Bessie and Dodie, sixteen and
nine years old respectively, were with her, and the three of them were
under the protection of her eldest son Oliver, a dreamy, frail young
man of twenty-one.

When Indian summer ended abruptly in early November, the
family's activities had moved inside the small house with its sod brick
walls and roof and its dirt floor. Very little light penetrated the one
tiny window, but Oliver had learned to extract the maximum amount
of heat from the small stove, and they had passed the minus thirty degree evenings quite happily listening to Oliver read out loud or play
his violin and watching him draw simple scenes on his sketch pad.
True, he had to get up during the night to bank the fire, and true, the
girls woke each morning with eyelashes frozen together and hair stuck
to the pillow with frost, and true, their food had to be thawed each
morning before they could eat breakfast, but that was happening to
everyone. When Oliver walked to town for the mail, he reckoned they
were doing almost as well as anybody else.

One day in January, while walking home from Lloydminster, Oliver
froze some toes on one foot. Any old prairie hand could have predicted it. Thin English boots were no substitute for the less elegant
but much more sensible mocassins that most people wore. The toes
would not heal, and Oliver became unable to keep up with the firewood. To compound the problem, the sod brick walls of the hut were
shrinking in the severe cold, and the space that appeared between the
walls and the roof gradually became big enough for a man to put his
head through.

The Holtby girls took over the responsibility for the fire,
manoeuvring the poplar poles onto a sawhorse and bucksawing them
into lengths. But it was bitterly cold outside and the girls' clothing was
inadequate, so they began to bring whole logs into the house to buck
them. Sawhorse and wood took up most of the room, and the fire's
constant need for more and more fuel filled all their time. Then a new
crisis loomed: their food supply dwindled until they had only beans
and tea left.

The wretched hut and its occupants huddled alone on the prairie,
their only hope being to reach their nearest neighbour two miles

away. Kate bundled the two girls in as many clothes as they could wear
and took them outside. The only thing she could see in the direction
of the neighbour's shack were bluffs of bare poplars standing in forlorn clumps here and there. Pointing the girls in the general direction
of the neighbour's place, she urged them forward, but before they
were out of sight, she lost her nerve and called them back. The risk
that she would lose them was too great. That night Kate Holtby
prayed. She could think of nothing else to do.

James Salter's homestead lay farther from town, beyond the
Holtbys'. Because one of his team of horses had finally succumbed to
months of poor feed and inexpert care, Salter was riding the survivor
into town to buy a replacement on the morning after Kate's night of
prayer. In the days before roads crosshatched the prairie, anyone wishing to get to town rode in as straight a line as he or she could reckon.
In winter, anonymous poplar bluffs and look-alike knolls provided the
only navigational markers on the vast expanse of white snow, and they
were imprecise. Salter was lost. When he spotted the Holtby place, he
thanked his lucky stars, for he knew that these unknown fellow colonists would let him warm himself at their fire and help him get his
bearings. When Kate opened the door to Salter's knock, she knew he
had been sent from heaven.

Dr. Amos came as soon as Salter reached him with the news.
Oliver's toes were gangrenous and, in addition, he had scurvy. Scurvy
could be treated with lime juice and a decent diet, but only amputation
would relieve the pain in Oliver's toes. Next day a land guide came
with a big sleigh and moved the whole family to the tents in town,
where they joined a growing number of people in need of government
help.

Mr. Speers had known since he visited the colony in October that
many of the colonists were reluctant to accept help. At a town meeting
he had asked about their true condition. Did they need assistance?
Was there any destitution? Were they in want?

> I desired them to be honest with themselves and give me
> the facts. I might say there is a reserve about these English
> people and I am frequently confronted with their pride.

One woman declared that she would not become "the object of
charity," but Speers reckoned that twenty-three families would
need some government help—money, housing, food or just encour-

agement. And as the weather worsened, he predicted, these numbers would grow.

At first, most of those who needed assistance remained in their own homes and were supplied with basic foodstuffs delivered by the NWMP. A system of liens against land was proposed by the department in order to pay for the assistance, a provision that most of those receiving help insisted upon in any case. The NWMP were cautioned to obtain these guarantees when they distributed the food. But in January, the land agent was told not to make people pay for the rations they had received. "Under very special instructions from [Deputy Minister] Smart, no destitution should be permitted to exist among these people." Though seventy liens were taken throughout the winter, none were registered. But when other needy settlers not associated with the Barr Colony applied for liens, they were refused. As Speers said in a memo, "The privilege is for the British Colonists who came here last spring."

The "privilege" extended only to the provision of food. Daniel Swan had six children and a daughter-in-law with two babies. He had settled near Saskatoon because it was too expensive in the colony. With tears streaming down his face, he told a government agent that the $1200 he had brought with him had been spent, and he was faced now with having to sell his cattle at half their value in order to raise some cash. The department supplied him with oatmeal and flour but refused his request for money.

Henry Bowra did not resort to tears. He was indignant. Owing to illness in November, the fifty-seven-year-old farmer had been forced to request a government donation of food for his young wife and four small children. The food, duly delivered by the NWMP, plus his own potatoes and some help from the neighbours, had lasted him until Christmas.

When the heavy snow came, the cow died. And when the neighbours heard that the government had sent food, they stopped helping. Bowra had sixty-five cents left from the $1000 he had brought with him. It was the stinginess of the food supply that enraged Bowra the most. "Verily," he wrote, "we do better than that in England." He was in desperate straits when he sent a letter to NWMP Inspector McGinnis, by then the commander in Battleford.

Since Christmas ('Merry Xmas' save the mark) I have had the pleasure of seeing my children feeding sumptuously at the Canadian Government Expense on dry bread and oats one meal and for a change, oats and dry bread at the next, the mother and I looking on and sipping hot water discoloured with a few leaves of tea.

Bowra demanded to know if this was the way the government treated unfortunates cast on their hospitable shores. He professed to prefer complete starvation.

In fact I shall prefer dying right out with my dear little ones than continuing to try and drag out in this torture for another three or four months. . . . Will the government provide food or not. Kindly spare us half measures. An early reply will oblige.

More food arrived immediately, and since Bowra refused to move his family to the barracks, the department arranged with Peter Paynter to provide necessities, including a stove. No lien was taken.

Although most of the colonists were able to supply themselves with food, their diets were by no means luxurious. Store supplies had been very low at the beginning of winter owing to the delivery scow being frozen in the river. Once the freight sleighs were able to get through from Saskatoon, the variety of food available improved, but the prices were ruinous.

Everyone who could afford beef and pork kept frozen carcasses hanging where meal-sized pieces could be sawed off when needed. The Topotts ate a steady diet of rabbit, by far the most plentiful meat available, cooking it in delectable ways that the English did so well. When a storm prevented hunting, they existed on dry bread. Jim McCormick and his three partners stored all the garden produce that had survived the September frost in their cellar and faced the winter knowing that there were 963 cabbages waiting to be eaten.

A few lucky people like the Bodens had a cow still producing milk. After several unsuccessful attempts, the brothers learned how to churn butter and make Devonshire cream. The majority of the colonists, however, settled for beef drippings rendered from suet. William Topott even tried diluted mustard in an attempt to make dry bread more interesting. As spring approached, the supply of stored vegetables dwindled, meat could not be kept frozen hard and freighters could not navigate the softening trails. The supplies of food grew dangerously low, leaving many colonists to exist for weeks on oatmeal and dry bread.

From his Portland, Oregon, home, Isaac Barr, who had dropped the honorific "Reverend," was quoted in a Minneapolis newspaper regarding the plight of destitute colonists. It was not his fault that "many of the emigrants misrepresented their financial condition," he said, citing an instance where a man with eleven children confessed on arrival in Saskatoon that he had only £6, not £600 as he had claimed. "I was also imposed upon by a number of worthless characters who were permitted to join the colony because they brought letters of reference from excellent authorities," he complained.

With Barr eschewing all responsibility for the condition of the settlers and Lloyd concerning himself with liquor licences and disreputable notaries public, it was fortunate that the government was there to provide assistance. The total amount was surprisingly small. Seven hundred dollars was spent in Lloydminster and a further seven hundred in Battleford. No money was spent on able-bodied men and boys who had been expected to find work, the most needy being given jobs building the immigration hall at twenty to thirty cents an hour. A recuperating Oliver Holtby watched the men working on the hall bring their nails into the government tent to heat them on the stove, then dump the hot nails into their aprons and go out to start work again.

When Bob Holtby returned from working near Edmonton in April, he found the hall finished and his family ready to move from the government tent. They returned to the sod house, living there while Bob and Oliver built a log house based on the buildings Bob had seen while he was away. The sod house became a stable.

The livestock in the Britannia Colony fared very poorly over the winter. Seventy-five per cent of the horses died due to "carelessness, lack of feed, inattention and exposure." A government suggestion in the fall that the livestock be moved up to Onion Lake to be cared for by experienced ranchers had been largely ignored. Few settlers had succeeded in growing a crop, and the resulting shortage of oats was especially hard on the horses. And many people had resorted to cutting dead grass in the fall to feed their cattle, with predictably poor results.

It did not surprise government officials to be asked for help again as spring approached. Lloyd suggested that the NWMP barracks be built to provide work. Several colonists asked for seed, a request that was opposed until Speers insisted that it was absolutely essential. No seed had been produced in the colony the summer before, and now it was impossible for people to travel to Battleford or Saskatoon for seed since there were so few healthy teams and the roads were in such poor condition. The department agreed to supply seed oats at fifty cents a bushel and seed potatoes at one dollar, with payment due the following autumn.

But the department stood firm in its refusal to give any financial assistance. The widow Budden had settled near Battleford with her daughter and five sons, two of whom were old enough to qualify for land. She had lost the money she had invested with Barr and had spent her remaining $1500 getting through the winter. The October fires had destroyed half of her hay, two of her horses had died of swamp fever and a third by "falling down a hole," but Mrs. Budden's request that the government sell her a team on installments was turned down.

But spring was in the air, and that was enough to inspire optimism. Even though the snow lay deep after a three-day storm in mid-March, the Bodens' chickens started to lay again. Then the snow began to melt. Now neither sleigh nor wagon would do. Wagons on wheels and people on foot dropped through the snow crust into pools of water caught between the snow and the frozen ground beneath. Every tiny crevice ran with water. Big Gully Creek overflowed its banks and turned the Gully Flats into a lake. Freight lay stranded along the trail. There was no flour available, and no mail could get through. A tobacco famine added insult to injury. Everyone was anxious to get out on the land, but no one could move very far while this state of affairs existed.

Lloyd and his followers had turned their attention to matters farther afield. New groups of colonists were due to leave Britain any day, the most important being the people who had signed up with Barr the previous spring. One of the purposes of Lloyd's circular letter, written in the summer of 1903, had been to inform and encourage this second group. In addition, Lloyd had written to the *Church Family Newspaper* in Britain in February 1904 to welcome to the colony "any readers . . . who would send . . . an undoubted reference from their clergyman of sobriety, integrity and general usefulness." Undeterred by his mentor's fall from grace, Barr's advance man, the Reverend Doctor John Robbins, had been recruiting in London all winter long, and a colonist named Griffen with credentials from Lloyd was reported to be recruiting there as well.

Interested emigrants could obtain information from several sources. William Hutchinson's newspaper articles and Harold Phillpotts's published letters provided practical advice and no small amount of propaganda to eager readers in the Old Country.

"Do not come in a large party. Too many people at once tend to drive up prices. Bring at least $1000; learn to bake bread before coming; learn to cook and to handle a gun for sport and food; come with a partner since many jobs can not be done alone; leave behind all furniture, crockery and heavy tools; and most important of all, do not listen to anyone else's advice," Hutchinson advised. He went on to warn against succumbing to "false reports, misleading statements and exaggerated rumours," which he said were purposely circulated "to prevent settlers coming through to the Colony."

In his circular letter, Lloyd had suggested that the settlers go by rail to Edmonton and then travel to the colony via the North Saskatchewan River, probably with a mind to avoiding the defection of people in Saskatoon and Battleford as they made their way overland. He suggested that the new colonists take the CPR main line to Calgary and then travel to Edmonton on the spur line. If they waited until the river was high in the spring, they could get to Fort Pitt by barge, and from there to Lloydminster by wagon.

The Battleford and Saskatoon newspapers waged war against the Edmonton scheme all through the spring of 1904. An editorial in the *Saskatchewan Herald* pointed out that there was no settlement along most of the route and therefore no one to help people in trouble on the river. The writer fulminated about the audacity of the people of Edmonton, who were encouraging this enterprise, and reminded his readers of the disaster that had resulted when Edmonton promoted itself as a route to the Klondike. The same issue of the newspaper quoted a Barr colonist who had made several trips down the river the summer before and wished to point out the disadvantages of the route—river pilots were hard to find; water came over the bow of the scows; scows had to be unloaded every time they struck a rock or a sandbar, and when it rained, everything got wet.

Ignoring the concerns of the two towns and undeterred by the department's insistence that the new group, whichever route they chose, would be treated as "ordinary settlers," Lloyd peppered officials with letters. In February he asked, unsuccessfully, for a capitation grant to bring out the new immigrants, and he announced his intention to meet them at seaboard when they disembarked. He informed the department that he had arranged for the newcomers to arrive in late April or early May. He was determined that a two-man welcom-

ing committee would meet settlers coming via Saskatoon and requested that the department supply the committee with a salary and
board for their trip.

On April 27, 1904, the *Herald* published a letter to the editor from a
Barr colonist whose pen name was *Verite Sans Peur*. The author fear-
lessly took issue with Lloyd, the men around him and the recruiting
pamphlet. After pointing out the lack of real information about the
killing frosts, the heavy snows and the presence of mosquitoes, he
went on to attack the idea of encouraging settlers to come by river,
calling it "one of the craziest ideas that ever entered into a sane man's
head." His final criticism was aimed at one of the men who planned to
welcome settlers coming through Saskatoon. "[Nathaniel Jones] is a
gentleman, a very genial old fellow, late manager of a safe company
in Manchester, but absolutely ignorant of anything pertaining to a
farm."

To critics like this, Jones was typical of the people in Lloyd's circle.
He had concerned himself solely with the affairs of the town, neglect-
ing his own homestead, which he had lived on only briefly for two
months in the fall of 1903. Jones was the sort of colonist Speers was
referring to when he said he was not optimistic about "those who have
hived at Lloydminster."

> They are a literary people and cultured and doubtless the
> social condition has kept them to some extent contented.
> They have musical societies and many organizations, and
> hold very many meetings . . . but as I have suggested to
> them publicly, that they have to dispense with leaders and
> make an individual effort to improve their farms, to become
> producers.

While the people on the land faced the challenges of their second
year on the prairie, the literary and musical events in the village continued. With the air of a society columnist reporting on the activities
of the elite, William Hutchinson described a "dance and entertainment" given by a few "prominent" women in the colony. There were
songs and sketches and, just before the dancing began, a "capital set of
tableaux." After a few verses of "The Maple Leaf Forever," the heavy
curtains draping the platform were opened to reveal John Bull and
Uncle Sam holding a copy of Canada's national anthem. And lest
someone in the audience should wonder about the significance of a

scene with only an Englishman and an American in it, the tableau was entitled "Canada."

Ivan Crossley did not attend the entertainment. It had been months since he had seen anyone but the occasional passerby, but he had survived the winter, living alone on Mr. Hall's quarter section and looking after his herd of good Hereford cattle. By April Crossley had saved enough money to put $100 down on a team of oxen, promising to pay the balance of $70 within twelve months. He bought a wagon on credit, convincing the agent that he was trustworthy even though he was not legally of age. Then he hired himself out with his wagon and his oxen, whom he called Moses and Aaron, to work the freighter route from Fort Pitt. They were ready to go as soon as the ice was out of the river.

In a letter written that spring to Madeleine, Bernard Boden said, "I have been told that if a man out here can get through his first year alright he ought to do well as by that time he is thoroughly acclimated." Percy and Bernard had survived the winter. Their oxen had matured and become quiet and willing workers. With stronger animals and a lighter plough, the two men finally were able to carve a straight furrow. Bernard's letters were overflowing with optimism as he described the euphoria he felt at being able at last to break the land: "Twenty-six furrows equals thirteen rounds equals half an acre broken."

The geese were flying north. There were ducks on the lakes, frogs in the sloughs, crocuses in the fields and mosquitoes everywhere. Mr. Speers had watched the Barr colonists struggle to build on the experiences of the past months. His assessment was terse but filled with admiration: "The people on the farms are doing well and will develop into first class settlers."

Epilogue

NO ONE WHO CAME TO THE LLOYDMINSTER DISTRICT AFTER 1903 EXPERIENCED conditions as difficult as those encountered by the Barr colonists. The people who arrived the following spring, whether they came through Battleford or Edmonton, benefitted from the lessons learned the year before. The trek route had been repaired in advance and bridges put in place at the difficult crossings: the distances between the government tents were shorter, and the camps were supervised by resident farmers who were recent arrivals themselves and sympathetic to the problems of the inexperienced newcomer. The settlers who floated down the river from Edmonton on barges encountered none of the usual problems associated with that route and arrived without incident, the only exception being a man who drowned when he and the horse he was riding from Fort Pitt to Lloydminster were swept away while fording the flood-swollen Big Gully Creek.

Settlers who waited until the railway came through in 1906 had virtually no trouble at all. It made Ivan Crossley shake his head.

> They came right up to Lloydminster and jumped off where we had trekked 200 miles not so many years before. Well there were uncles and aunts and grandmothers able to come out then. . . . Time went on and we were able to buy more supplies and things got better . . . and prices got less and people weren't trying to skin you all the time.

The delay in the building of the railroad angered many who had been promised jobs constructing the line and who realized that without a railroad it would be difficult to send produce to market. But very few settlers were able to grow enough grain to sell in those first years, and the lack of transportation to market was a small problem compared to the shortage of consumer goods that persisted until the railroad came through. After that momentous day, the variety of available building materials, foodstuffs and clothing increased as dramatically as the prices charged for them fell.

Many of the new settlers were British, and most of them had heard about the Barr Colony from the extensive newspaper coverage given the original colonists. As one observer said,

> The notoriety which the Barr Colony and its affairs gained in England did more perhaps than the whole output of immigration literature distributed prior to 1903 to attract British attention to the Northwest Territories.

In addition to the people who heard about Canada in this manner, there were relatives and sweethearts who had been waiting to join their loved ones in the colony ever since the S.S. *Lake Manitoba* had sailed. The train brought Bernard Boden's fiancée, Madeleine, who had waited for four years until Bernard was able to support her, and Ethel May Armstrong, who arrived from Leeds with her piano to marry Bob Holtby, by now living with his brother Oliver in the log cabin on the homestead. Bob's mother, Kate, and sisters Bessie and Dodie had been in Toronto for two years living with his father, but the parents' marriage was past salvaging. In 1906, Kate and the two girls left Robert Holtby behind in the city and came back to live on the homestead. They were accompanied by the eldest Holtby daughter, Kitty, who had come from England to join them in Toronto.

Kitty did not think very much of Lloydminster at first, but she changed her mind when she met Frank Jones, one of Nathaniel's sons, and she married him not long afterward. That seemed to start everyone leaving the Holtby home. Bessie met Ivan Crossley when she was riding into town on top of a load of hay and married him the next year. Ivan had been joined by his brother Guy three years before, and the two had farmed adjoining homesteads. Guy bought Ivan's land when Ivan and Bessie moved into town to run a livery business. Six weeks after Ivan and Bessie's wedding, May and Bob got married and set up their own household. When Dodie moved into Lloydminster to live with Ivan and Bessie, her mother and her brother Oliver were left to live alone in the log cabin that had replaced their sod shack.

Oliver's talents lay in painting and playing the violin, not in farming. He and his mother lived on "bread and scrape" for years until they moved into town themselves. Although her grandchildren remember her fondly, Kate was not demonstrative, and she seemed stiff and tightly contained in the lace-collared black silk dresses she affected. When her estranged husband, Robert, made the first of several visits to Lloydminster to see his children, she stayed inside the house lest she encounter him accidentally on the street.

Robert's brother Willie, his wife Agnes and their three sons returned to the colony one year after they had left in haste for England. The two Holtby families were neighbours, but Kate and Agnes were very cool to each other. Family legend had it that each refused to forgive the other for agreeing to come to Canada.

There was a saying that the best cure for the kind of homesickness that afflicted many women was a trip back to the Old Country, and it was generally true. The fortunate ones were able to return home for a visit, and when they came back to the prairies, they settled in more contentedly. But Isaac Barr had been correct about those who were not able to take the "cure" when he wrote in the fall of 1902, "I believe that homesickness lasts much longer with women than with men, and that some of them carry the longing for the scenes of their youth to their graves."

There was a longing for things British among many of the men as well, but they expressed their homesickness in a determination to keep Lloydminster as British as possible. Many married within the colony or brought back a woman from home. Stanley Rackham waited until he was thirty-five, but he finally found the perfect British bride on one of his trips back to England. British brides were brought to farms with names like "Ridgeway Farm," "Stretton" and "Marland Hill Farm." English relatives reading these genteel names must have imagined their loved ones living on well-groomed estates.

When the owners of those Canadian farms heard that Britain had declared war on Germany in the summer of 1914, an impressive contingent, including many family men approaching middle age, joined the British or the Canadian army to defend Mother Britain and the Empire. Among their numbers were Jim McCormick and Jim Ashton, both of whom attained high rank and won the Distinguished Service Order.

It is not surprising that George Lloyd was rejected when he volunteered for service in World War One. The reverend gentleman was fifty-three years old. He had left Lloydminster in 1905 when his contract with the Colonial and Continental Church Society ended and become principal of Emmanuel College in Prince Albert. All through an illustrious career that culminated in his consecration as Bishop of Saskatchewan in 1922, he continued to stir up controversy with his lifelong commitment to keeping Canada for the British.

His unsettling reputation was reflected in the variety of feelings he inspired among the colonists. As an elderly man, Oliver Holtby described Lloyd "as a tower of strength during those first days," and Ivan Crossley said Lloyd was loved by all. But their verdicts may have been softened by time. In 1903, opinion regarding Lloyd was more likely to agree with that of Charles Marlow, who said that although Lloyd was a good pastor, he seemed unfortunate in his numerous business affairs and caused a lot of confusion. Mounted policeman A. C. Macdonald was more harsh when he remarked that Lloyd would have made a "splendid grand inquisitor." A correspondent from the colony writing to the *Saskatchewan Herald* was only a little kinder when he said, "The people now think they jumped from the pan into the fire when they threw over Rev. Barr for Rev. Lloyd."

Lloyd and the committee had sought to remove Barr's name from any association with the colony. But people persisted in using his name. From 1903 to the present, when colonists and outsiders speak of the founding of Lloydminster, they refer to "the Barr Colony."

The man who had organized this massive undertaking was the only one of the principals who left no written material upon which he could be judged. After spending a few months demanding immigration bonuses from the federal government and granting interviews from the safe side of the American border, he seemed to disappear. It was not until his biographer, Helen Evans Reid, found his family in Australia more than sixty years later that it was revealed that Barr had married Christina Helberg in Nebraska, had two sons by her and then emigrated to that most distant part of the Empire to participate in a new—and unsuccessful—settlement scheme.

In the years following 1903, the vilification of Barr, which had begun in the press, was perpetuated by some of the colonists and certain writers, not the least of whom was George Exton Lloyd. But Barr was not an evil man. Not one of the Canadian government officials, who might well have been trying to vindicate themselves when testifying before a British parliamentary committee investigating block and group settlements, accused him of dishonesty. James Mavor, a University of Toronto professor hired by that same committee to visit and assess the colony, blamed the colony's difficulties on the ineptitude of the English settler and the isolation of the colony site, not on any sinister activities of Mr. Barr.

Isaac Barr was a brilliant promoter whose pamphlets stirred up the dreams of many more people than he had ever thought possible. As the size of the group increased, Barr's inability to organize and to delegate was complicated by his last-minute efforts to provide enough money to see his plan through and his people settled. His biographer portrays him as a peace-loving man who backed away from confrontation, thus explaining convincingly his sudden abdication of leadership when he realized he no longer had the confidence of the people. Two thousand greenhorns had been organized into a colony in a short time and had struck off across the prairie to an isolated patch of ground determined to accept advice from no one. When things started to go wrong, the colonists, the newspapers and the government of Canada looked for a scapegoat and found him easily in Isaac Barr.

Despite its difficult beginnings, the Barr Colony town of Lloydminster and the nearby communities of Marshall and Lashburn became the centre of a successful agricultural district, but one divided by a provincial border. When the provinces of Alberta and Saskatchewan were created in 1905, the territorial border was moved east to the Fourth Meridian, which ran right through the middle of Lloydminster.

The naive group that came to save "Canada for the British" established farms and businesses, and most of them thrived. When people laughed at how green they had been, the Barr colonists liked to tell the story of Joseph Hill, a Cockney pork butcher who had never done any farming before he came to Canada.

Joseph Hill was forty-nine when he and his family emigrated with Mr. Barr. He came because it was very hard to feed and shelter his brood in England and he worried about what would happen when he became too old to work. He and his wife had a daughter and five sons, three of whom were grown men, which allowed the family to file on an entire section. They built a log house and were well advanced in breaking the land when they received a letter saying that half their section belonged to some Swedes. Since they wanted their four quarters to be together and they had used up all their money, the Hills had to move to town, live in the government tents and send the three grown sons out to work in order to feed the family through the winter.

In the spring they filed on new homesteads. Their horses having died, it was not until 1905 that they got very much land broken, and their first crop was not planted until 1906. By then they owed a lot of money. The 1907 crop was killed by frost, but the 1908 crop was so good that they paid all their debts and had money left over. The Barr colonists liked to talk about the awards that Joseph Hill and his sons won for growing oats, including the world championship in 1914, and they liked to say that there were others among them who had done just as well.

At the Public Archives of Canada in the records of the Department of the Interior is a set of documents called "The Barr File." Among many other things, it contains a satirical composition entitled "History of the Barr Movement" by George Morris. It is the story of the Barr Colony written in the form of a chapter of the Bible. Verse eleven reads as follows:

> And it came to pass that the first year was not joyous but grievous; nevertheless in time the children of England obtained for themselves houses and lands, such as they could not have obtained whence they came, and their children's children dwelt in the land and waxed strong and became a great nation such as had not been seen aforetime.

Notes

BF   Barr File, Public Archives of Canada
BPSC   Bruce Peel Special Collection Library, University of Alberta
SABR   Saskatchewan Archives Board, Regina
SABS   Saskatchewan Archives Board, Saskatoon
SPL   Saskatoon Public Library
USSC   University of Saskatchewan Special Collections

I have chosen throughout the book to use the form "Northwest" for North-West Mounted Police, Northwest Territories, the Northwest, the North-West—all of which are used in various sources.

CHAPTER I

The Department of Immigration, File 194804, Department of the Interior, hereinafter BF, is in the Public Archives of Canada. The file contains department correspondence, cables, telegrams and some newspaper clippings.

Sifton's immigration policy: Hall, "Clifford Sifton: Immigration and Settlement Policy."

Industrialists' endorsement: Barr pamphlet 2, p. 19, BPSC, SABS.

Apparent government endorsement of scheme: Holmgren, "Isaac M. Barr and the Britannia Colony," p. 25, BPSC. Letter to Editor, *Hornsby and Finsbury Park Journal*, August 23, 1902, BF. Just to Preston, August 25, 1902, BF.

Barr's letterhead in author's collection. Copies in BPSC, SABS.

Lloyd checks Barr's credentials: Lloyd, "The Trail of 1903," BPSC.

Number of farmers: Ivany, "The History of the Barr Colonists as an Ethnic Experience: 1903-1928," p. 111-12, BPSC, calculates that 22.1 per cent of the adult men were farmers because they listed agricultural occupations. The author would set a lower figure. In the *Manitoba* passenger list, source of Ivany's information, Ivan Crossley, the author's grandfather, was listed as a farmer, but his farming experience consisted solely of helping his uncle grow peaches in Florida. Thomas Edwards described himself as a farmer, but his daughter told the author that when he was given one of his parents' farms to manage, he neglected his work so badly that his parents sent him abroad.

The colonists' romantic vision of rural life may have led them to describe themselves as farmers in advance. Patrick Dunae, in " 'Making Good': The Canadian West in British Boys' Literature, 1890-1914," wrote that British youth of this era received a very positive picture of farming and ranching life in the Canadian West. Historian Dr. Lewis G. Thomas, in his notes on this manuscript, argued persuasively that British idealization of the rural way of life was a powerful motive for emigration.

Sifton's version of events: *Hansard*, July 10, 1903.

CHAPTER II

Condition of the trail: Reid, *All Silent All Damned*, p. 81. Pick, *Next Year*, p. 107, SPL. Crossley interview.

Parker's report: *Saskatchewan Herald*, November 12, 1902.

Barr's Prince Albert experience: Barr to Preston, August 5, 1902, BF. Murray, "The Early History of Emmanuel College." *Manitoba Free Press*, April 16, 1903. Reid, pp. 24-25.

Agricola is now Willingdon, Alberta.

Lloyd's insistence on an exclusive reservation: Lloyd to Smart, November 14, 1902, and Preston to Smart, November 21, 1902, BF.

Barr agrees to conditions for land grant: Holmgren, p. 42.

Holtby family decision to emigrate: Bailey and Bailey, "Our Neighbours, The Oliver Holtby Story." Bick interview. Boan, "Sod Hut Pioneer." Robert Holtby, "Day by Day, A Diary of a Journey, March 30-July 22, 1903," pp. 1-2, BPSC. William Holtby diary in Bette Slater private collection. Slater interview.

Largest body of British subjects: Quoted by Hutchinson, "In Western Canada," *Sheffield Weekly Telegraph*, May 16, 1903, BPSC, SABS, SABR.

His weekly articles provide rich detail.

Barr's finances: Reid, pp. 100-102.

Barr's help to Welsh doctor: Hutchinson to Barr, June 11, 1903, BF.

Canadian Co-operative Home Farm pamphlet in Barr correspondence file, BPSC, SABS.

Hospital Insurance circular, BPSC.

Hospital ticket in Nicol papers, SABR.

Lloyd becomes chaplain: *London Times*, January 15, 1903. His letter under CCCS letterhead, December 1902, BPSC.

Letter from Barr to Crossley in author's collection. Copies in BPSC, SABS.

CHAPTER III

Big reservations: *Saskatchewan Herald*, February 25, March 4 and 11, 1903.

Department's concern about preparations: Preston to Scott, February 12, 1903, BF. Smart to Sifton, March 2, 1903, BF. Sifton to Smart, March 2, 1903, BF. Barr to Smart, March 4, 1903, BF. Sifton to Smart, March 5, 1903, BF.

Douglas Party: Holmgren, pp. 67, 71. Barr to Douglas, February 11, 1903, BF. Smith to Scott, March 6, 1903, BF.

Special treatment for Barr Colony: Speers to Scott, March 9 and 30, 1903, BF. Jones to Smart, March 5, 1903, BF. Department memo, April 9, 1903, BF.

Sailing date changes: Barr pamphlet 2, pp. 2, 3. Smart to Preston, December 12, 1902, BF. Preston to Smart, December 31, 1902, BF. Smart to Scott, February 19, 1903, BF. Jones to Smart, March 5 and 6, 1903, BF. *London Times*, January 15, 1903. "Notice to Members of Colony," February 3 and March 10, 1903 and "Notice from Elder Dempster," March 11, 1903, Barr correspondence file, BPSC.

Carlyle-Bell: Speers to Smith, October 30, 1903, BF.

Topott family: Interview in USSC, used with the permission of Helen Evans Reid.

Barr's reply to Jones: Barr to Jones, February 24, 1903, BF.

Isabel Crossley died the year after Ivan emigrated without seeing him again.

Reasons for male emigration: Barr to *Hornsey and Finsbury Park Journal*, undated and October 4, 1902, BF. Copping, *The Golden Land*, p. 75. Hiemstra, *Gully Farm*, pp. 2-5.

Remittance men: Rendell, "Letters from a Barr Colonist," p. 18.

Home Farm Pamphlet.

Reasons for female emigration: Ivany. Jackel, ed. *A Flannel Shirt and Liberty: British Emigrant Gentlewomen in the Canadian West, 1880-1914*, pp. xiii-xvii. Barr pamphlets 1, p. 3, and 2, p. 13.

The number of boys who accompanied Laura Sisley is variously reported as twelve (Wetton), fourteen and three (*Manitoba Free Press*, April 17, 1903, and December 1903).

Lake Megantic settlers: *Manitoba Free Press*, April 7, 1903.

Although most Barr colonists sailed on the *Lake Manitoba*, those who wished to be on the land early sailed on other ships of the Elder Dempster line—the Lakes *Champlain*, *Montrose*, *Erie* and *Megantic*. A few sailed after the *Manitoba* on the *Lake Simcoe*, and they conducted their land journey with such dispatch that they arrived at the colony site ahead of the main body of settlers. It was this group that would be recognized on a 1978 commemorative certificate as the "Advance Party."

Euston station: an unidentified newspaper clipping, BF.

CHAPTER IV

Barr and the biscuit: Crossley interview.

English superiority: E. W. Thomson, *Boston Evening Transcript*, November 21, 1903, BF.

"Dead-uns," etc.: Quoted in *Weekly Telegraph*, August 6, 1903.

"Englishmen need not apply.": Jackel, p. xx.

Barr forced to include Canadians and Americans: Smart to Scott, March 3, 1903, BF. Department memo, April 9, 1903, BF.

Barr's right to assign lands: Smith to Scott and Scott to Smith, March 18, 1903, and Chisholm to Smart, May 6, 1903, BF.

Departmental preparations: *Manitoba Free Press*, March 30, 1903, BF. Smith to Scott, April 9, 1903, BF. Sifton, *Hansard*, July 10, 1903.

Reuters dispatch: Preston to Smart, April 15, 1903, BF.

Bread incident: Crossley memoir in author's collection. Holtby diary, p. 23, BPSC. Lloyd. Reid, p. 68.

CHAPTER V

Press coverage of journey: *Manitoba Free Press*, April 16, 1903. *Minneapolis Journal*, April 13 and 15, 1903. *The* (Winnipeg) *Telegram*, April 14, 1903.

Barr's special car: Bromhead to Scott, March 14, 1903, BF.

Hiring the doctors: Lloyd, "The Trail of 1903." Marion Lloyd, "The British Colony," BPSC.

Barr hires teamsters: Barr to Indian agent in Battleford, April 15, 1903, BF.

Bromhead's warnings: Bromhead to Barr, April 15, 1903, BF. *Manitoba Free Press*, April 6, 1903.

Robbins's promises: *Ibid.*, April 16, 1903.

Rough train trip: Laura Sisley quoted in Foster, "Group of 'raw Englishmen' Braved Canadian West."

Wealth of the colonists: *Toronto News*, quoted in Reid, p. 70. *Manitoba Free Press*, March 30 and April 3, 1903.

Reuters dispatch: Preston to Smart, April 15, 18 and 21, 1903, and Smith to Smart, May 2, 1903, BF.

Boden writes to Madeleine: Boden letters, April 7 and 12, 1903, BPSC, SABS.

CHAPTER VI

Bell tents: Campbell, *The Silent Song of Mary Eleanor*.

Special treatment of Barr colonists: Smart to Smith, June 15, 1903, BF.

Saskatoon described: Kerr and Hanson, *Saskatoon: The First Half-Century*, p. 49. Anderson, *The Yellowhead Trail in Manitoba and Saskatchewan*, p. 36. Lloyd, "The Trail of 1903."

Department in control: The colonists were aware that the government had taken over. As early as April 19, Bernard Boden told his fiancée that he suspected the government had taken control out of Barr's hands.

Mass meetings: Speers to Smith, April 22, 1903, BF. *Minneapolis Journal*, April 23, 1903. *Manitoba Free Press*, April 23, 1903. Lloyd, "The Trail of 1903." Speers to Scott, April 30, 1903, BF. *Saskatchewan Herald*, April 8, 1903.

"Barr, Barr, wily old Barr": Reid, p. 77, cites Pick, who attributes this song to a man "dying" of sea sickness on the *Manitoba*. Heath, in "Protest Songs of Saskatchewan," cites Pick as well and notes that Guy R. Lyle, compiler of the Barr Colony Collection (BPSC), differs with Pick as to the melody used. Pick says it was "The Nautch Girl," while Lyle says it might have been "The Rajah of Bong."

Description of store tent: *Manitoba Free Press*, April 22, 1903.

The fate of Lloyd's $300 gift from the colonists: When Lloyd bought a team from Jack Barr, he paid in part with an I.O.U. for $300. Jack gave the I.O.U. to his brother Isaac in return for Lloyd's $300, which Isaac had been holding for safekeeping. Isaac should then have returned the I.O.U. to Lloyd, but he did not, although he was asked for it on several occasions. Three months later, according to Lloyd, Isaac cashed the I.O.U. at a bank in Saskatoon. The bank then asked Lloyd for $300 plus interest. This may explain, in part, why Lloyd felt such animosity towards Barr for the rest of his life.

Sifton's opinion of government assistance: Hall, p. 75.

Drunkenness: Hiemstra, p. 61-65.

Speers's comments on the English: Speers to Smith, April 22, 1903, BF.

Democrat (wagon): According to Dr. Thomas, a democrat is a passenger wagon with two seats, one in front of the other. A buggy has only one seat.

CHAPTER VII

Plans for the trek: Barr, "To all members of British Colony who have entered for homesteads," in Barr correspondence file, BPSC. Crossley memoir. *Weekly Telegraph*, May 16, 1903.

Use of soap: *Weekly Telegraph*, September 19, 1903.

Settlers deserting: *Manitoba Free Press*, April 22, 1903. *Saskatchewan Herald*, March 23, 1904. *Weekly Telegraph*, November 5, 1903. Smith to Preston, June 13, 1903, BF.

Criticism of colonists: *Ibid.*, May 4, 1903.

Chisholm versus Barr: Chisholm to Smart, May 6, 1903, BF. *Saskatchewan Herald*, May 6, 1903. Holmgren, pp. 98-99. Holmgren mistakenly places the Clinkskill meeting in Battleford instead of Saskatoon.

Barr's activities in early May: Barr to Smart, May 18, 1903, BF. Rackham diary, May 9 and 14, 1903, BPSC, SABS. Reid, p. 94.

NWMP hats: According to Dr. James Boulton, the mounted police began to wear Stetson hats officially at about the time the Barr colonists arrived.

CHAPTER VIII

Barr's 1902 visit to Paynter: Barr pamphlet 2, p. 17. Crossley memoir.

Topott family: Reid interview. Martha need not have worried about wolves. Since the demise of the buffalo herds, wolves had disappeared from the area.

Barr's return trip to Battleford: Chisholm, May 16, 1903, BF. Lloyd, in "The Trail of 1903," mistakenly says that Barr was still travelling with the women's ox-wagon cavalcade. McCormick diary, pp. 11-15, BPSC. Reid quotes Mrs. Topott incorrectly when she says that Barr visited them just before the baby was born, i.e., before May 15; in the interview with Reid, Mrs. Topott states that Barr visited them at least ten days after her baby was born. Rackham, May 20 and 25, 1903. Clive Tallant, "The Break with Barr: An Episode in the History of the Barr Colony," BPSC.

Barr embattled: Smart to McCreary, May 8, 1903, BF. Speers to Scott and Barr to Smart, May 18 and 27, 1903, BF. Speers to Scott, June 17, 1903, BF. Crossley interview. Reid, pp. 93-94.

Confrontation in Battleford: Chisholm to Smart, May 6, 1903, BF. Ashton memoir, BPSC. Chisholm to Smith, May 16, 1903, BF. Smith to Scott, May 17, 1903; Scott to Smith, May 18, 1903, and Smith to Scott, May 19, 1903, BF. Crossley interview. Ivany. Catherine Jones, "The Jones Story," BPSC. Lloyd, "The Trail of 1903." James Hanna McCormick, *Lloydminster*, SPL, BPSC, SABS. Reid. *Saskatchewan Herald*, May 20, 1903. Slater interview.

Contrary to the original plans, the rest of the committee of twelve was appointed, not elected.

The practice of referring to Barr as "I. M. Barr," not "the Reverend Barr," "Mr. Barr," "Isaac Barr" or even just "Barr," began about this time and persisted in the speech and writing of Lloyd and others for the rest of their lives. It was as if the terse name was all they could bear to say.

Lloyd's telegram: Text quoted in Smith to Scott, May 19, 1903, BF.

Barr is allowed no access to his books: Speers to Scott, May 30 and June 17, 1903, BF. Lloyd, "The Trail of 1903."

Barr's final days in the West: Holmgren, pp. 110-11. *Saskatchewan Herald*, June 3, 1903. *Hansard*, July 10, 1903. *Toronto News*, June 8, 1903.

Frederick Haultain was the premier of the Northwest Territories; George Bulyea was the minister of agriculture.

CHAPTER IX

Dodie Holtby memories: Boan.

Condition of the homesteads: *Weekly Telegraph*, October 3, 1903. Foster, p. 7. Crossley interview.

Bodens' oxen: Boden, May 24, 1903.

Doing things the hard way: Bob Holtby, "Recalling the Old Days," speech in possession of Mildred Beamish.

Picnic atmosphere: Langley to Smith, July 15, 1903, BF. Boden, July 2, 1903.

NWMP maintain order: Rackham, July 1, 1903.

"Scandal rife": McCormick diary, p. 30.

Lack of water: Barr pamphlet 2, p. 3.

The committee criticized: Speers to Smart, June 23, 1903, BF. Langley to Smith, July 15, 1903, BF. Marlow to Lambert, September 24, 1903, BF.

Naming the town: George Ives, a bright and witty 109-year-old when interviewed, described the tent meeting he attended near his homestead. Flamanck proposed the name "Lloydminster," Ives's father seconded the motion and the fifteen men present said "Aye."

A crupper is a strap placed under the animal's tail to keep the saddle from slipping over its head when it bucks.

Criticism of postmaster: Marlow to Lambert, September 24, 1903, BF.

Seeding: Because Lloydminster was judged to be too far north for the successful growing of the varieties of wheat then available, oats were the crop of choice. If the cold weather came before they ripened, they could be cut green and used for livestock feed.

Lloyd's attitude towards non-English settlers: "There is a determination on the part of Mr. Lloyd and the more active part of his committee that no other than English people shall be admitted.", Langley to Smith, July 15, 1903, BF.

Lloyd's circular letter of July 1903: Lloyd publications file, BPSC. Lloyd's figure of 600 was deceptive. Almost half of the registered homesteaders were on land outside the colony, had not arrived from Britain yet or were among the single men working in Manitoba for the first year.

Barr's financial problems: Tallant, p. 44. *Hansard*. Smart to McClary, August 24, 1903, BF.

CHAPTER X

Colonists ill-prepared: Speers to Scott, July 24, 1903, BF.

Lloyd's plans for town: Holmgren, p. 137. Lloyd. Speers to Scott,

June 13, 1903, BF. According to Speers, the deputy minister only
   agreed to the development of the town site "to promote social and
   religious intercourse in winter months."
When the town site was surveyed, it was discovered that the twenty-
   eighth township line did not coincide with the Fourth Meridian as
   anticipated. A narrow strip of land two lots wide was left over.
   Lloyd bought the land, called the Gore, from the CPR and had it
   surveyed into lots, which sold quickly. The proceeds went to the
   committee to pay bills.
Barr's house-building advice: Barr pamphlet 1, pp. 10-11.
The interior walls of several houses were papered with the saffron-col-
   oured covers from the *Farmers Advocate.*
Women's duties: Boden. Hutchinson, July 9, 1903.
Jobs: Snow report, July 6, 1903, BF. Speers to Scott, April 4, 1904, BF.
Carlyle-Bell: Speers to Smith, October 30, 1903, BF. Speers to Scott,
   October 30, 1903, BF.
Two factions: *Ibid.*, Marlow to Lambert, September 24, 1903, BF. *Bos-
   ton Evening Transcript*, November 21, 1903.
Houses in town: Lloyd described houses like Jones's soddery in a letter
   he wrote to Prime Minister Sir Wildred Laurier. The houses
   looked like Irish cabins, he said, but "men coming as we do from
   some of the finest towns in England are not by any means ashamed
   of them." Lloyd to Laurier, January 15, 1904, BF.
Speers's Report: Speers to Scott, October 30, 1903, BF.

CHAPTER XI

When Laura Sisley's money ran out, she operated the local post office
   and gave music lessons. Later, she supported herself by keeping
   house for one or another of the boys she had helped to establish.
Flamanck controversy: Minutes of Village of Lloydminster, March 11,
   1904, from papers of Nathaniel Jones (hereinafter called Jones papers), contributed by Mildred Beamish.
Herbert Hall: He was a fifth-generation Canadian, a graduate of agricultural college and Lloyd's lifelong friend. He was hired as a farming instructor for the colony, but when all his possessions were
   destroyed in a prairie fire, he moved into town and established a
   general store in partnership with George H. Scott.
Factional disputes and liquor licences in Speers to Scott, October 30,
   1903, BF. *Weekly Telegraph*, April 16, 1904. Letter to Postmaster

General, Lloyd to Haultain, March 4, 1904, Jones papers. Minutes of village meetings on March 5 and 11 and May 30, 1904, Jones papers. *Saskatchewan Herald*, May 5, 1904.

Winter aid to colonists: Speers to Scott, October 30, 1903, BF. Speers to Chisholm, January 15, 1904, BF. Speers to Scott, April 4, 1904, BF. Bowra to McGinnis, January 9, 1904, BF. Clipping from Minneapolis newspaper, March 15, 1904, BF.

Livestock: Speers to Scott, April 4, 1904, BF.

New recruits: *Saskatchewan Herald*, March 23, 1904. Preston to Scott, March 24, 1904, BF. The department instructed its man in London not to interfere with Griffen but to keep clear of any responsibility in connection with the colony.

According to *The Canadian Encyclopedia*, the Edmonton route to the Klondike was the route of the "foolhardy," many of whom took two years to reach the gold fields.

"Those who have hived in Lloydminster": Speers to Scott, April 4, 1904, BF. According to his "Application for Patent," Nathaniel Jones finally moved onto his land in February of 1905 shortly before his wife, Elizabeth, arrived from England. He and three of his sons filed on a whole section, which they finally proved in 1908.

EPILOGUE

New arrivals: *Saskatchewan Herald*, March 30, May 11 and 31, 1904. Crossley memoir.

Notoriety of colony: Edmund A. Oliver, "The Settlement of Saskatchewan to 1914," BPSC.

Homesickness: *Hornsey and Finsbury Park Journal*, October 4, 1902, BF.

British brides: Ivany, p. 53.

Assessment of Lloyd: Marlow to Lambert, September 24, 1903, BF. Holmgren, p. 7. *Saskatchewan Herald*, March 30, 1904. Macdonald made his remark to Professor James Mavor, himself on less than cordial footing with the Anglican priest in question.

Assessment of Barr: Holmgren, pp. 154, 163-69. Reid, pp. 96 and 102-103.

Sources

Abbreviations

BF   Barr File, Public Archives of Canada
BPSC   Bruce Peel Special Collection Library, University of Alberta
SABR   Saskatchewan Archives Board, Regina
SABS   Saskatchewan Archives Board, Saskatoon
SPL   Saskatoon Public Library
USSC   University of Saskatchewan Special Collections

Articles

Anonymous. "The Mother's Duty." *The Independent*, August 15, 1907.

————. "A Sketch of the Life of The Right Reverend George Exton Lloyd, M.A., D.D., L.L.D. Bishop of Saskatchewan, 1922-1931." *Canadian Churchman*, March 3, 1949. Letter to Editor by Marion Lloyd published April 21, 1949.

Bailey, H. T. and M. H. Bailey. "Our Neighbours, The Oliver Holtby Story." *Lloydminster Times*, 1949.

Beal, Bob, and Rod Macleod. "North-West Rebellion." In *The Canadian Encyclopedia*, 2d ed., 1511. Edmonton: Hurtig Publishers, 1988.

Bergman, Brian. "Isaac Barr's Battered Dream." *Alberta Report*, August 6, 1984.

Berton, Pierre. "Klondike Gold Rush." In *The Canadian Encyclopedia*, 2d ed., 1143-44. Edmonton: Hurtig Publishers, 1988.

Boan, Dorothy. "Sod Hut Pioneer." In *My Canada*, edited by Glenn Keith Cowan. Toronto: Irwin Publishing, 1984.

Brown, Peggy. "Rackham Family." In "The Fort Pitt Trail," compiled by Dorcas Alma Hewitt, 1968.

Butts, Edward. "Almighty Voice." In *The Canadian Encyclopedia*, 2d ed., 66. Edmonton: Hurtig Publishers, 1988.

Dunae, Patrick A. " 'Making Good': The Canadian West in British Boys' Literature, 1890-1914." In *Prairie Forum* 4, no. 2 (Fall) 1979: 165-81.

Foster, Keith. "Group of 'Raw Englishmen' Braved Canadian West." *Western People*, January 6, 1983.

G. F. B. "In the Wilderness, 'The Promised Land.' " *Lloydminster Times*, July 26, 1978.

Hall, D. J. "Clifford Sifton: Immigration and Settlement Policy." In *Settlement of the West*, edited by Howard Palmer. Calgary: Cowprint Publishing Co., 1977.

Heath, T. G. "Protest Songs of Saskatchewan." *Saskatchewan History* 25 (1972): 81-91.

Holtby, Robert. "Recalling the Old Days." *Lloydminster Times*, July 17, 1963.

Hutchinson, William. "In Western Canada." Series published in *The Sheffield Weekly Telegraph*, London, England, 1903-6, BPSC.

Illustrated War News. Toronto: The Grip Printing and Publishing Co., 1885. Souvenir Number in Special Collections, University of Victoria.

Lester, Carl. "Dominion Land Surveys." *Alberta Historical Review* 11, no. 3 (Summer 1963).

Lyle, Guy R. "Eye Witness to Courage." *Saskatchewan History* 20 (Autumn 1967): 81-107.

———. Review of *All Silent, All Damned: The Search for Isaac Barr*, by Helen Evans Reid. *Saskatchewan History* 23 (Winter 1970): 31-34.

Murray, J. E. "The Early History of Emmanuel College." *Saskatchewan History* (Autumn 1956): 81-101.

Notes and Correspondence. *Saskatchewan History* 6 (1953).

Oliver, Edmund H. "The Settlement of Saskatchewan to 1914." *Proceedings and Transactions of the Royal Society of Canada*. 3d series, 20 (May 1926): 63-67.

Palmer, Howard. "Immigration and Ethnic Settlement, 1880-1920." In *Peoples of Alberta*, edited by Howard and Tamara Palmer. Saskatoon: Western Producer Prairie Books, 1985.

Portman, Jamie. Review of *All Silent, All Damned: The Search for Isaac Barr*, by Helen Evans Reid. *Herald Magazine*, July 18, 1969.

Reinhardt, Dorothy. "My Grandpa—Nathaniel Jones." In "The Britannia Story." Dorothy Jones Reinhardt collection.

Rendell, Alice. "Letters from a Barr Colonist." *Alberta Historical Review* (Winter 1963): 12-27.

Tallant, Clive. "The Break with Barr: An Episode in the History of the Barr Colony." *Saskatchewan History* 6 (Spring 1953): 41-46.

———. "The North-West Mounted Police and the Barr Colony." *Saskatchewan History* 7 (Spring 1954): 41-46.

Woodcock, George. "Doukhobors." In *The Canadian Encyclopedia*, 2d ed., 616-17. Edmonton: Hurtig Publishers, 1988.

Yanyu, Susan. "Pioneers Remember Early Days in Barr Colony." *Lloydminster Times*, July 26, 1978.

Books

Anderson, Frank W. *The Yellowhead Trail in Manitoba and Saskatchewan*. Saskatoon: Frank W. Anderson, 1979.

Book of Common Prayer. London: The Musson Book Company Ltd., n.d.

Broadfoot, Barry. *The Pioneer Years 1895-1914*. Toronto: Doubleday Canada Ltd., 1976.

Campbell, Marjorie Wilkins. *The Silent Song of Mary Eleanor*. Saskatoon: Western Producer Prairie Books, 1983.

Copping, Arthur E. *The Golden Land*. Toronto: The Musson Book Company Ltd., 1911.

Dion, Joseph F. *My Tribe. The Crees*. Calgary: The Glenbow Museum, 1979.

Dempsey, Hugh A., ed. *William Parker, Mounted Policeman*. Edmonton: Hurtig Publishers, 1973.

Dunae, Patrick. *Gentleman Emigrants*. Vancouver: Douglas and McIntyre, 1981.

Hampsten, Elizabeth. *Read This Only to Yourself*. Bloomington: Indiana University Press, 1982.

Hiemstra, Mary. *Gully Farm*. London: J. M. Dent & Sons Ltd., 1955.

Hopwood, Victor G., ed. *David Thompson Travels in Western North America, 1784-1812*. Toronto: Macmillan of Canada, 1971.

Jackel, Susan, ed. *A Flannel Shirt and Liberty: British Emigrant Gentlewomen in the Canadian West, 1880-1914*. Vancouver: University of British Columbia Press, 1982.

Kerr, D. G. G. *A Historical Atlas of Canada*. Toronto: Thomas Nelson and Sons (Canada) Ltd., 1959.

Kerr, Don, and Stan Hanson. *Saskatoon: The First Half-Century*. Edmonton: NeWest, 1982.

MacGregor, J. G. *The Battle River Valley.* Saskatoon: Western Producer Prairie Books, 1976.

Macleod, R. C. *The North West Mounted Police 1873-1919.* Ottawa: The Canadian Historical Association Booklets, 1978.

MacPherson, Ian. *The Co-operative Movement on the Prairies, 1900-1955.* Ottawa: The Canadian Historical Association Booklets, 1979.

McCormick, J. Hanna. *Lloydminster or 5,000 Miles with the Barr Colonists.* London: Drane's (Ye Olde St. Brides Presse), 1924.

McLaren, Angus. *Birth Control in Nineteenth-Century England.* London: Holmes and Meier, 1978.

Martin, Chester. *Foundations of Canadian Nationalism.* Toronto: University of Toronto Press, 1955.

Page, Robert. *The Boer War and Canadian Imperialism.* Ottawa: The Canadian Historical Association Booklets, 1987.

Pick, Harry. *Next Year.* Toronto: Ryerson Press, 1928.

Reid, Helen Evans. *All Silent, All Damned: The Search for Isaac Barr.* Toronto: Ryerson Press, 1969.

Roberts, Sarah Ellen. *Of Us and Oxen.* Saskatoon: Modern Press, 1968.

Russell, E. T. *What's in a Name*, 3d ed. Saskatoon: Western Producer Prairie Books, 1980.

South from Lloydminster. Book Committee of Southminster and Furness Ladies Clubs, 1973.

Thomas, Lewis H. *The North-West Territories 1870-1905.* Ottawa: The Canadian Historical Association Booklets, 1970.

Thomson, Don W. *Men and Meridians: The History of Surveying and Mapping in Canada*, vol. 2. Ottawa: Queen's Printer, 1967.

Wetton, C. *The Promised Land*, 2nd ed. Lloydminster: *The Lloydminster Times*, 1979.

Correspondence, Diaries and Journals

Barr, Isaac M. Pamphlets, Circulars, Letters, Material about Barr and Testimonials. BPSC.

Boden, Bernard d'Este. Letters dating from April 7, 1903-January 6, 1907. BPSC.

Holtby, Robert. Day by Day. A Diary of a Journey, March 30-July 22, 1903. Copy in BPSC.

Holtby, William. Diary. Bette Holtby Slater collection.

Lloyd, G. E. Letter under Colonial and Continental Church Society

letterhead. December 1902. BPSC.
McCormick, James Hanna. Barr Colony: Diary of a Trail Journey. BPSC.
Rackham, Stanley. Diary, November 1, 1900-December 31, 1911. BPSC, SABR.

Government Records

Canada. Department of the Interior. File 194804. PAC.
———. House of Commons. *Official Report of the Debates, Ninth Parliament.* Ottawa, 1903.
Minutes and Correspondence of Village of Lloydminster, 1904. Papers of Nathaniel Jones. SABR.

Newspapers

Lloydminster Times.
London Times.
Manitoba Free Press.
Saskatchewan Herald.

Pamphlets

Barr, I. M. *British Settlements in North Western Canada in Free Grant Lands, Canada for the British.* (Before September 30, 1902), BPSC.
———. *British Settlements in North Western Canada in Free Grant Lands: Report of my Journey to the Saskatchewan Valley, N.W. Canada to Select Land for the First British Settlement.* Christmas 1902, BPSC.
———. *British Settlements in Canada. The Canadian Co-operative Home Farm No. 1.* BPSC.
———. Hospital Insurance Circular. Dorothy Reinhardt collection.
"Sketch of the Life of The Right Rev. Geo. Ext. Lloyd, M.A., D.D., L.L.D. Bishop of Saskatchewan, 1922-1931." Study pamphlet for boys 12-15. BPSC.

Theses and Manuscripts

Ashton, E. J. "An Immigrant Looks Back." Photocopy. BPSC.
Crossley, F. Ivan. "My Life and Experiences with the Barr Colony." 1960. Author's collection.
Hamilton, Z. M., compiler. "Place Names of Saskatchewan." 1949.
Holmgren, Eric J. "Isaac M. Barr and the Britannia Colony." Master's

thesis, University of Alberta, 1964. BPSC.

Ivany, Kathryn. "The History of the Barr Colonists as an Ethnic Experience: 1903-1928." Master's thesis, University of Alberta, 1985. BPSC.

Jones, Catherine. "The Jones Story." BPSC.

Lloyd, George Exton. "The Trail of 1903." 1940. BPSC.

Lloyd, Marion. "The British Colony." BPSC, SABR.

Interviews

Beamish, Eric, and Leona Beamish. Interview with author. Lloydminster, Saskatchewan, April 27, 1989.

Bick, Muriel Crossley. Interview with author by letter, July 1989.

Crossley, F. Ivan. Interview with Helen Evans Reid. Kelowna, British Columbia, June 18, 1963, USSC.

Davie, Isobel Jones, and Mary Jones Fuller. Interview with author by letter, September 1989.

Fisher, Madeline Edwards, and Russell Fisher. Interview with author. Edmonton, Alberta, May 1, 1989.

Ives, George. Interview with author. Aldergrove, British Columbia, January 23, 1991.

Lyle, James Kenneth. Interview with author. Victoria, British Columbia, March 1989.

Slater, Bette Holtby. Interview with author. White Rock, British Columbia, July 5, 1990.

Steer, Paul. Interview with author. Victoria, British Columbia, January 27, 1989.

Stevenson, Emma. Interview with author. Victoria, British Columbia, January 27, 1989.

Topott, Martha (Mrs. William). Interview with Helen Evans Reid. Location unknown, 1963, USSC.

Acknowledgements

SEVERAL MEMBERS OF MY FAMILY ASSISTED ME IN THIS PROJECT. MILDRED Beamish, Eric Beamish, Leona Beamish, Muriel Bick, Bruce Boan, Jack Boan, William Crossley, Isabel Davie, the late Mary Fuller, Zaida Gilchrist, Hazel Holtby, Jack Holtby, Dorothy Reinhardt, John Scott and Bette Slater shared memories, artifacts, letters, genealogical tables and photographs of their parents and grandparents. Leola Crossley provided tremendous assistance with promotion.

I would like to thank the following people for the special information they shared. Dr. Diane M. Secoy, Professor of Biology, University of Saskatchewan, explained the mysteries of snake migration; Dr. James Boulton provided information on mounted police headgear; Archdeacon John Lancaster shared his knowledge of clerical dress; Bill Cookson reminisced about Liverpool's Princes landing stage; Mark Nixon discussed the eating habits of expatriate English folk, and Ken Lyall pondered the mysteries of compass deviation.

The people who staff the archives, libraries and museums of Canada were helpful and gracious. I thank them all, and more specifically do I thank Kathy Classen, Historical Cultural Supervisor, City of Lloydminster; Wayne Crockett, Saskatchewan Archives Board, University of Saskatchewan; Jeanine Green, Bruce Peel Special Collections Library, University of Alberta; Barbara Lyall, Vancouver Island Regional Library; Guy R. Lyle, retired archivist, compiler of the Barr Colony Collection at the University of Alberta and Barr Colony descendant; Shirley A. Martin, Adam Shortt Library of Canadiana, University of Saskatchewan; Marian J. Powell, Legislative Librarian, Saskatchewan Legislature, and Ivan J. Saunders, Saskatchewan Archives Board, University of Regina.

Three professionals in the field of historical writing deserve special thanks. Dr. Michael Bliss gave me an invaluable boost at the beginning of the project. Barry Broadfoot was generous with his vast knowledge of Western Canada and with witty reminders of writers' frailties. Dr. Lewis G. Thomas, Professor Emeritus of History, University of Alberta, read an earlier version of the manuscript for accuracy. His comments often took the form of short essays on aspects of prairie history that eloquently reflected a lifetime of thought and study. Any mistakes or misinterpretations remaining in the manuscript are mine alone.

The people at Douglas and McIntyre are friendly and very professional. I would like to thank Rob Sanders, Barbara Pulling and Janice Bearg in particular.

My husband, Dick, is amazingly tolerant of things historical. I am very grateful for his encouragement, his wisdom and his companionship.

INDEX

Absentee claims, 31, 38

Advance agents, 29, 36-37, 46, 63, 65, 77, 87. *See also* Bromhead, W. S.; May, Charles; Robbins, Dr. John

Advance party, 42, 46, 110, 126. *See also* Pioneer Party

Alberta Territory. *See* Northwest Territories

Alcohol, 62, 81-82, 106, 137, 153, 189, 193, 199, 200

Alkali flats, 112-13

All-British Colony, 1, 5, 58, 59, 74, 75, 92, 108, 143; offices, 33, 34-35, 58

Amos, Dr. W. W., 76, 106, 108, 136, 142, 185, 187, 188, 194, 196. *See also* Doctors

Anglican Church. *See* Church of England

Armstrong, Ethel May, 205

Ashton, E. J. (Jim), 18-19, 34, 41, 54, 60, 80-81, 84, 94, 96-97, 111, 116 122, 152, 159, 170, 187, 206

Assiniboia Territory. *See* Northwest Territories

Assiniboines. *See* Native people

Athabasca Territory. *See* Northwest Territories

Baggage, 1-2, 47-48, 96-97, 112, 120; missing, 96, 97, 100, 107- 8, 162; on ship, 52, 54, 56, 68-69, 70, 72

Bain wagons, 1-2, 96-97

Bank of British North America, 122, 139, 178

Bannock, 114, 131

Barges (scows). *See* River barges

Barr, Isaac Montgomery, 1, 3, 8, 33, 34, 36, 53, 58, 87, 126, 149, 154, 200, 206; admiration of the British by, 6, 8, 9; and alcohol, 71, 136; as Anglican priest, 5-6, 7, 10, 16; assessment of, 14, 23-25, 207; attitude towards Cana-

dians and Americans of, 20-21, 27, 58-59; attitude towards Europeans of, 10, 11, 13; and Chisholm, 60, 123, 126, 136-37; colonization scheme of, 3, 9- 13, 15; and CPR, 16, 31, 130, 161; credentials of, 12-14, 15; disappearance in Saint John of, 67, 68, 71; early life of, 5-6, 13-14, 23; finances of, 25, 27, 29, 30, 31-33, 34, 36, 37, 38, 42, 46, 98-101, 141, 161, 162, 207; financial advice to colonists of, 35, 48-49, 102, 103; in headquarters camp, 126-27, 135, 136, 146; and Lloyd, 13-15, 128, 207; in Ottawa, 19, 23, 24-26, 76-77; promises and plans of, 2, 6-8, 9-13, 20, 22, 26, 29-30, 42, 47, 48, 56, 60, 65, 75-76, 78, 87-88, 89, 91, 107-8, 110, 114, 150, 153, 154, 161, 167-68, 187; after resignation, 140-41, 142-43, 162, 199, 207; resignation of, 135-36, 138-39; in Saskatoon, 88, 96, 97, 104, 108; visits Canada in 1902, 13, 16, 19- 26. *See also* Barr colonists, complaints of; Immigration, Department of; Syndicates

Barr, J. S. (Jack), 23, 32, 36, 101-2, 103, 178

Barr colonists, 50, 52, 80, 92, 118, 122; advice, willingness to take, 107-8, 107, 152, 160; agricultural experience of, 9, 15, 24, 32, 35, 41, 59, 61, 94; children of, 48, 54, 55, 58, 91, 109, 110, 134, 137, 174, 188, 190; class consciousness of, 79, 84, 105, 119; complaints of, 57-58, 83, 87, 96, 99, 126-27, 128, 130, 135-36, 148; desertion by, 75, 106-7, 118-19, 124-25, 126, 138, 140, 143; emigration, preparation for, 29, 41-42, 47-48, 50; emigration, reasons for, 15, 27, 42-45; as farmers, 150-52, 159-61, 164-65, 179,